23.93

TEACHING FOR OUTCOMES IN ELEMENTARY PHYSICAL EDUCATION

A Guide for Curriculum and Assessment

B+T

Christine J. Hopple, MS

3/99

Human Kinetics

Library of Congress Cataloging-in-Publication Data

Hopple, Christine J., 1962-
Teaching for outcomes in elementary physical education : a guide for curriculum and assessment / Christine J. Hopple.
p. cm.
Includes bibliographical references.
ISBN 0-87322-712-3
1. Physical education for children--Curricula. 2. Physical education for children--Evaluation. I. Title.
GV443.H66 1995
372.86--dc20

94-10391
CIP

ISBN: 0-87322-712-3

Acquisitions Editor: Scott Wikgren; **Developmental Editor:** Julia Anderson; **Assistant Editor:** Julie Marx Ohnemus; **Copyeditor:** Anne Mischakoff Heiles; **Proofreader:** Pam Johnson; **Typesetting and Layout:** Kathy Boudreau-Fuoss; **Text Designer:** Doug Burnett; **Cover Designer:** Jack Davis; **Illustrator:** Mary Yemma Long; **Printer:** United Graphics

Printed in the United States of America 10 9 8 7 6 5 4 3

Human Kinetics
Web site: http://www.humankinetics.com/

United States: Human Kinetics, P.O. Box 5076, Champaign, IL 61825-5076
1-800-747-4457
e-mail: humank@hkusa.com

Canada: Human Kinetics, Box 24040, Windsor, ON N8Y 4Y9
1-800-465-7301 (in Canada only)
e-mail: humank@hkcanada.com

Europe: Human Kinetics, P.O. Box IW14, Leeds LS16 6TR, United Kingdom
(44) 1132 781708
e-mail: humank@hkeurope.com

Australia: Human Kinetics, 57A Price Avenue, Lower Mitcham, South Australia 5062
(08) 277 1555
e-mail: humank@hkaustralia.com

New Zealand: Human Kinetics, P.O. Box 105-231, Auckland 1
(09) 523 3462
e-mail: humank@hknewz.com

Contents

What You Need to Know About *Teaching for Outcomes in Elementary Physical Education*

Let's face it—accountability and assessment are two terms we can't ignore in elementary physical education. More and more, we are asked to delineate exactly what students are learning in our programs. We have to assess and report students' progress toward goals or outcomes the state and district develop, and our plans focus heavily on improving instruction and assessment methods in order to meet these goals.

These demands keep our field dynamic, but at times bring some frustrations. Although good books have been written about curriculum, there has been a lack of information about methods of assessment that are both practical and meaningful for teachers and students. Many of us have found the information we learned in our college tests and measurement class just doesn't seem to work in the "real world" of teaching children in elementary physical education. Somehow, the grade letters *A* to *F* are more applicable than *T*-scores and *Z*-scores; finding out how far students can throw a softball seems less important than helping them learn to throw it well, and who has the time to use and record the data from all those skill tests, anyway?

Fortunately, the demands for accountability and assessment also have a positive side. This is an exciting time in elementary physical education. We are spelling out just what we expect students to learn from physical education. Educators who know how things work "in the trenches" are challenging the beliefs that assessments don't work in elementary PE or just aren't worthwhile. Recently, national and state conferences for physical education and district programs throughout the country have offered a variety of sessions on developmentally appropriate physical education, assessment, and related outcomes for learning. Groups of physical educators have met to work through these issues, and a growing number of elementary physical educators are developing and implementing assessment tools.

This book brings you the best of this new thinking. It was developed with the help of many elementary physical educators and the guidance offered by the National Association of Sport and Physical Education (NASPE) statements on the "Physically Educated Person" and "Benchmarks" (Franck et al., 1992). It is divided into two parts. Part I, "Outcomes and Assessment in Elementary Physical Education," addresses the critical link between planning and assessment. It presents ideas on the purposeful planning of a curriculum, explanations of the new assessments, and perhaps most importantly, strategies to help you work effectively and efficiently with these new concepts. In the first part I hope to dispel the attitude that assessment is only something teachers do after instruction so they can give a grade to students.

In Part II, "Sample Assessment Tasks and Curriculum Ideas," you'll find the practical, hands-on information that you can use in the day-to-day planning, instruction, and assessment of your program. Each chapter in Part II addresses a specific group of skills or concepts in the elementary physical education curriculum. You'll read the nitty-gritty information that we teachers love. You'll find sample unit outcomes, assessment tasks, and ideas that you can use when developing lessons for these skills concepts. Two appendixes provide additional information that you may find useful—sample grade-specific unit outcomes and a listing of NASPE's Benchmarks.

Because your teaching situation, your philosophy, and your students are unique, no educational format is entirely applicable for all teachers. Therefore, *Teaching for Outcomes in Elementary Physical Education* doesn't try to offer a lock-step method for everyone to follow. It does, however, provide you with information and ideas that you can choose from, use, or modify to more fully meet your students' needs. I hope that by the end of this school year this guide will have a well-worn look, with pages crinkled, your notes in the margins, items crossed out, and ideas added. I'll be disappointed if it ends up on the shelf looking as new as the day you bought it!

I also hope that reading this resource is just the first step in the process of planning, instructing, and assessing the important outcomes of your curriculum. I want this book to be a springboard for developing your own outcomes, assessment tasks, and activity ideas; for talking with colleagues in your area; and even for discussing your work with classroom teachers in other content areas. After all, the issues of accountability, developmentally appropriate content, and assessment affect all teachers today, not only physical educators.

Because we at Human Kinetics are dedicated to the mission of helping you help children become physically educated, we invite you to share with us your questions or comments. We're not just publishers of books—we're also experienced physical educators. You can write us at the United States Physical Education Association (USPE), Human Kinetics, P.O. Box 5076, Champaign, IL 61825-5076 or call us at 800-373-USPE. We may not always have the answer you're looking for, but we'll do our best to help you find it!

Christine Hopple

Acknowledgments

This resource, a long time in coming, still wouldn't be in this form today without the time, energy, support, and dedication of the following professionals. They all helped make a stronger and better guide, whether by reviewing the progressions, giving feedback, pushing me to consider things differently, suggesting activities, or just listening to me when the going got tough (possibly the most difficult job of all!). Space does not permit listing the many individual contributions, but I offer to each person a simple, sincere "Thanks—for your support."

Julia Anderson
Developmental Editor
Human Kinetics
Champaign, IL

Kakki Aydlotte
J.C. Hening Elementary School
Midlothian, VA

Dianna Bandhauer
Lecanto Primary School
Lecanto, FL

Mike Cain
Elementary Curriculum Director
Unit 4 Schools
Champaign, IL

Tess Costello
Bottenfield Elementary School
Champaign, IL

Marian Franck
Chair, NASPE Outcomes Committee
Willow Springs, PA

Kathy Goodlett
Ruby Shaw Elementary School
Mesquite, TX

Rose Goodman
Westview Elementary School
Champaign, IL

George Graham
Department of Health, Physical Education, and Recreation
Virginia Polytechnic Institute and State University
Blacksburg, VA

Linda Haluska
Manatee County School Board
Bradenton, FL

Manny Harageones
Consultant, School Improvement
Florida Department of Education
Tallahassee, FL

Don Hellison
College of Kinesiology
University of Illinois-Chicago
Chicago, IL

Tom Holton
Supervisor, Physical Education
Marion County School Board
Ocala, FL

Vicky Hopple
Oak Hill Elementary School
Oak Hill, FL

Prillie Huls
Garden Hills Elementary School
Champaign, IL

Mary Kennedy
Garden Hills Elementary School
Champaign, IL

Jean King
Director, Center for Applied Research and Educational Improvement
University of Minnesota
Minneapolis, MN

Marian Kneer
Western Springs, IL

Mark Manross
Madison, WI

Bill Meadors
Kentucky Wesleyan University
Owensboro, KY

Carol Meyer
Evaluation Specialist
Beaverton School District
Beaverton, OR

Pam Milchrist
Health and Physical Education Department
Sacramento State University
Sacramento, CA

Bobbie Monroe
Chiddix Junior High School
Normal, IL

Jodi Peebles
Ft. McCoy Elementary School
Ft. McCoy, FL

Susan Peterson
Department of Kinesiology
University of Nevada-Las Vegas
Las Vegas, NV

Rae Pica
Moving and Learning Center
Barnstead, NH

Allan Sander
College of Education and Human Services
University of North Florida
Jacksonville, FL

Larry Satchwell
Shiloh Elementary School
Lithonia, GA

Sue Schiemer
Bloomsburg Elementary School
Bloomsburg, PA

Lynn Srull
Jefferson Middle School
Champaign, IL

Jeff Starwalt
Human Kinetics
Champaign, IL

Gail Webster
Department of Health, Physical Education and Recreation
Kennesaw State College
Marietta, GA

Jill Whitall
Department of Kinesiology
University of Maryland
College Park, MD

Scott Wikgren
Human Kinetics
Champaign, IL

Sincerely,
Christine J. Hopple
Human Kinetics

PART I

Outcomes and Assessment in Elementary Physical Education

In this part of the book, you'll read about the ideas that led to the recent focus on outcomes for learning, and the new assessments of performance and portfolio tasks. You'll learn about the National Association of Sport and Physical Education's work to determine, through their outcomes document (Franck et al., 1992), what the goals of a "physically educated person" are: what students should know, be able to do, and value after participating in quality physical education programs.

In chapter 1 you will find direction for purposeful planning of the desired goals and outcomes of your curriculum. You'll be introduced to the basic tenets of *designing down* the curriculum, a process to ensure that what you teach students actually helps them reach the goals you desire. Practical hints and strategies will help you polish and fully define what you want your students to accomplish, and you'll discover how NASPE's Outcomes Project (Franck et al., 1992) can give you direction in this process.

Chapter 2 discusses the assessments of performance and portfolio tasks and the concept of authentic assessment. Physical educators in many areas of the country already are reinterpreting assessments to give the word new meaning. This chapter will answer some of the nitty-gritty questions about assessment: What is a portfolio? How can I make one? How do students submit work for a portfolio? How do I score them? The chapter includes hints on developing the rubrics, or scoring scales, for these assessments and other practical strategies to make using these assessments easier.

CHAPTER 1 Designing Curricular Outcomes

Because many state departments of education and school districts are either restructuring or planning to restructure their education systems based on the learning outcomes that students should achieve, we as physical educators are seeking to become familiar with the tenets of this reform movement, and to learn how we can design and plan course activities so our students can meet whatever outcomes we set for them.

The Movement to Restructure Education

One response to the concerns about the quality of our nation's educational system has been an educational movement to designate specific outcomes, or goals, of learning. In the past 10 years this reform movement has moved from implementation at just the school and school district levels to a current emphasis on a national scale. Experts in such diverse subject areas as mathematics, science, reading, and physical education, in addition to entire state departments of education (including those in Pennsylvania, Kentucky, Virginia, Connecticut, and Minnesota) now seek to implement outcomes reform. Chances are high that your school district or state will join others that seek to clearly define what students should learn and be like once they graduate from school.

To describe this movement toward outcomes, it is easier to start with what it is *not*, rather than what it is. It is not a new method for teaching (such as "cooperative learning"), not a new content area for the school curriculum, and not even a program. It *is* "a way of designing, developing, delivering, and documenting instruction in terms of its intended goals and outcomes" (Spady, 1988, p. 5).

This reform challenges us to approach education with a whole new mind-set. It requires us to be open-minded and to think differently about how we plan, instruct, and assess our students. It asks that we think beyond separate, sometimes unrelated, facts and skills and focus on what students will actually learn and—more importantly—be able to do with that learning when they graduate from high school.

Elementary, middle school, and high school educators are being asked to work together to help students meet and demonstrate broad, exit-level *outcomes*: that is, end results or goals created perhaps by a school district or state department of education, or in a given subject area. These outcomes are meant to reflect the skills and knowledge that students will need to be successful in their adult lives; as such, outcomes become the focal point for the instructional decisions made at each level of schooling (Brandt, 1992a; Spady, 1988).

Examples of these broad, exit-level outcomes are illustrated in Kentucky's Basic Communication and Math Skills Goal Area (see Figure 1.1), one of six framework areas developed by the state Department of Education (Kentucky Department of Education, 1991). In Kentucky, students will be expected in the future to show mastery of such desired outcomes before they can graduate from high school, instead of meeting the traditional *x* number of credit hours needed to graduate requirement. Other states likely will adopt an outcomes-related approach and requirements before the 21st century.

Four Principles of the Movement Toward Outcomes

Four principles underlie the philosophy of reforming education to focus on outcomes. These principles include clarity of focus, expanded opportunity, high expectations, and designing down (Brandt, 1992a; Spady, 1988). Each is explained below.

1. *Clarity of focus*. All phases of the curriculum-designing process—planning, instruction, and assessment—and the decisions made at each of these stages should clearly focus on the exit-level outcomes students are expected to meet. These outcomes become the goals toward which instructors teach and test.

Council on School Performance Standards

A List of Valued Outcomes for Kentucky's Six Learning Goals

Goal 1: Basic Communication and Math Skills

1. Accessing sources of information and ideas: Students use research tools to locate sources of information and ideas relevant to a specific need or problem.
2. Reading: Students construct meaning from a variety of print materials for a variety of purposes through reading.
3. Observing: Students construct meaning from messages communicated in a variety of ways for a variety of purposes through observing.
4. Listening: Students construct meaning from messages communicated in a variety of ways for a variety of purposes through listening.
5. Quantifying: Students communicate ideas by quantifying with whole, rational, real, and/or complex numbers.
6. Computing: Students manipulate information and communicate ideas with a variety of computational algorithms.
7. Visualizing: Students organize information and communicate ideas by visualizing space configurations and movements.
8. Measuring: Students gather information and communicate ideas by measuring.
9. Mathematical reasoning: Students organize information and communicate ideas by algebraic and geometric reasoning such as relations, patterns, variables, unknown quantities, and deductive and inductive processes.
10. Classifying: Students organize information through development and use of classification rules and classification systems.
11. Writing: Students communicate ideas and information to a variety of audiences for a variety of purposes in a variety of modes through writing.
12. Speaking: Students communicate ideas and information to a variety of audiences for a variety of purposes in a variety of modes through speaking.
13. Visual arts: Students construct meaning from and communicate ideas and emotions through the visual arts.
14. Music: Students construct meaning from and communicate ideas and emotions through music.
15. Movement: Students construct meaning from and communicate ideas and emotions through movement.
16. Using electronic technology: Students use computers and other electronic technology to gather, organize, manipulate, and express information and ideas.

Figure 1.1 *Kentucky's Goal 1 exit-level outcomes.*

Note. *From* Transformation: Kentucky's Curriculum Framework, Volumes I and II. *Reprinted with permission of the Kentucky Department of Education.*

2. *Expanded opportunity*. All students should be given enough time and opportunity to learn and practice the knowledge and skills they need to achieve the expected outcomes. Care is taken to assure that students have mastered the appropriate prerequisite skills and knowledge for moving to higher levels; as needed, students receive a second chance to work and master the content.
3. *High expectations*. All students should be expected to accomplish the important outcomes that are within their reasonable grasp. Teachers use a variety of strategies to help students meet these expectations: Students not only know what the expectations are, but also realize that support is there to help them reach these outcomes.
4. *Designing down*. When designing an outcomes-related curriculum, teachers must begin with the outcomes they want for students and plan backward. By *designing down* from the graduation-level outcomes, teachers ensure that the outcomes at lower levels are in line with the exit goals that have been set. Like with planning a vacation, it always helps to know the destination. This makes it easier to decide the route, how many days to take, and what stops to make along the way. Also, by designing down, teachers at all levels gain a sense of exactly why they are teaching specific content and how far they expect students to travel. Knowing exit outcomes beforehand gives planning, instruction, and assessment a purpose beyond simply offering lessons and units.

Designing Down and Delivering Up

After the exit-level outcomes for an educational system are determined by a state department of education, school district, or school, designing down is used to determine the lower-level outcomes for program, course, unit, and lesson levels (see Figure 1.2). In outcomes terminology, the overall statewide, school district, or schoolwide Grades K-12 outcomes are called *exit* outcomes. The next lower level is called the *program* level, and it defines the overall Grades K-12 outcomes for a given program or subject area (e.g., physical education program, mathematics program, reading program). Outcomes are then developed for these programs at the elementary, middle school or junior high, and high school *course* levels. (You will find the term "course" consistently used in this guide to define what we usually think of as a "program".) *Unit* and *lesson* outcomes designing then follows from the course outcomes (see Figure 1.3).

Exit outcomes
↓
Program outcomes
↓
Course outcomes
↓
Unit outcomes
↓
Lesson outcomes

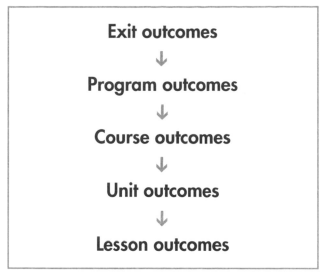

Figure 1.2 *Designing-down sequence.*

The more specific outcomes (developed from the exit, Grades K-12 outcomes) at the program, course, unit, and lesson levels are termed *enabling outcomes*, or *benchmarks*. Enabling outcomes help to break the larger, overall outcomes into smaller, more manageable chunks. Because benchmarks, or enabling outcomes, at each level develop from (and after) the exit-level outcomes, they always assume those broad outcomes as the ultimate focus. As you might expect, you will have many progressively more specific benchmarks as you design down, with the largest number of enabling outcomes at the lesson level.

Once planning has helped establish the enabling outcomes at each of these levels, instruction is then *delivered up* by the teacher: That is, students begin instruction in kindergarten and progress upward. By the time students have finished Grade 12, they should have mastered the desired exit outcomes for Grades K-12.

Implications of Physical Education Restructuring

The widespread move toward restructuring education gives physical educators a common basis for communicating not only among colleagues in the field, but also with teachers of other subjects. This restructuring allows teachers to have a hand in their destiny, so to speak, in implementing outcomes-related programs. Understanding this movement toward outcomes is crucial for physical education to

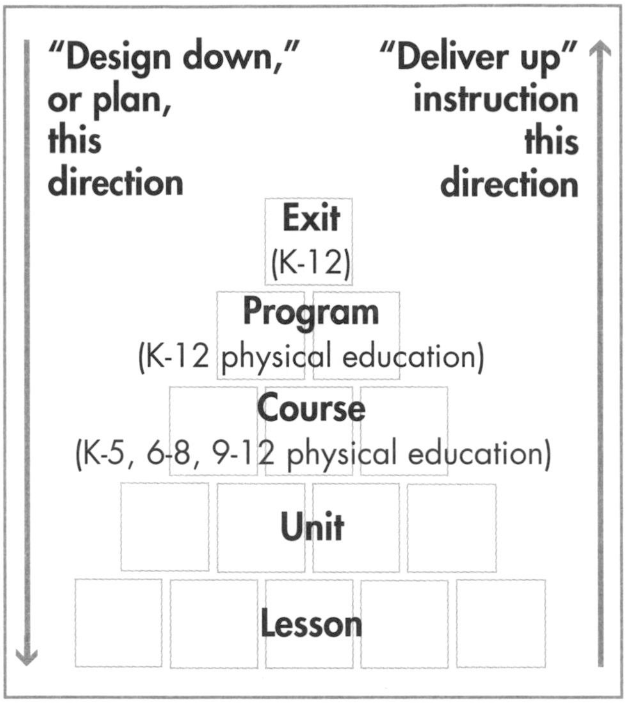

Figure 1.3 *Designing down to levels of enabling outcomes.*

be an integral part of an outcomes-related system, and knowing how to design down becomes an important strategy toward this goal.

Even where a district or state is not yet participating in an outcomes-related model, the concepts of defining outcomes and designing down can help teachers improve planning, instruction, and assessment in physical education. After an introduction to the process of designing down at the program, course, unit, and lesson levels we will look at strategies to make this restructuring practical and efficient.

Designing Down to Program Outcomes

Designing down to the program level involves developing exit outcomes for the subject area—physical education—for Grades K-12 (see Figure 1.4). Sometimes these program outcomes are developed by a state department of education, in some places by a curriculum committee in a school district, and sometimes even by specialists in the subject areas, such as by the National Association for Sport and Physical Education. Grade K-12 program outcomes should specify what one expects students to have learned and be able to do with that learning in physical education by the time they complete high school.

Why Is This Important?

When program outcomes are developed cooperatively by teachers at the elementary, middle, and high school levels, instruction at each of the levels can become an integral and unique piece of the larger puzzle that will fit together without overlap and missing pieces. Without these outcomes for physical education being designated and developed in the continuum of Grades K-12, it becomes easy to lose sight of the important contributions each piece makes to a student's total education. Also, in a climate of increased economic accountability, program outcomes give physical educators an important tool to justify and support the vital place physical education has in a curriculum.

Where Do I Begin?

Before you begin, optimally, program-level K-12 outcomes will have been developed cooperatively by a committee of physical educators from the elementary, middle, and high school levels. As a start toward producing defined goal statements, a committee may want to see whether the state or school district has already developed exit-level outcomes or a framework to use for designing down program-level outcomes.

A second important resource that the committee should review is the *Outcomes of Quality Physical Education Programs* developed by the National Association of Sport and Physical Education. I will refer to this document collectively as the Outcomes Project (Franck et al., 1992). It is a

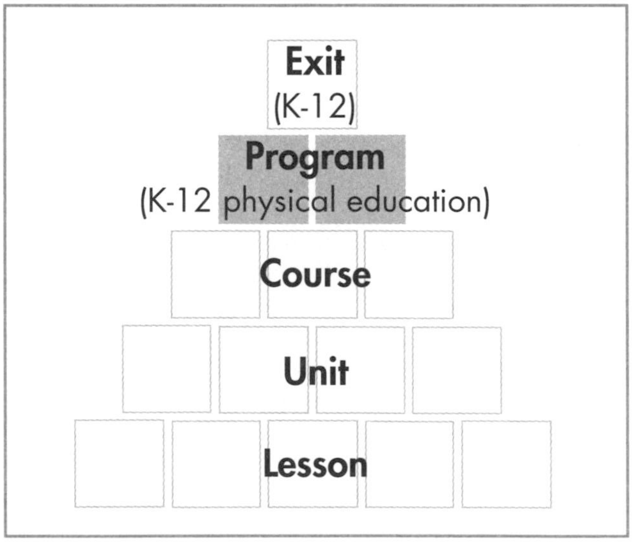

Figure 1.4 *Designing down to the program level.*

helpful series of statements for physical educators to use in designing down, and I will explain it more fully.

Physical Education Outcomes

A group of professional physical educators has developed a set of program-level, K-12 outcomes through the work of NASPE's Outcomes Committee (Franck et al., 1992). This committee defined the skills, knowledge, and values that a "physically educated person" should have at graduation from high school in order to lead a physically healthy and productive life.

NASPE's *Outcomes of Quality Physical Education Programs* begins with the "Definition and Outcomes of the Physically Educated Person" ("Outcomes" statements). This first part defines the skills students should have, what it means to be physically fit and to participate in physical activity, the concepts they should know, and the attitudes and values students should develop as a result of participating in quality physical education programs (see Figure 1.5). These statements can become, or serve as, program-level K-12 outcomes of physical education.

The second part of NASPE's document is called "Benchmarks for Physical Education" (Franck et al., 1992, p. 8). Although the NASPE Benchmarks are not specific to designing down at the program level, I will introduce them now to give you a sense of the whole document. Whenever I refer to the Benchmarks in NASPE's Outcomes Project, the word will be capitalized; here, the term takes on a specific meaning. You'll find that some NASPE Benchmarks are statements of very specific competencies and others are broader combinations of skills or concepts that physically educated people should acquire and understand at various occasions in their school careers (Franck et al., 1992). The Benchmarks are designed for every other grade level, beginning with kindergarten. You'll find an example of NASPE's Grades 5-6 Benchmarks in Figure 1.6, and the Benchmarks for Grades K, 1-2, 3-4, and 5-6 are in Appendix B.

The Benchmarks were neither meant to include all the competencies students will achieve at the given grade levels nor meant to be systematically designed down from the 20 outcome statements. You'll find that the statements apply to what students might learn in one lesson, one unit, or even over a period of a year or more. Nonetheless, taken together they can be useful as an overall gauge, or measuring stick, of what your students should know, be able to do, and value throughout their school physical education career. To help you use them as an assessment tool, the relevant Benchmarks have been referenced to different examples of assessment tasks, which you will find later in this guide.

The Benchmarks have greatest impact not used in isolation but in conjunction with the designing down of a curriculum. For example, if you are a specialist seeing your elementary students one day a week, you surely would find it difficult to have students meet every Benchmark at each grade level. So, which Benchmarks do you expect students to achieve? Which ones are realistic? Considering your own beliefs along with the needs of your physical education district, community, and students, what additional skills, concepts, and values—not even listed in the NASPE Benchmarks—should students be able to meet? By designing down from the program outcomes, you will be able to answer these questions more easily.

Where Do I Go From Here?

Once program-level outcomes have been developed, or NASPE's 20 outcomes have been adopted just as they are, you can further design down outcomes to the elementary, middle, and high school *course* levels—and then beyond to *unit* and *lesson* levels. Although this text specifically emphasizes designing down to the elementary course level, the processes are similar at the middle and high school course levels. Program statements from the Outcomes Project (Franck et al., 1992) will be used as a basis for providing examples.

Designing Down to Elementary Course Outcomes

One of the most crucial—though often overlooked—steps in designing an elementary physical education course curriculum is stating the outcomes or goals precisely (see Figure 1.7).

Besides defining what students should learn at the specific course level, developing course outcomes can help you tie the curriculum together, rather than having a multitude of units and lessons that are more random than rational. You want to know why courses are being taught and what they are helping students to accomplish. Some teachers may think that determining these outcomes is too theoretical or just not important ("After all, I know in my head what the reasons

Definition and Outcomes of the Physically Educated Person

A Physically Educated Person

HAS learned skills necessary to perform a variety of physical activities

1. . . .moves using concepts of body awareness, space awareness, effort, and relationships.
2. . . .demonstrates competence in a variety of manipulative, locomotor, and nonlocomotor skills.
3. . . .demonstrates competence in combinations of manipulative, locomotor, and nonlocomotor skills performed individually and with others.
4. . . .demonstrates competence in many different forms of physical activity.
5. . . .demonstrates proficiency in a few forms of physical activity.
6. . . .has learned how to learn new skills.

IS physically fit

7. . . .assesses, achieves, and maintains physical fitness.
8. . . .designs safe, personal fitness programs in accordance with principles of training and conditioning.

DOES participate regularly in physical activity

9. . . .participates in health enhancing physical activity at least three times a week.
10. . . .selects and regularly participates in lifetime physical activities.

KNOWS the implications of and the benefits from involvement in physical activities

11. . . .identifies the benefits, costs, and obligations associated with regular participation in physical activity.
12. . . .recognizes the risk and safety factors associated with regular participation in physical activity.
13. . . .applies concepts and principles to the development of motor skills.
14. . . .understands that wellness involves more than being physically fit.
15. . . .knows the rules, strategies, and appropriate behaviors for selected physical activities.
16. . . .recognizes that participation in physical activity can lead to multicultural and international understanding.
17. . . .understands that physical activity provides the opportunity for enjoyment, self-expression, and communication.

VALUES physical activity and its contributions to a healthful lifestyle

18. . . .appreciates the relationships with others that result from participation in physical activity.
19. . . .respects the role that regular physical activity plays in the pursuit of life-long health and well-being.
20. . . .cherishes the feelings that result from regular participation in physical activity.

Figure 1.5 *Kindergarten to 12th grade program outcomes for physical education.*

Note. *From* Outcomes of Quality Physical Education Programs *by M. Franck, G. Graham, H. Lawson, T. Loughrey, R. Ritson, M. Sanborn, and V. Seefeldt (the Outcomes Committee of NASPE), 1992, Reston, VA: National Association for Sport and Physical Education. Copyright 1992 by NASPE. Reprinted by permission.*

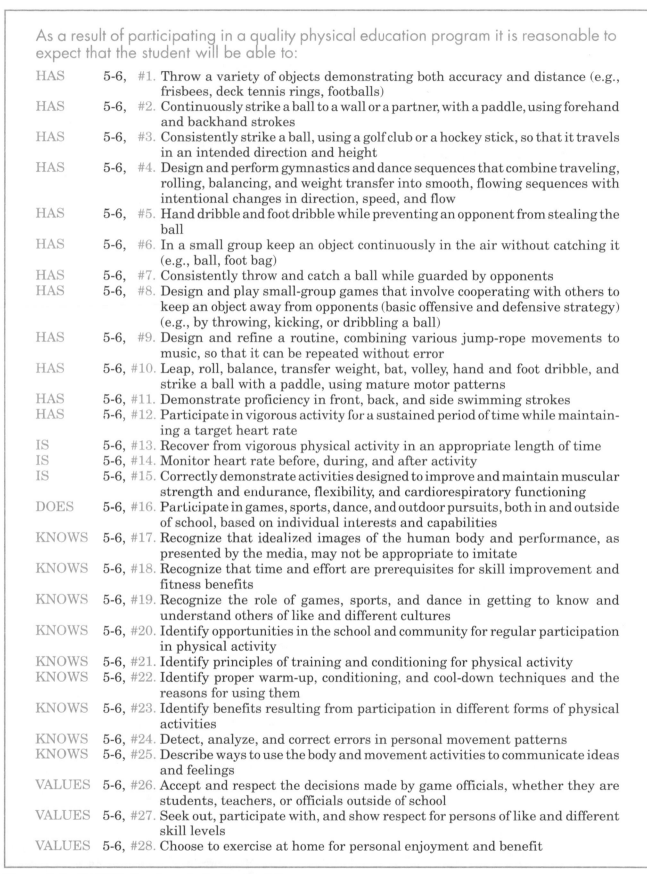

As a result of participating in a quality physical education program it is reasonable to expect that the student will be able to:

HAS	5-6, #1.	Throw a variety of objects demonstrating both accuracy and distance (e.g., frisbees, deck tennis rings, footballs)
HAS	5-6, #2.	Continuously strike a ball to a wall or a partner, with a paddle, using forehand and backhand strokes
HAS	5-6, #3.	Consistently strike a ball, using a golf club or a hockey stick, so that it travels in an intended direction and height
HAS	5-6, #4.	Design and perform gymnastics and dance sequences that combine traveling, rolling, balancing, and weight transfer into smooth, flowing sequences with intentional changes in direction, speed, and flow
HAS	5-6, #5.	Hand dribble and foot dribble while preventing an opponent from stealing the ball
HAS	5-6, #6.	In a small group keep an object continuously in the air without catching it (e.g., ball, foot bag)
HAS	5-6, #7.	Consistently throw and catch a ball while guarded by opponents
HAS	5-6, #8.	Design and play small-group games that involve cooperating with others to keep an object away from opponents (basic offensive and defensive strategy) (e.g., by throwing, kicking, or dribbling a ball)
HAS	5-6, #9.	Design and refine a routine, combining various jump-rope movements to music, so that it can be repeated without error
HAS	5-6, #10.	Leap, roll, balance, transfer weight, bat, volley, hand and foot dribble, and strike a ball with a paddle, using mature motor patterns
HAS	5-6, #11.	Demonstrate proficiency in front, back, and side swimming strokes
HAS	5-6, #12.	Participate in vigorous activity for a sustained period of time while maintaining a target heart rate
IS	5-6, #13.	Recover from vigorous physical activity in an appropriate length of time
IS	5-6, #14.	Monitor heart rate before, during, and after activity
IS	5-6, #15.	Correctly demonstrate activities designed to improve and maintain muscular strength and endurance, flexibility, and cardiorespiratory functioning
DOES	5-6, #16.	Participate in games, sports, dance, and outdoor pursuits, both in and outside of school, based on individual interests and capabilities
KNOWS	5-6, #17.	Recognize that idealized images of the human body and performance, as presented by the media, may not be appropriate to imitate
KNOWS	5-6, #18.	Recognize that time and effort are prerequisites for skill improvement and fitness benefits
KNOWS	5-6, #19.	Recognize the role of games, sports, and dance in getting to know and understand others of like and different cultures
KNOWS	5-6, #20.	Identify opportunities in the school and community for regular participation in physical activity
KNOWS	5-6, #21.	Identify principles of training and conditioning for physical activity
KNOWS	5-6, #22.	Identify proper warm-up, conditioning, and cool-down techniques and the reasons for using them
KNOWS	5-6, #23.	Identify benefits resulting from participation in different forms of physical activities
KNOWS	5-6, #24.	Detect, analyze, and correct errors in personal movement patterns
KNOWS	5-6, #25.	Describe ways to use the body and movement activities to communicate ideas and feelings
VALUES	5-6, #26.	Accept and respect the decisions made by game officials, whether they are students, teachers, or officials outside of school
VALUES	5-6, #27.	Seek out, participate with, and show respect for persons of like and different skill levels
VALUES	5-6, #28.	Choose to exercise at home for personal enjoyment and benefit

Figure 1.6 *NASPE's Benchmarks for Grades 5-6.*

Note. *From* Outcomes of Quality Physical Education Programs *by M. Franck, G. Graham, H. Lawson, T. Loughrey, R. Ritson, M. Sanborn, and V. Seefeldt (the Outcomes Committee of NASPE), 1992, Reston, VA: National Association for Sport and Physical Education. Copyright 1992 by NASPE. Reprinted by permission.*

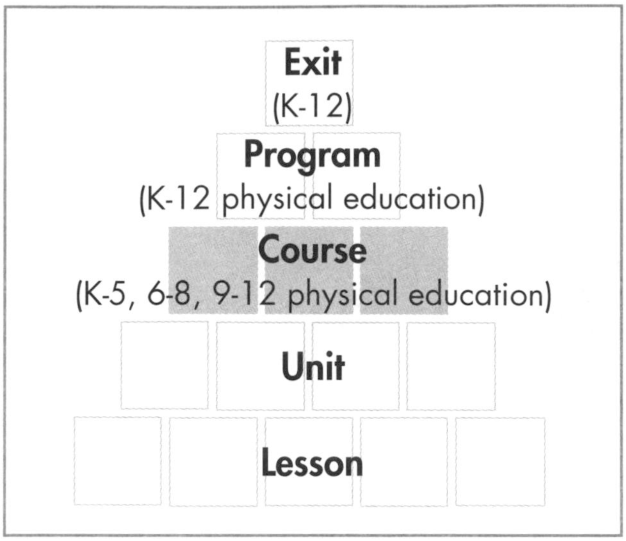

Figure 1.7 *Designing down to elementary course outcomes.*

are, and that's what's important"), but there are benefits of going through this process.

Why Is This Important?

One benefit to writing down these broad course outcomes is that you can use them to show parents, the principal, school board members, and other classroom teachers what you are trying to accomplish. This helps you be viewed as accountable! In fact, just going through the developing process will start you thinking about and examining your curriculum in terms of course outcomes. Your planning and instruction become stronger and tighter. It's like having a garage sale—you get rid of things that just aren't worth the space or don't work any more, and you're left with the possessions that are most important to you. Deciding on the written outcomes for your elementary course is an important first step in having a defensible and well thought-out curriculum that will accomplish what you want it to.

Where Do I Begin?

Whatever program outcomes you are using, it is helpful to have them in front of you as you begin to design down to your course outcomes, making the design more specific to your situation. Start the process by trying to answer the question: "What do I want my students to be able to do, know, and be like when they leave elementary school?" Even though you may have a general sense of the answer, putting this in writing can be difficult! State your answer in broad terms, keeping in mind that you want to describe student outcomes in terms of the whole elementary school experience in physical education, and not one specific unit (such as soccer). It helps to remind yourself of the overall categories or framework areas underlying your curriculum's organization. For example, what should students know, be able to do, and be like as regards manipulative skills? nonmanipulative skills? Do you expect students to think critically to solve problems? What do you want them to value about physical education and activity?

An example of some elementary course outcomes designed down from NASPE's program outcomes is shown in Figure 1.8. As you can see, these broad statements extend NASPE's broader K-12 statements to give them meaning in terms of one specific elementary course. Whether you work from outcomes developed by NASPE, your state, or the district, the course outcomes you develop, or design down, for your K-6 curriculum should reflect the K-12 program level.

What Else Can Help With This Process?

Although designing these course outcomes will take time, the hours you spend can be stimulating and thought-provoking. Here are some hints to help you in this process.

1. Work with another physical education teacher(s). Two or three of you can bounce ideas off each other and discuss them. Working also with teachers at the middle or junior high school and high school course levels helps ensure that course outcomes complement each other and are not unnecessarily repeated at each level. Working with other teachers, when it is possible, often helps make your final product that much stronger.
2. Keep in mind that the number of contact days you have with students affects what you can expect of them. Your course outcomes statements will be broad; still, the number of times you instruct students weekly may influence how students develop.
3. Realize that producing good outcomes statements probably won't happen in a day, so don't feel bad if you can't polish them off quickly. Put them aside and return to them at another time. Reflect, revise, reflect!
4. Get feedback. Once you have a good outline, show it to your district supervisor, principal, other physical educators, and perhaps even a

NASPE outcomes program A physically educated person	Sample elementary course outcomes By the end of elementary school, the students should be able to
HAS learned skills necessary to perform a variety of physical activities.	1. design, refine, and perform movement sequences that focus on the use of one or more concepts of body awareness, space awareness, effort, and relationships, when alone and with others; 2. modify performance of skills using the different movement concepts of body awareness, space awareness, effort, and relationships; 3. competently use individual locomotion, nonlocomotor, and manipulative skills in a variety of appropriate practice situations; 4. design, refine, and perform movement sequences that use combinations of locomotor and nonlocomotor skills, when alone and with others; 5. competently combine various locomotor, nonlocomotor, and manipulative skills in order to play or to design small-group games.
IS physically fit.	1. work toward achieving and maintaining physical fitness; 2. participate in appropriate assessment of personal fitness levels.
DOES participate regularly in physical activity.	1. participate in health-enhancing physical activity at least three times weekly, either in or out of school.
KNOWS the implications of and the benefits from involvement in physical activity.	1. recognize the commitment and benefits associated with participation and improvement in physical fitness and skill development activities; 2. recognize the safety factors associated with participating in physical activities in and out of physical education class; 3. apply cues and principles relative to specific manipulative skills to improve skill performance; 4. apply strategies and rules necessary for safe and skillful involvement in game situations; 5. understand the basic concepts of physical fitness and personal wellness and the relationship between the two; 6. recognize the opportunities for enjoyment, self-expression, and communication that can be found through participation in physical activities.
VALUES physical activity and its contributions to a healthful lifestyle.	1. exhibit respect and consideration toward the self and others as needed for successful participation in physical activities in and out of physical education class; 2. appreciate the relationships and benefits that result from working and participating with others in and out of physical education class; 3. respect the role physical activity plays in achieving and maintaining personal fitness and well-being; 4. cherish the feelings that can result from regular and successful participation in physical activity, in and out of school.

Figure 1.8 *Sample elementary course outcomes.*

classroom teacher or some parents with whom you work well. These people offer a different perspective, and can help you make sure that the outcomes say what you mean for them to say. They can inform you whether the outline is straightforward and easy to understand.

Once you have completed writing the course outcomes, give them to your superintendent, supervisor, principal, parents, and classroom teachers in your school. Use them at the beginning of the year to let parents know about the curriculum. Print them in the school newsletter. If you have a school handbook for parents, include them there. It is to your advantage to let others know what you are doing.

Designing Down to Unit Outcomes

Once you have designed your course outcomes, you can use them to design down to the next level, the unit level (see Figure 1.9). Here, you start getting quite specific by delineating how students will move toward the course outcomes you have already designed. This is where you really start seeing the course outcomes in action.

Why Is This Important?

Unit outcomes are the integral link—the bridge—between the future (course outcomes) and the present (lesson outcomes). Without this bridge, students would end up participating in a number of units and activities that had no particular reason for being in the curriculum other than a teacher's whim, the season of the year, or available equipment. Defining unit outcomes helps you to look critically at what you are teaching and determine if it really helps your students progress.

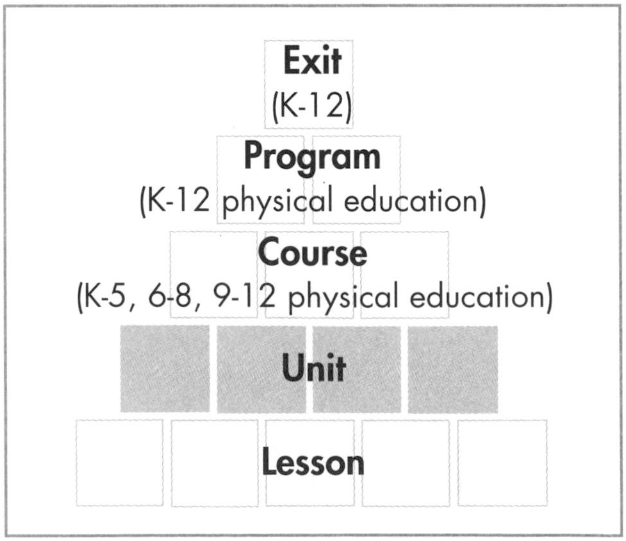

Figure 1.9 *Designing down to unit outcomes.*

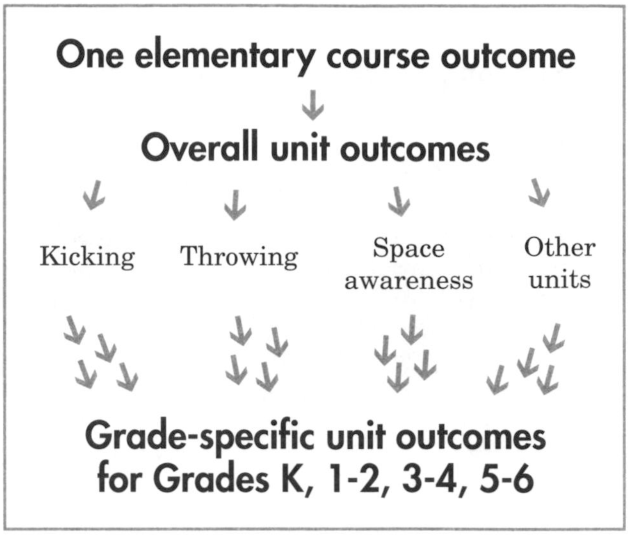

Figure 1.10 *Several overall and grade-specific unit outcomes can be developed from one course outcome.*

Where Do I Begin?

There are two levels of unit outcomes: the first is the overall unit outcomes and the second is grade-specific unit outcomes. An *overall unit outcome* describes what students should be able to do for a specific unit (e.g., soccer, gymnastics, throwing and catching) by the end of elementary school. *Grade-specific unit outcomes* further define overall unit outcomes by outlining what students should be able to do in that unit at specific grade levels. Thus, from each course outcome, a number of overall unit and grade-specific outcomes can be developed (see Figure 1.10).

To design your overall unit outcomes, take one of your elementary course outcomes and ask yourself, What does this outcome mean in terms of my kicking unit? my gymnastics unit? my other units? What should students be able to do in these units—relative to this course outcome—before they leave my school? After going through the process of developing overall unit outcomes from each course outcome, you will have a list of outcomes specific to each unit in your curriculum. Examples of overall unit outcomes designed down from two particular course outcomes in Figure 1.8 are shown in Figure 1.11.

Next to be developed are grade-specific unit outcomes. Here, break down an overall unit outcome *by grade level* (K, 1-2, 3-4, and 5-6) into the specific skills and competencies students should accomplish. The grade-specific unit outcomes will directly affect the lesson outcomes that you develop from them. Figure 1.12 shows a listing of some sample grade-specific unit outcomes designed from one overall unit outcome for a unit of soccer (or kicking and punting). These examples do not include all the grade-specific unit outcomes for this unit; certainly, others would be derived from additional overall unit outcomes you have designed.

Note that listing outcomes by grade level doesn't necessarily mean that all students in a class will achieve them in these specific grades; some children will reach them sooner than others. As a teacher using a developmentally appropriate curriculum, it is important to remember that the grade-specific outcomes you develop are only guidelines as to when most students should achieve the outcomes. Each student should be taught to his or her actual skill level, no matter what the grade number. Remember also that the given grade-specific outcomes are only examples. Your outcomes will vary, depending on your students, how often you see them for physical education, for what length of time you instruct, and so forth.

Sample elementary course outcomes By the end of elementary school, the students should be able to	Sample overall unit outcomes By the end of elementary school, in the named unit the students should be able to
(HAS) 2. modify performance of skills using the different movement concepts of body awareness, space awareness, effort, and relationships;	Soccer—kick, dribble, and punt, using the force, pathways, and speed appropriate to the situation and necessary for control; dribble, kick, and pass, using a variety of relationships with others. Throwing and catching—throw a variety of objects (such as Frisbees, foam footballs), using the appropriate force and speed for accuracy and distance; vary relationships with others to throw and catch more successfully. Dribbling—dribble while using the force, pathways, and speed appropriate to the situation and necessary for control; vary relationships with others to participate more successfully in dribbling activities.
(HAS) 5. competently combine various locomotor, nonlocomotor, and manipulative skills in order to play or to design small-group games.	Soccer—design and play a small-group game incorporating the skills of kicking and passing, receiving, collecting, and punting to keep the ball away from defenders and move it toward a goal area. Throwing and catching—design and play small-group (e.g., 2-on-2) keep-away type games using the skills of throwing, catching, and running to keep the ball away from a defender and move it toward a desired position. Dribbling—design and play a small-group game using the skills of dribbling, throwing, and catching to keep the ball away from a defender and move it toward a goal area.

Figure 1.11 *Sample overall unit outcomes designed down from course outcomes.*

Sample elementary course outcome	Sample overall unit outcome	Sample grade-specific unit outcomes
By the end of elementary school, the students should be able to	By the end of elementary school, in the named unit the students should be able to	By the end of Grades 5-6 the students should be able to
(HAS) 2. modify performance of skills using the different movement concepts of body awareness, space awareness, effort, and relationships.	Soccer—kick, dribble, and punt, using the force, pathways, and speed appropriate to the situation and necessary for control; dribble, kick, and pass, using a variety of relationships with others.	• dribble and change speeds at the signal, • dribble with a group in a boundaried area, without losing control of the ball and avoiding contact with others or defenders, • use the inside of the foot to dribble and kick a leading pass to a partner, and • use the force necessary to punt a ball to targets at varying distances.
		By the end of Grades 3-4 the students should be able to
		• dribble while changing pathways and directions at the signal, • dribble in a group in a boundaried area without losing control of the ball and colliding with others, • use the force necessary to punt a ball as high and as far as possible, and • dribble and then kick the ball to a large target area from a distance of choice, using the instep.
		By the end of Grades 1-2 the students should be able to
		• dribble and slowly jog around stationary obstacles while using the inside of each foot, and • run up to and kick a stationary ball as far as possible with the instep.
		By the end of kindergarten the students should be able to
		• walk and "roll" the ball forward using the inside of each foot.

Figure 1.12 *Sample grade-specific outcomes for one overall unit outcome in soccer.*

What Can Help With This Process?

Developing your overall and grade-specific unit outcomes will take some time and effort. Here are some hints that may help you in this process:

1. Set realistic overall and grade-specific unit outcomes for the number of contact days you have with your students. For example, if you see students 2 days a week, it may not be feasible for them to combine kicking, passing, and receiving skills to design and play a small-group game by the end of elementary school. Perhaps they will only be able to master putting together a few skills. View this as a limited result not of your teaching but of the time you have to work within. Let's face it: It doesn't make sense to expend your time and effort on designing down if you create an unrealistic framework for teaching. (Perhaps you can use this limitation to advantage as a justification for allotting physical education more contact hours.)
2. Don't reinvent the wheel. You can modify some of the overall unit outcomes that you develop for use with a variety of units. For example, perhaps for one unit you expect students to be able to design and play a small-group game, using kicking skills and dribbling and throwing, and another using dribbling and throwing skills. See if you can adapt the overall unit framework you develop for your kicking unit to fit your dribbling and throwing unit as well. Another example would be overall unit outcomes for behaviors and relationships with others: Very likely you would expect these outcomes to apply to all your units.
3. Group together all the overall unit outcomes by unit before you begin to develop grade-specific unit outcomes. This way, all the outcomes pertinent to each specific unit are in one place, instead of spread among the different course outcomes. For example, once you have the overall unit outcomes for kicking, list them together (by computer, if possible) and then turn to developing the grade-specific unit outcomes for kicking.
4. The task of creating outcomes at the unit level probably takes longer than any other step in the designing-down process. It may take all year to develop all your grade-specific unit outcomes, especially if you work on each unit as it occurs during the year. That's OK: It isn't an overnight process. Once you begin designing down, you may even find it necessary to revise something. This is part of the process!
5. Don't think that you have to throw away your entire present curriculum. You want to keep an open, clear mind and not limit your thinking to what you are doing now. One reason to look at course outcomes in terms of each unit, even if it seems repetitious, is to ensure covering all angles. That way nothing falls through the cracks.
6. Use a computer, if possible, so you can revise your writing, separate the outcomes by unit, and experiment with ease.

Where Do I Go From Here?

When you have developed the overall and grade-specific unit outcomes, give yourself a pat on the back—the hardest part is over! Use the grade-specific unit outcomes to communicate with parents about what children will learn in physical education for the next nine weeks, for example. Perhaps list the grade-specific unit outcomes students will be working on and insert this into students' report cards, a letter to parents, or the school newsletter. You also can use these outcomes as a basis for formal assessment. In the second part of this guide you will read about specific performance and portfolio tasks to assess grade-specific unit outcomes. And not least, you can use these unit outcomes to design down to the lesson level—the last step in the process.

Designing Down to Lesson Outcomes

The last step in the designing-down process is developing lesson outcomes (see Figure 1.13). Lesson outcomes are the most specific level, relating directly to the teaching you do every day with your students. In this section, you will find information to help you design down to the lesson level, including how the "learnable pieces" in the second part of this guide fit into this process.

Why Is This Important?

Designing down to the lesson level assures you that class content each day helps move students in the intended direction. There will be a purpose planned for each of your lesson outcomes. It's that final step toward putting into action all your plans.

Where Do I Begin?

Developing lesson outcomes involves further defining your grade-specific unit outcomes in realistic terms of what your students can achieve in a

(30-minute) lesson. Put another way, if someone asked "What did your students really learn today?" you should be able to answer in very specific terms: that is, your lesson outcome or outcomes. Lesson outcomes should clearly specify the focus of your instruction and your students' learning, whether it be related to a physical skill, cognitive concept, or student attitude or behavior.

To aid you in developing lesson outcomes at each grade level, you will find what are called *learnable pieces* listed later in this guide for each of the different themes (e.g., kicking, throwing, space awareness, cardiorespiratory fitness). A learnable piece, like a lesson outcome, is a specific focus for what students can realistically achieve in a lesson.

In discussing lesson outcomes Graham (1992) states, "'Children will learn to volley a ball' is not only general but unrealistic for 30-minute lessons. [But] 'the children will learn to bend their knees as they receive and volley a ball' provides a specific guideline for observation" (p. 24). Specifying learnable pieces (e.g., bending the knees) gives the children and you something specific to practice, focus on, and observe.

Consider another example of how a learnable piece works, using the theme of throwing and catching (e.g., a softball unit). You wouldn't expect that children should be able to catch different objects with perfect form as a lesson outcome in Grades 1-2. These youngsters should, however, be expected to work on the learnable pieces for that skill: the ability to have the thumbs together if the ball is above the waist and the pinkies together if it is below the waist. Thus, an appropriate lesson outcome or objective might be "Students will learn to put their fingers in the correct position (thumbs together if above waist, pinkies together if below waist) when catching appropriate objects," rather than "Children will learn to catch different balls."

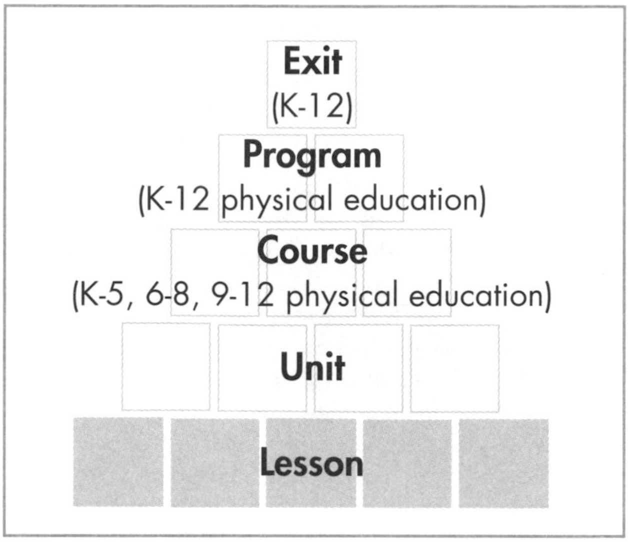

Figure 1.13 *Designing down to lesson outcomes.*

What Can Help With This Process?

Developing lesson outcomes, or objectives, in terms of learnable pieces requires us to think much more specifically. In some cases, it requires thinking differently about what we are teaching and what students are learning in each lesson. To aid you in the process of developing these lesson outcomes, here are some hints.

1. Don't be an "objective junkie." Don't accumulate more lesson outcomes in one unit than you can reasonably instruct toward or students can reasonably achieve. Just as you should hold realistic expectations for how many grade-specific unit outcomes can be achieved at the different grade levels, you must do the same for the lesson outcomes in a particular unit. Hopefully, you will have a match between the number of lesson and grade-specific unit outcomes you can achieve—if you were realistic at the higher level of outcomes you set.

If you do find that you have written more lesson outcomes than can be achieved in the number of days you have for that unit, you'll need either to add days for the unit or to cut back lesson outcomes. If you choose to decrease the number of lesson outcomes, you still will need to make sure that your grade-specific and overall unit outcomes reflect this lesser number. Although it may be difficult, holding yourself and your students accountable for only what you can realistically achieve is a key to having a meaningful program and achieving what you expect.

2. Children should not be expected to master a large number of learnable pieces in each lesson. Try to have your objectives cover only one or two learnable pieces in a lesson, rather than to overload students with information and give them more than they can handle at one time.

For example, the learnable pieces for overhand throwing at Grades 1-2 include

- side to target
- down, back, and up
- hand up

- step with the opposite foot, and
- throw hard.

It would be an instructional nightmare to teach students all five learnable pieces in one lesson—or even in five lessons. It is more realistic to introduce these various learnable pieces to students at different times during the first and second grade, giving them ample time to practice and master each. This isn't to say that you should never give students two pieces in one lesson; whether you would depends on the specific learnable pieces and on your students. After your students have practiced and mastered a specific piece, you might revisit it, expecting them to show you this later in combination with another learnable piece. These are guidelines for working with learnable pieces: unfortunately, there isn't one specific answer to the questions of how many and for how long. Only you can answer these, guided by your students, situation, and teaching style.

3. After developing your lesson outcomes, be flexible and ready to change them when necessary. For example, once you begin teaching students in a specific unit, you may find you have assigned too many lesson outcomes for each grade level. Or, perhaps students master the lesson outcomes faster than you had expected. Be open to adjusting the time you spend on a particular lesson and unit, according to your students' needs. You can never go wrong when you think first of what and how your students are doing! Also, keep notes on how your students are doing with the lesson and unit outcomes: These will come in handy when you teach the same unit the following year.

Where Do I Go From Here?

Believe it or not, that is the whole process of designing down! Once you've done it, not only can you treat yourself for a job well done, but you can also use what you have developed to instruct. Later you can assess students' progress toward these outcomes. In the following section you'll be introduced to the performance assessments of portfolio and performance tasks, which tie in closely with outcomes-related curriculums. You'll also find ideas to simplify assessing students in both lesson and unit outcomes in realistic and meaningful ways. Furthermore, you'll find specific examples of performance and portfolio tasks developed for each theme for the different grade levels. Hopefully, you will be able to easily implement these, making your outcomes-related curriculum complete.

CHAPTER 2 Performance Assessments

To no one's surprise, ever more educators today are calling for more meaningful and worthwhile assessment methods (Hebert, 1992; Wiggins, 1992). Physical educators are not alone in asking for more practical, relevant assessment tools to measure how students apply knowledge and skills. While not a cure-all, performance assessments are a possible solution to many of the questions that teachers have regarding assessment.

What Are Performance Assessments?

Performance assessments are an authentic, practical way of determining whether students are progressing toward the outcomes they are expected to achieve. They can provide a rich picture of what students actually know and can do, relevant to the outcomes that figure importantly for success later in life. These new forms of assessment complement an outcomes-related curriculum and recent terminology has been developed to describe them, terms that have implications for us as physical educators: *authentic performance assessments*, *performance tasks*, *portfolio tasks*, and *rubrics*. Each of these are explained now in more detail.

Authentic Performance Assessments

Performance assessments are measures in which students actually demonstrate the behaviors that the teacher wants to assess (Meyer, 1991). For example, if a classroom teacher wants to find out how well students write short stories, she would ask them to write a short story—not simply to take a multiple-choice test on writing skills—in order to most accurately evaluate their skills. If an art teacher wants students to be able to correctly form a pottery bowl, then a performance assessment would have the students actually make the bowl—not answer questions about or write down the process on paper.

In physical education a simplified example of a performance assessment might be this: You want to find out how well students can throw a ball overhand. To make this assessment you would have students actually throw balls overhand. Realistically, there aren't many other methods to find out whether students can do this. In these three examples—writing, making pottery, and overhand throwing—the focus is on having the students actually demonstrate the skills the teacher wants to assess.

Although the concept of performance assessments is not entirely new to physical educators, what is innovative is the concept of *authentic performance assessment*. An assessment is seen as authentic when the student completes or demonstrates the desired behavior in a more real-life situation, rather than in a contrived context (Meyer, 1991). It requires that students apply what they have learned to situations that relate directly to their present or future everyday life. Thus, an authentic context is one that is relevant, meaningful, and motivating to the student—not something done just to "get it over with," or "because they have to." An authentic performance assessment is itself a part of the whole learning process. It is not tacked on to the end of instruction with results that may or may not actually mean something.

Authentic performance assessments are very different from such traditional forms of performance assessments as fitness, skills, and multiple-choice rules tests, which ask that students perform in controlled, isolated contexts (see Figure 2.1). This is not to say that traditional tests have no place or purpose in an educational setting; however, many people now question the overreliance on these assessments and whether they even measure how students are moving toward broad educational outcomes. Today, many educators are looking at assessments of performance and portfolio tasks as ways to assess students' progress in physical education more authentically.

Performance Assessments

Traditional	Authentic
Fitness tests	Performance tasks (including student-designed games and sequences)
Skills tests	Portfolio tasks
Rules tests	

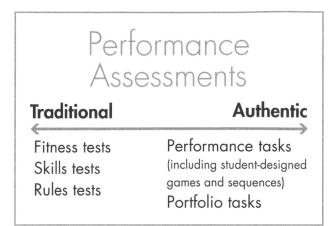

Figure 2.1 *Examples of authentic and traditional assessments in physical education.*

Performance Tasks

A *performance task* is a type of performance assessment in which students physically perform the skill or desired product that is to be assessed. In physical education, skill and fitness tests are examples of performance tasks that traditionally have been used. Even with these, however, there is a call for more relevant and authentic performance tasks that teachers can easily use in their physical education programs.

As an example of an authentic performance task in elementary physical education, let's say that you want to assess students' abilities to move in time with music in a 4/4 meter. Rather than requiring all students to learn and perform a specific folk dance that you assign, a more authentic context would be having groups of students choose the way they would like to move to music that they, possibly along with you, choose. To fulfill the general criteria you set (for how many counts students must move, the number of locomotor movements to use, etc.), some students might design and perform a jump-rope routine, others a dance to rap, a Harlem Globetrotters basketball routine, or an aerobic exercise routine. You allow students to demonstrate the desired skills in a context that is more meaningful and interesting to them. Later in this guide you will find additional examples and practical strategies for using performance tasks in physical education.

Portfolio Tasks

A *portfolio task* is another type of performance assessment, which is part of a collection of student work gathered over a period of time, usually a school year. Think of it as a scrapbook of their learning. Included in a portfolio might be specific tasks of students' work in and outside of class, attitude surveys, fitness test scores, photos of students taken in physical education, and anecdotal records that you add.

Teachers can use portfolios to check their students' understanding and progress, find out what students are thinking, communicate with parents, and evaluate the effectiveness of their teaching and curriculum (Frazier & Paulson, 1992; Schiemer, 1993; Wolf, LeMahieu, & Eresh, 1992). Portfolios have long been used in arts programs, and are being used increasingly by other classroom teachers. By planning and structuring assignments carefully, physical educators can use portfolios to effectively assess students, especially in the cognitive and affective domains. You will find more specific ways to do this in Part II.

Rubrics

A *rubric* is a scale of criteria that explains in detail the possible levels of performance for a portfolio or performance task. A rubric usually has three to five different levels; a 3-point scale, for example, might consist of criteria at levels of "needs improvement," "acceptable," and "exemplary." A student's performance on a task would be compared to the criteria at each level to determine her particular level. As you can imagine, the more specific and detailed the rubric is for a task, the better.

As an example of a rubric, you might give third-grade students a portfolio task asking them to list what hints to remember to kick a ball successfully. Their performance could be measured by a 3-point rubric, such as the one in Figure 2.2.

Implications of Performance Assessments

Authentic performance assessment measures, including portfolio and performance tasks, are important, meaningful methods of measuring students' progress toward real-life outcomes that can't always be measured by standardized tests. Educators increasingly see these measures used for assessment. It makes sense that we physical educators also explore the merits and uses of these tools in the gymnasium. Performance and portfolio tasks are explored next in terms of elementary physical education to give you information that will relate directly to using the examples you will find later in this guide.

Exemplary

- Student clearly described the elements critical to the performance of the skill.
- Student used appropriate terminology and vocabulary.
- Student provided at least two appropriate examples.

Acceptable

- Student provided partial information on the elements critical to skill performance.
- Student's responses reflected weak or nonexistent use of appropriate terminology and vocabulary.
- Student provided at least one appropriate example for each category.

Needs Improvement

- Student displayed minimal use of critical elements, terminology, and vocabulary, or did not respond at all.
- Examples provided by the student were not appropriate.

Figure 2.2 *Example of a scoring rubric for a portfolio task.*

Note. *From "Beyond the Traditional Skills Test" by S. Schiemer, 1993,* Teaching Elementary Physical Education, *4(2), p. 10. Copyright 1993 by Human Kinetics. Reprinted by permission.*

Using Performance Tasks for Assessment

Good teaching is inseparable from good assessing.
Wiggins, 1992

Even though assessment, whether performance or portfolio tasks, sounds good in theory, as teachers we know that it's not always easy to put into practice. Let's face it—assessing children is just not easy when you teach 10 classes a day, have no breaks between these classes, and see your students only 1 or 2 days a week. Not to mention that perhaps you teach outdoors, without a desk at which to sit and record results of assessment. And probably you don't have much planning time to work with the results. Despite these real problems, however, the solution is not to discard assessment altogether, as unfortunately has happened in many situations, but rather to find worthwhile alternative ways to assess in the time you have. Performance tasks are among these alternative measures.

Why Is This Important?

Given the increased emphasis on accountability handed us by legislators, parents, and the community, physical educators must explore and begin to use different methods of assessment. Gone are the days when using physical fitness tests sufficed to justify and account for our programs. If we truly want to prepare physically educated students, we must use other newer means of assessment, such as performance tasks, to demonstrate to administrators, parents, the community, and ourselves that the students in our charge actually are learning the necessary course, unit, and lesson outcomes.

Besides demonstrating your accountability, using performance tasks can help you make informed decisions about instruction, decisions that ensure your teaching is based upon the real, not presumed, needs of your students. Using performance tasks essentially keeps you from teaching in a vacuum without ever knowing what your instruction is—or isn't—actually accomplishing. The results from these assessment tasks can be used as a more meaningful basis of communication with parents about their child's progress in physical education. These assessments can help you make decisions about your overall program and teaching effectiveness.

Because performance tasks are designed from, and along with, the important outcomes you are teaching toward, they will look very similar to your instruction. You will be "teaching to the test," but that's OK, given that authentic assessment tasks really are an extension of what you are teaching. You want students to know and be able to do the very tasks you use to assess them. Performance tasks, in reality, allow assessment to become an integral part of (not apart from) your instruction. Later we provide some strategies to make using performance tasks more manageable and easier than you thought possible!

Where Do I Begin?

We suggest that you begin by using the performance tasks that fit the level that is most comfortable and realistic for you and your situation.

For example, it may be impractical to assess all your students at the end of each unit of instruction, at least when you first begin using the tasks. To help you decide on how often and what grade levels to assess, think about the following options:

1. Assess only one or two specific grade levels when you start using the performance tasks, until you

get used to using and working with them. Think about assessing the same grade level(s) that your state Department of Education specifies if it has a statewide testing program.

2. When you can, use one performance task to assess outcomes from more than one unit. For example, instead of giving a formal performance task from each of the themes of rolling, balancing, and weight transfer, give one performance task that applies skills in all three areas. Many concepts from the themes of effort, space awareness, body awareness, and relationships can be combined with tasks from other skills.
3. Instead of giving students a performance task to assess achievement for each unit, alternate between a performance task for one unit and a portfolio task for the next.

Once you decide at what grade level(s), how often, and which specific performance tasks to assess, you will need to develop a rubric, or scoring scale, to use in evaluating these tasks. Here are some hints to help in this process.

Hints for Developing Performance Task Rubrics

In working with performance tasks, both creating the task and defining the rubric for it are difficult, and it's debatable which one takes more time or effort. One certainty, however, is that without clearly defined criteria your performance task will not be workable or worthwhile.

We suggest that you first design three, rather than five, levels of scoring criteria for each performance task you use for assessment: outstanding, acceptable, and deficient. Then decide the characteristics you want for each of these levels (a rubric varies from teacher to teacher, depending on values and what he or she expects from students). To aid you in developing the scoring criteria for each rubric, we have given "rubric clues" for each of the theme performance and portfolio tasks you will find later in this guide. These clues are meant to stimulate your thinking about how and at what level you would classify a student's performance.

For example, the Grades 5-6 performance task for the theme of kicking (see p. 128) involves a small group (2-on-2, 3-on-3) of students of similar skill level who design and play a game using the skills of kicking and punting toward a goal area. An example of a 3-point scoring rubric, based on the rubric clues for this task, is shown in Figure 2.3.

Assessment Rubric: Kicking and Punting (Grade 6)

Outstanding. The student clearly and consistently demonstrates the ability to

- cooperate with others and help create the rules and boundaries for the game,
- work with others in a (physically and verbally) positive manner,
- abide by group decisions when playing,
- use the offensive strategies of keeping the body between the ball and the defender and of creating space by moving to get open, and
- use the defensive strategy of keeping the body between the opponent and goal.

Acceptable. The student usually shows the ability overall to

- cooperate with others and help create the rules and boundaries for the game,
- abide by and accept decisions of the group (any challenging is done in a nonthreatening manner),
- keep the body between the ball and the defender and to move to pass and receive the ball, and
- keep the body between the opponent and goal.

Deficient. The student

- does not cooperate with others in a positive manner,
- contributes barely or not at all to developing the rules and boundaries for the game,
- has difficulty in abiding by and accepting decisions made by the group, and may interact with others in a nonpositive manner,
- when on offense, is consistently unable to (or doesn't try to) use the offensive strategies of keeping the body between the ball and the opponent or of moving to open spaces, and
- when on defense, is consistently unable to keep the body between the opponent and goal.

Figure 2.3 *Sample scoring rubric for a student-designed game.*

In this example, students are held accountable not only for acceptable work toward physical skills, but also for their social skills. Outstanding social skills coupled with poor physical skills do not gain a student an "outstanding" effort; conversely, neither do outstanding physical skills coupled with poor social skills. As a teacher you will need to determine what is outstanding, acceptable, or deficient work.

A different scoring rubric might be developed for the performance task of students who design, refine, and perform a movement sequence. In this example using the theme of space awareness in Grades 3-4 (see p. 57), students are asked to design, refine, and perform a movement sequence with a partner using at least two directions and two levels, as well as a definite beginning and ending shape. The rubric clues focus on meeting the predefined criteria for the sequence and on a smooth performance. Figure 2.4 is an example of a scoring rubric for this task.

Assessment Rubric: Space Awareness (Grades 3-4)

Outstanding. The sequence clearly shows

- two (different) directions and two levels,
- a definite beginning and ending,
- excellent refinement: no visible breaks in continuity and smooth transitions between movements.

Acceptable. The sequence shows

- one or two different directions or levels,
- a beginning and ending shape, although they may not be held long enough,
- an attempt at refining the sequence: breaks in continuity and smoothness may appear by one or both partners.

Deficient. The sequence

- lacks any planned directions, levels, or a beginning and ending shape, and
- no or few attempts have been made to refine the sequence: One or both partners have repeated losses of execution, smoothness, or memory.

Figure 2.4 *Sample scoring rubric for a student-designed sequence.*

These are some hints you can use when designing your rubrics:

1. Decide what errors are most justifiable for assigning a student's performance to one or another level. It may be easiest to first ask what constitutes an outstanding performance of a task. Use each of the clues to flesh this out. Next ask yourself what you consider definitely unacceptable, then acceptable. Keep in mind the details. What happens, for example, if a student shows acceptable work for one clue, such as physical skills, but is deficient in another, such as cooperation and social skills? Do students need to be acceptable in both areas to receive an overall acceptable rating? Anticipate these situations and determine your answers beforehand.
2. When designing criteria, be as specific as you can: Another teacher reading your rubric should be able to rate your students' performance in the same way you would. This helps ensure that you are as objective as possible, so that each student's work is judged by the same criteria.
3. If you really get stuck, experiment. If you like the idea of using the performance tasks but just aren't sure how to develop criteria at each level, try either to begin by designing a criteria with only two levels or to design a rubric and make it a pilot test before you begin using it "for real." It may be a year until you teach that unit again, but it certainly will ease the pressure on you and your students.
4. "Recycle" rubrics whenever possible. You may find you can use the basic criteria of a rubric for more than one assessment task. For example, the task of designing and playing a small-group game, such as with kicking, is also used in this guide as a basis for performance assessments in the themes of throwing, dribbling, volleying, and striking (at Grades 5-6 level). Criteria you develop also can be used to assess students in other areas. You can approach the tasks involving movement sequences similarly. When you ask students to design, refine, and perform a movement sequence, you may find that the criteria you've developed for one task apply as a skeleton on which to develop criteria for another.

Hints for Assessing Performance Tasks

After designing the task's rubric, you're ready to assess! Although it takes some time to get used to performance tasks, before long you will come to view them as an important part of your teaching—not something that just "takes up too much time." Some strategies to simplify assessment and make it more practical follow.

1. *Use performance tasks for informal, as well as formal, assessment.* For example, you will probably want to assess students' progress towards grade-specific unit outcomes at the end of a particular unit of instruction, but there are other uses for the tasks, as well.

- Use a performance task as an informal preassessment as you begin instruction in a particular unit. Say you are beginning a dribbling (basketball) unit. You have a vague idea of your second graders' skill level, but you're not exactly sure—it's been almost a year since you taught them this unit. By observing them in the given performance task of dribbling first with one hand, then the other, while standing in self-space, you can quickly ascertain their skill level. You could reassess them formally, at the end of the unit, using the same task.
- Consider using a performance task as a quick preassessment a day or two before you begin a unit. This sounds like added work, but consider: We tend to begin units on Monday and end them on Friday. Often that Friday is given to play or choice time. Why not use the last 6 or so minutes of that class to have students quickly do the performance assessment for their grade level for the next unit? Of course, this may not work for every task, but where it is appropriate not only will you know better where to begin instruction the following Monday, but you will be able to answer students' ever-present question "What are we going to do on Monday?"

2. *Use assessment stations when possible to simplify and quicken assessments.* By using stations you can focus attention on a few students at a time, instead of on the whole class. Take the performance task for Grades 1-2 for the theme of jumping and landing. It asks that students jump forward over a self-turned short jump rope while in self-space. When formally assessing second graders doing this task, you could easily set up different fitness stations to music. One might be where students jog around the blacktop area or gym; one could be for long-rope jumping and another for short-rope jumping using different tricks (introduced earlier in class, and posted on cards); another might be a jump-the-shot station. Students could stop when you stop the music, and rotate stations when the music begins again. With five stations you can easily assess about five students at your assessment station: The students probably won't even know they are being assessed. If necessary, have a parent help monitor students at the other stations.

If you can't use stations and students are working in a large group, consider giving four to six students pinnies to wear, flags to stick in their belts, or some other markers to help you keep an eye on them as they move about. When their assessment is done, they can pass along a pinnie or flag to another student.

3. *When recording results, write down the names of students who can't perform the task, rather than the students who can.* Those whom you record performed at a deficient level; the other students (minus any whom you marked as absent) performed the task at an acceptable level. (This should simplify your work.) If your scoring rubric (scale) has more than two levels (e.g., outstanding, acceptable, deficient), you may want to mark only those students who perform at either extreme; the others, minus absentees, would be at the acceptable level. You can use a simple form, such as the one in Figure 2.5 (see Figure 2.6 for a blank copy). An alternative is to have one box for each of your rubric criteria levels, and write students' names in the appropriate box as you observe their performances.

4. *Allow yourself enough time to assess.* Don't feel pressured or wait to get it all in at the last minute. Plan some extra time in each unit for assessment. Remember that some tasks may take more than one class period to assess. It would be difficult, for example, for a group of four students to design, refine, and perform a movement sequence combining locomotor and nonlocomotor movements in one lesson (see locomotor skills theme in chapter 5, Grades 3-4, for a complete task). Designing and refining this routine can be part of your instruction; you would then assess the students during the performing segment.

5. *Have students write their games or sequences on paper* for any performance tasks requiring these designs. These written versions can be references when you assess their actual performances, and you can later add them to their portfolios.

Unit	Kicking	Kicking	Kicking
Rubric level	Class: Peebles	Class: Ketcham	Class: Samuel
Outstanding	Larry, Sue, Rosie, Dianna, Mark, Scott, George, Vicky, Manny, Harriet	Trinesha, Adjahnae, Barry	
Acceptable	(fill in all other names of students in class later, if desired)		
Deficient	Trent, Lisa	Johnny B.	
Absent	None	Marcus, John W.	

Figure 2.5 *Sample form for recording performance assessments.*

Unit			
Rubric level	Class:	Class:	Class:
Outstanding			
Acceptable			
Deficient			
Absent			

Figure 2.6 *Form for recording performance assessments.*

Once I've Assessed Students, Then What?

After you have assessed students' performances by the criteria outlined in your scoring rubric, you can use the results in various ways, depending on your needs and situation. You might use the results to alter future instruction or enter the specific results of the performance tasks into your students' portfolios. Entering the results can help you—and parents—easily track a student's performance. You can use a large graph to list each task throughout the year (make a master and copies of it): A parent or other volunteer can record the level at which each student performed the task on these graph sheets (see Figure 2.7). Figure 2.8 is a blank form that you can use.

If you don't use portfolios, you might wish to create a master form listing each of the performance tasks students completed during the past 9 weeks, as well as their levels of work in particular tasks (see Figure 2.9). This information can be included on students' report cards. Again, if this takes too much time, use a volunteer or computer to help you fill out the forms. It may be that all you need to do is check off boxes to show how well the students performed, adding a comment as necessary.

You may wish to use the assessments as a basis for assigning grades. You will find assessments can help you give more specific information to parents about a child's performance in physical education.

It may take time before the tasks become a normal part of your teaching routine that you adapt to your situation, but, hopefully, you soon will view performance tasks for assessment as a necessary and important part of teaching—one that you can't do without!

Using Portfolio Tasks for Assessment

Portfolios are being used by more and more classroom teachers as an authentic form of assessment showing examples of students' learning during the school year. They are seen as meaningful not only for teachers but also for students, who get to see the improvement they made over time. Physical educators can take advantage of these benefits that their colleagues have discovered through using portfolios. By collecting portfolio tasks completed by students, as well as such other information as fitness scores, performance task scores, and anecdotal records, physical educators will have a useful assessment tool.

Why Is This Important?

Two important benefits of using portfolios and portfolio tasks in physical education are that they can become meaningful educational tools for your students and also helpful means for you to gather information. By assessing the tasks students submit to their portfolios, you have a basis for charting the progress of individual students, gauging the understanding of a particular concept by a class as a whole, and revising your following day's instruction to more effectively meet your students' needs. Portfolios are also effective tools for communicating with parents, evaluating teaching, and making your program more accountable and familiar to others.

Where Do I Begin?

Using portfolios in physical education presents unique challenges to the physical education specialist. For example, the many students you may see in one day can make assessing large numbers of portfolios problematic. Physical educators without an indoor teaching area may have difficulty finding a place where students can work on or even store portfolio tasks. And how can you find time to fit portfolio work into a 30-minute class period? Such logistical problems create the need for physical education teachers to adapt the idea of a portfolio to their specific setting. Next we present some strategies to help you solve some important concerns that you need to address before beginning to use the portfolio tasks as part of your instruction.

What Is a Portfolio Physically Made of? Because you want students to be able to collect and keep a variety of papers in their portfolios, it is important that they be sturdy enough to last over a year and large enough to handle many papers. Some classroom teachers have students bring in a common two-pocket folder; others give each student a regular or legal-size manila folder to use as a file (staple the sides closed if you wish). These can be ordered in quantity through the school. Allow students to personalize their folders by coloring them or gluing pictures on them. The folders can be reused by the same students the next year to save on costs. You can also use large (18×12-inch) pieces of construction paper, which, when folded in half, can hold numerous pieces of paper.

If possible, have both the folders and construction paper laminated so they hold up better. Also, make sure that the student's name (last name first) is written on the portfolio in a common, visible area

Student *Mark Manrove* Class *Sanders*

Grade *2*

Date	Performance task in unit	Rubric level O	A	D	Comments
9/10	Body awareness	✓			
10/18	Space awareness	✓			Moves well to open spaces.
11/20	Kicking		✓		Sometimes uses toe to dribble.
1/18	Throwing			✓	Doesn't keep side to target.

Figure 2.7 *Sample performance assessment record.*

Student ______________________ **Class** ______________________

Grade __________

Date	Performance task in unit	Rubric level			Comments
		O	A	D	

Figure 2.8 *Performance assessment record.*

Student ______________________ Class ________

Grade ______________

Dear Parent or Guardian: Below you will find the scores from assessments your child took during the past 9 weeks in physical education. If you wish to discuss any of these, I would be glad to meet with you. Please contact me at school, 333-3333.

Thank you, C. Hopple

Test	Description	Level of performance	Comments
Kicking	2-on-2 small-group game	O	Shows good teamwork!
Throwing	2-on-1 small-group game	A	
Dance	small-group sequence	A	

O = outstanding A = acceptable D = deficient; needs improvement

Figure 2.9 *Sample report card for performance task.*

(such as the upper left-hand corner) for easy reference by you and the student.

What Should Go In a Portfolio? You will find the portfolio handy for collecting not only work students do during class, but also their out-of-class or homework assignments. These can include journal logs, fitness logs, self-reflections, work sheets, and even notes a student wants to write to you. In addition, you may find the portfolio handy for keeping profiles of students' physical fitness scores, a checklist of the "learnable pieces" for different skills they have mastered, and records of the performance tasks you give during class.

How Can Portfolios Be Organized and Stored? Though you likely will have your own organizational habits that work best for your situation, we do suggest that you file the portfolios for each class alphabetically (by last name) in a crate or sturdy box with handles (for easy carrying). Mark each crate or box so students can easily find the one for their own class, and store the files on an accessible shelf or cabinet in your room or in the gymnasium.

How Can Students Submit Work for Their Portfolio? How you deal with the submitting of work to a portfolio may differ, depending on the protocols you set up with your students. Sue Schiemer, a physical education specialist in Bloomsburg, PA, uses portfolios extensively in her program and has her students submit their dated papers to her (as they begin class if there was a homework assignment, or at the end of class if there was an in-class assignment, such as developing a simple sequence and writing it down). She then clips or staples all the papers for each class together and later reviews them individually.

You may find it helpful to designate a large box or crate as an in-basket for portfolio work. Teach your students the protocol of putting their assignments, journal logs, or notes to you in this basket as they enter the teaching area; eventually, this will become an efficient process taking very little time. You may also want to put another in-basket on your desk so students can submit an item later if they forget to bring it to your class.

What Happens After Students Submit Work for Their Portfolios? We suggest that you first make provisions for assessing that work. Once you have done this, the work is ready to go in the portfolio itself. Again, you will most likely find the way that works best for you, but here are some ideas to get you started:

- File papers in a student's portfolio yourself.
- Enlist a parent, senior citizen, student, or other volunteer to file papers in the portfolio.
- Set aside the last few minutes of class to return students' papers; allow them to look them over and file them in their folders (have a student in each class retrieve and later return the box of files to where it is stored). Or, if you have a review, choice, or fitness day, instruct students in the protocol of coming up to you a few at a time, getting their papers, and filing them any time throughout the period (as long as they do it before the end of class).

How Many Portfolio Tasks Should I Give Students? The sample portfolio tasks given later in this guide are only suggestions for tasks at the different grade levels. They are there for you to pick and choose from; you certainly shouldn't feel that you need to give all of them to your students each year. Here are a few more options to keep in mind when using the portfolio tasks with your students:

- Begin using portfolios with only a few of your classes (for example, the fourth through sixth graders). Add the other classes as your experience grows in using portfolios.
- Don't feel that you have to give your students a portfolio task for each unit. Start with selected units or give a task for every other unit.
- Because a given portfolio task is often suggested for students in two grade levels (aside from kindergarten), consider assigning students in the fifth grade, for example, a portfolio task in one unit, and assigning students in the sixth grade a portfolio task in the next unit. Doing this keeps students from repeating the same portfolio task two years in a row, and it can also help with the amount of papers you assess or review at one time.
- Consider giving some of the tasks both before and after work in a specific unit, as a pre- and postassessment, to have an idea of how far students have progressed. This gives them a chance to see their improvement as well.

Are There Any Other Hints or Considerations for Working With Portfolios? Be sure to discuss the *portfolio protocols* you want students to use; make them a part of the routine. Change them as little as possible and make them as clear and simple to follow as possible. Discuss the confidentiality of each portfolio with students. Although privacy probably won't be a problem, assure students that what they write, especially in journals, is between you and them.

Hints for Developing Portfolio Task Rubrics

We suggest you assess the portfolio tasks according to three levels: outstanding, acceptable, and deficient. You as a teacher will need to decide for each portfolio task what constitutes work at each level. This rubric need not be extensive and involved; however, it should give you and others a clear picture of work criteria found at each level. As with the performance tasks, each of the portfolio tasks presented in this guide gives you specific rubric clues to use as a basis for making these decisions.

For example, let's take the Grades 1-2 portfolio task for the theme of jumping and landing (see p. 97). For this task, which we'll say is given to second graders at the end of the rope-jumping unit, students are asked to write hints to their friend Murgatroid. Murgatroid has never jumped rope before and needs some hints to improve as a short-rope jumper (Graham, 1992). Using the rubric clues that follow the task, you may decide to design your rubric similar to that shown in Figure 2.10.

You would then assess the level at which each student completes this portfolio task. As necessary, you may ask a student or two to explain their answers in order to see their reasoning. Depending on their answers, you may decide to give credit or not (perhaps these students were explaining a more advanced learnable piece). You, as the teacher, will decide what is acceptable and what is not. Here are a few more thoughts that may help you design and work with rubrics.

1. *Adapt the rubric clues to fit your situation.* Keep in mind that you may not want to work on all of the given rubric clues for a task. Perhaps you feel there are other criteria that belong in the

Assessment Rubric: Jumping and Landing (Grades 1-2)

Outstanding. The student can

- clearly name or describe three or more learnable pieces for short-rope jumping and
- use examples and terms appropriately.

Acceptable. The student can

- clearly name or describe two or three learnable pieces for short-rope jumping and
- give examples showing an overall use of appropriate terms, although there may be some errors.

Deficient. The student can

- name or describe one or no learnable pieces and
- use examples and terms with little appropriateness.

Figure 2.10 *Sample scoring rubric for a portfolio task.*

rubric. The process of designing a rubric and assessing a task isn't cut-and-dried; there aren't always right or wrong answers. You can and should adapt information to fit your situation. Only you can answer the question "What do I expect my students to know or be able to show by completing this task?" So don't hesitate to adapt the criteria to fit your program.

2. *Be ready to revise your criteria.* You may find that you need to revise your criteria at the three levels as you go along in the process. It's likely that you won't find the perfect rubric right away—working with this process takes some time and practice! It's just like teaching a new lesson: At first it is difficult, but it gets easier each time you present it.

3. *Begin with fewer levels.* In order to simplify the process until you feel more comfortable working with the rubrics, you may even consider creating only two levels of criteria—acceptable and deficient—by which to assess students.

Hints for Assessing Portfolio Tasks

Even though assessing students' portfolio tasks takes time, when it becomes part of your routine, you will view it as valuable and well worth the effort. In fact, once you start working with portfolios, you may wonder how you ever got along without them! So, to assess students' portfolio tasks efficiently, try these strategies.

1. *Don't assess every task in the portfolio.* Portfolios are an educational tool, not just an assessment tool. You may discover that it is not always important, or even helpful, to assess each piece of information in the portfolio.

For example, you might ask students to reflect at the beginning of the year on what they want to learn most in their physical education course. Or you might want to encourage them to "talk" to you midway through the year about how they feel they are doing in physical education. You would be interested in what they wrote, but assessing their statements individually would not be necessary or to the student's benefit. On the other hand, you should assess students on some portfolio tasks, such as those given in this guide. There are no cut-and-dried procedures for working with portfolios, though you will undoubtedly discover and use what is best for you and your students.

2. *Assess tasks as soon as possible after submission.* This way, you are most able to revise future lessons according to the students' needs, and students will receive feedback while they are still involved with the skills and knowledge.

3. *Use a stamp or other mark to designate the level a student's task was assessed.* For example, a rubber "smiley face" or other stamp can indicate an acceptable task; two can show an outstanding effort. Stamps are inexpensive, long-lasting, and take minimal time. If a student's task is deficient, you may not want to put any stamp on it, but instead write some quick notes about what could be improved: If students rework their task, you don't want to have to mark out a "deficient" stamp! Stickers, check marks, and gummy stars can also designate the level of achievement a student reaches.

Once I've Assessed Students, Then What?

Once you have assessed students on the task, the work can be returned to the portfolio. Allow students periodically to look through their portfolios; they especially enjoy seeing how they have improved from earlier work. Students should be allowed to resubmit work until they reach an acceptable or outstanding level.

You will find portfolios are also a great way to communicate with parents. Imagine sending home a portfolio after 9 weeks or the end of a semester, letting parents see what their child has been working on and learning in physical education. Not only can the portfolio contain the tasks, but also a student's fitness scores, self-reflections, and notes from you. Parents will have a good, all-around view of what their child can do and is like in physical education—and will probably appreciate the information. When you send home a portfolio, use a paper clip or staple near the fold to keep the papers in place and include a cover sheet explaining it. Encourage the student to describe what is in the portfolio to his or her parent (or guardian). Ask parents to write their comments and questions on this paper and to sign it at the bottom. Let them know you will get back with them to discuss concerns and set up a conference, if desired. After you review these cover sheets, add them to the portfolio.

Another interesting idea is to hold a "Portfolio Powwow" as part of a PTA function, parents' night, or even a parents' day (when parents can participate with their child in physical education). At this "Powwow," encourage students to sit down and show their parents what they have been working on in physical education before participating in fun, physical activities you may provide.

At the end of the year, you may allow students to take their portfolios home as a remembrance of their year in physical education, or you may keep it at school for the next year (this can save on time and supplies!). If you start students out with portfolio tasks in kindergarten or the first grade, you may want to think about making them a new folder when they start third grade.

As you probably now realize, the uses of a portfolio in physical education are many. The amount and kind of information you put in them are limited only by your time, effort, and creativity. Portfolios take some time up-front, but you will soon become so efficient working with them that you won't want to do without them. They can be a great source of information for you, your students, and their parents. They can make a lot of sense for your program!

PART II

Sample Assessment Tasks and Curriculum Ideas

In this part of the guide, you'll find hands-on information that will help you in the day-to-day planning, instruction, and assessment of your elementary physical education curriculum. This is the part of the book that you'll probably spend most of your time working with and poring over.

To make it easier to find information in Part II, I have grouped together similar skills and concepts from elementary physical education curriculums as chapters. You'll find a listing of these chapters and their component skills and concepts here. And because you may organize the year's curriculum differently than I have, some common units of instruction corresponding to the skills and concepts in these chapters are also listed here.

Chapter	Possible units
3. Safety and participation	
	Orientation and safety, throughout various units
4. Movement concepts	
Body awareness	Dance, gymnastics, locomotor skills
Space awareness	Dance, gymnastics, games, locomotor skills
Effort	Dance, gymnastics, locomotor skills
Relationships	Gymnastics, dance, throughout various units
5. Locomotor skills	
Locomotor movements	Locomotor skills, traveling
Chasing, fleeing, and dodging	Tag games
Jumping and landing	Jump rope, gymnastics
6. Nonlocomotor skills	
Rolling	Gymnastics, dance
Balancing	Gymnastics, dance
Weight transfer	Gymnastics, dance, locomotor skills
7. Manipulative skills	
Dribbling with the hands	Basketball, ballhandling skills
Kicking and punting	Soccer
Throwing and catching	Softball, bowling, football
Volleying	Volleyball
Striking with short-handled implements	Net games, tennis
Striking with long-handled implements	Hockey, softball
8. Fitness	
Introduction to fitness	Throughout various units
Cardiorespiratory fitness	Tag games, soccer, jump rope, fitness tests
Muscular strength and endurance	Gymnastics, tag games, jump rope, fitness tests
Flexibility	Gymnastics, dance, fitness tests
Training and conditioning	Throughout various units
Healthy habits	Throughout various units

For each skill and concept mentioned in the chapters of Part II, you'll find several similar elements to use when planning, instructing, and assessing students and your program. These elements are described in more detail now.

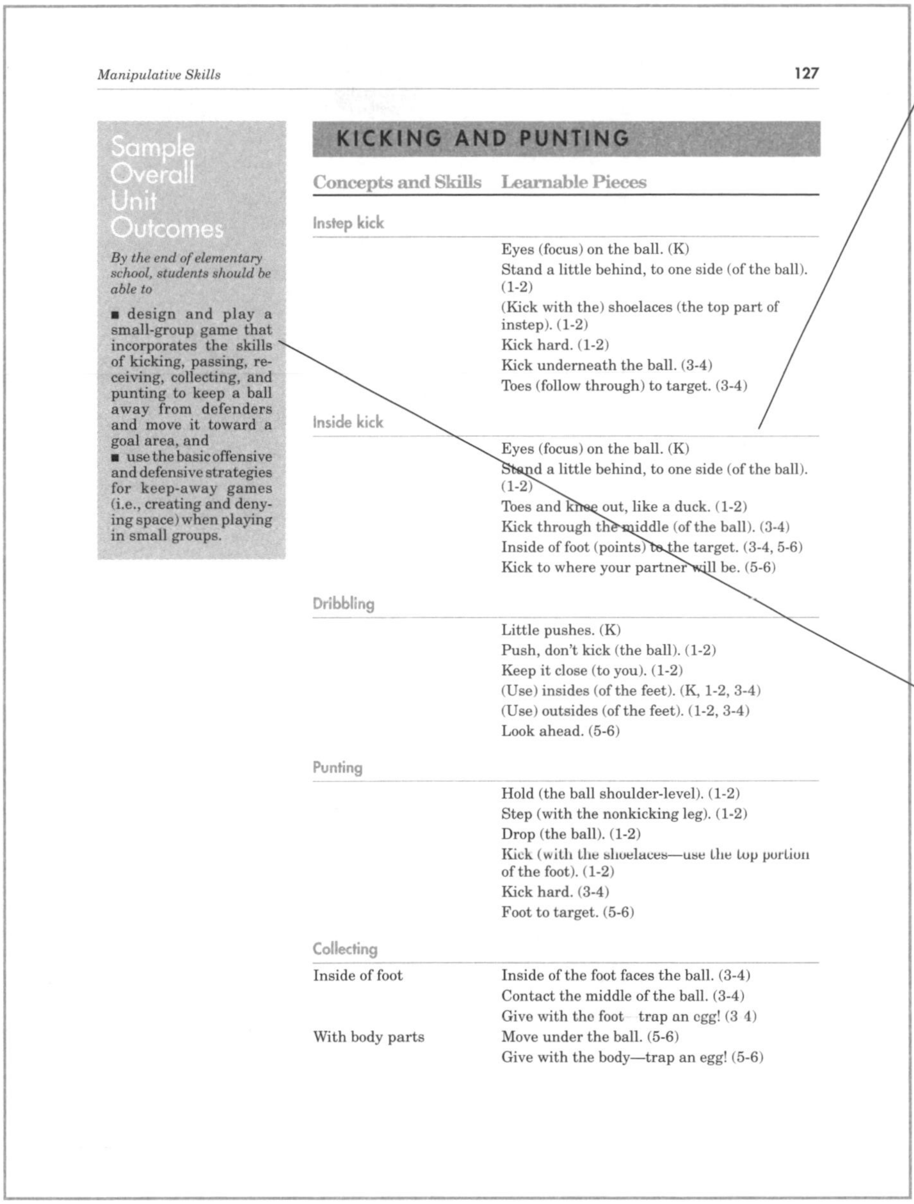

Manipulative Skills 127

Sample Overall Unit Outcomes

By the end of elementary school, students should be able to

- design and play a small-group game that incorporates the skills of kicking, passing, receiving, collecting, and punting to keep a ball away from defenders and move it toward a goal area, and
- use the basic offensive and defensive strategies for keep-away games (i.e., creating and denying space) when playing in small groups.

KICKING AND PUNTING

Concepts and Skills	Learnable Pieces
Instep kick	
	Eyes (focus) on the ball. (K) Stand a little behind, to one side (of the ball). (1-2) (Kick with the) shoelaces (the top part of instep). (1-2) Kick hard. (1-2) Kick underneath the ball. (3-4) Toes (follow through) to target. (3-4)
Inside kick	
	Eyes (focus) on the ball. (K) Stand a little behind, to one side (of the ball). (1-2) Toes and knee out, like a duck. (1-2) Kick through the middle (of the ball). (3-4) Inside of foot (points) to the target. (3-4, 5-6) Kick to where your partner will be. (5-6)
Dribbling	
	Little pushes. (K) Push, don't kick (the ball). (1-2) Keep it close (to you). (1-2) (Use) insides (of the feet). (K, 1-2, 3-4) (Use) outsides (of the feet). (1-2, 3-4) Look ahead. (5-6)
Punting	
	Hold (the ball shoulder-level). (1-2) Step (with the nonkicking leg). (1-2) Drop (the ball). (1-2) Kick (with the shoelaces—use the top portion of the foot). (1-2) Kick hard. (3-4) Foot to target. (5-6)
Collecting	
Inside of foot	Inside of the foot faces the ball. (3-4) Contact the middle of the ball. (3-4) Give with the foot—trap an egg! (3-4)
With body parts	Move under the ball. (5-6) Give with the body—trap an egg! (5-6)

Learnable Pieces

Gain an overall idea of the skills and concepts in each chapter by reading the list of relevant *learnable pieces* (also known as *cues* or *refinements*). You can use these learnable pieces as guides when you design down to the lesson outcomes for each of your units. They also are useful for emphasis during instruction. To make them more helpful, you'll find each learnable piece referenced to the grade level or levels where you'll find it described in this guide.

Sample Overall Unit Outcomes

A sample overall unit outcome sets the tone for what students should be able to demonstrate with a given skill or concept by the time they leave elementary school. This overall unit outcome serves as a guide for planning outcomes and assessments at the unit and lesson levels.

Grade Level

You'll find information under each skill or concept organized according to the grade levels of Grades K, 1-2, 3-4, and 5-6. In keeping with the philosophy of designing down, these grade levels are presented in reverse order, beginning with Grades 5-6 and concluding with kindergarten.

Sample Performance Task

An example of a performance task to use for assessing students in the skills and concepts also is given at the grade levels 5-6, 3-4, and 1-2, and—when appropriate—kindergarten. Because of the limited writing and verbal ability of kindergartners, as well as how fresh their introduction is to many of the skills and concepts in physical education, few assessments are given for these youngsters. Nor have performance assessments been presented for the cognitive concepts found in the chapter on fitness (chapter 8).

Sample Portfolio Task

Just as with the performance tasks, you will find portfolio tasks to use for assessing students in each skill or concept at the grade levels of 5-6, 3-4, and 1-2 (and kindergarten when appropriate). You'll also find several ready-to-use assessment sheets illustrating some portfolio tasks.

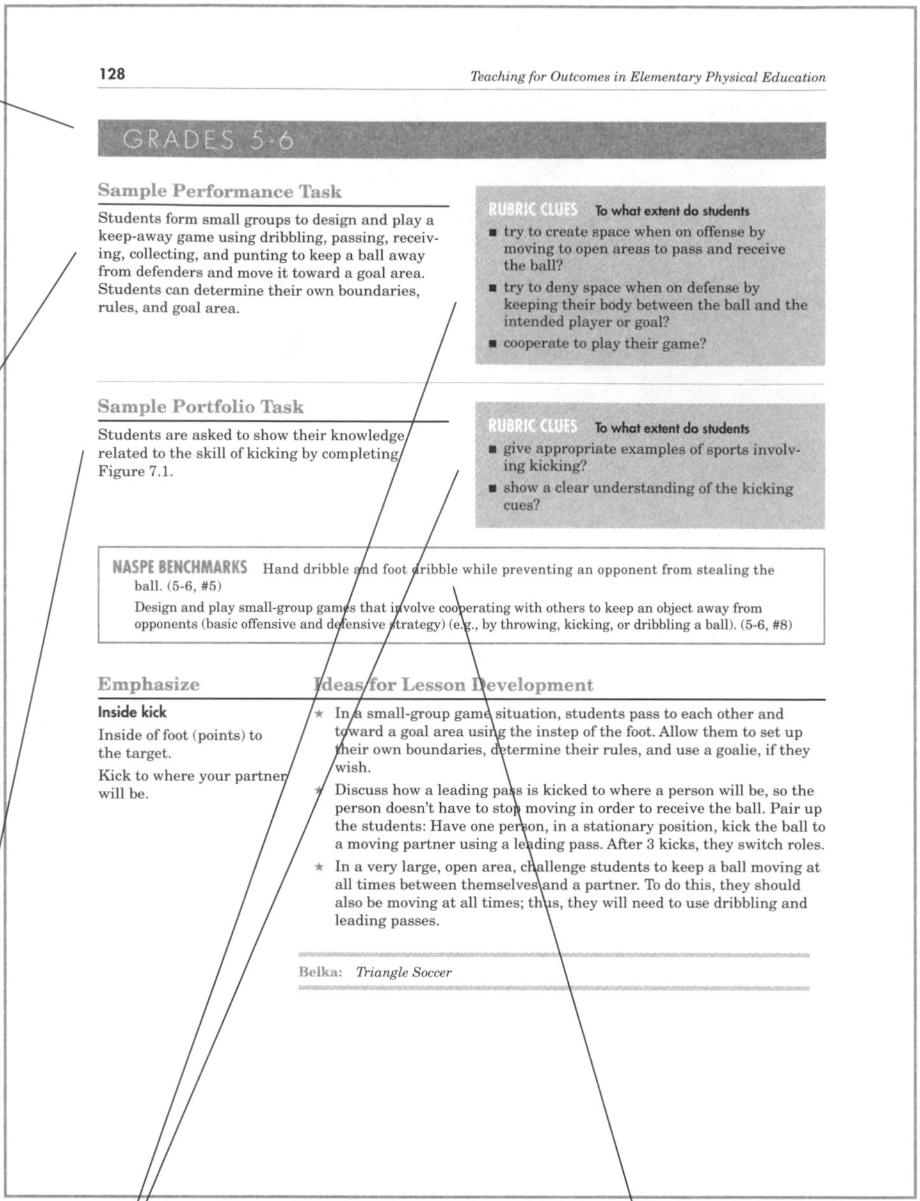

128 *Teaching for Outcomes in Elementary Physical Education*

GRADES 5-6

Sample Performance Task

Students form small groups to design and play a keep-away game using dribbling, passing, receiving, collecting, and punting to keep a ball away from defenders and move it toward a goal area. Students can determine their own boundaries, rules, and goal area.

RUBRIC CLUES To what extent do students

- try to create space when on offense by moving to open areas to pass and receive the ball?
- try to deny space when on defense by keeping their body between the ball and the intended player or goal?
- cooperate to play their game?

Sample Portfolio Task

Students are asked to show their knowledge related to the skill of kicking by completing Figure 7.1.

RUBRIC CLUES To what extent do students

- give appropriate examples of sports involving kicking?
- show a clear understanding of the kicking cues?

NASPE BENCHMARKS Hand dribble and foot dribble while preventing an opponent from stealing the ball. (5-6, #5)

Design and play small-group games that involve cooperating with others to keep an object away from opponents (basic offensive and defensive strategy) (e.g., by throwing, kicking, or dribbling a ball). (5-6, #8)

Emphasize

Inside kick

Inside of foot (points) to the target.

Kick to where your partner will be.

Ideas for Lesson Development

- ★ In a small-group game situation, students pass to each other and toward a goal area using the instep of the foot. Allow them to set up their own boundaries, determine their rules, and use a goalie, if they wish.
- ★ Discuss how a leading pass is kicked to where a person will be, so the person doesn't have to stop moving in order to receive the ball. Pair up the students: Have one person, in a stationary position, kick the ball to a moving partner using a leading pass. After 3 kicks, they switch roles.
- ★ In a very large, open area, challenge students to keep a ball moving at all times between themselves and a partner. To do this, they should also be moving at all times; thus, they will need to use dribbling and leading passes.

Belka: *Triangle Soccer*

Rubric Clues

These give you some ideas for criteria to use as the basis of your scoring rubric for each assessment task.

References to NASPE Benchmarks

Whenever you see the Benchmark box, you'll find a reference to the relevant Benchmark statement from NASPE's Outcomes Project (Franck et al., 1992). Many of the performance and portfolio tasks given here can help you assess whether students have reached these nationally approved indicators of achievement.

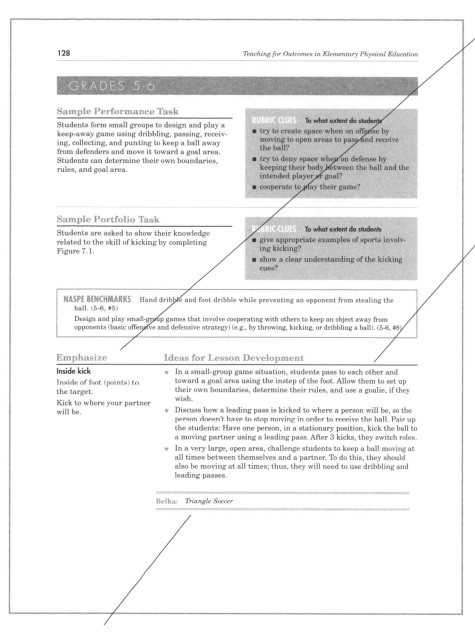

128 *Teaching for Outcomes in Elementary Physical Education*

GRADES 5-6

Sample Performance Task

Students form small groups to design and play a keep-away game using dribbling, passing, receiving, collecting, and punting to keep a ball away from defenders and move it toward a goal area. Students can determine their own boundaries, rules, and goal area.

RUBRIC CLUES To what extent do students

- try to create space when on offense by moving to open areas to pass and receive the ball?
- try to deny space when on defense by keeping their body between the ball and the intended player or goal?
- cooperate to play their game?

Sample Portfolio Task

Students are asked to show their knowledge related to the skill of kicking by completing Figure 7.1.

RUBRIC CLUES To what extent do students

- give appropriate examples of sports involving kicking?
- show a clear understanding of the kicking cues?

NASPE BENCHMARKS Hand dribble and foot dribble while preventing an opponent from stealing the ball. (5-6, #5)

Design and play small-group games that involve cooperating with others to keep an object away from opponents (basic offensive and defensive strategy) (e.g., by throwing, kicking, or dribbling a ball). (5-6, #8)

Emphasize

Inside kick

Inside of foot (points) to the target.

Kick to where your partner will be.

Ideas for Lesson Development

- ★ In a small-group game situation, students pass to each other and toward a goal area using the instep of the foot. Allow them to set up their own boundaries, determine their rules, and use a goalie, if they wish.
- ★ Discuss how a leading pass is kicked to where a person will be, so the person doesn't have to stop moving in order to receive the ball. Pair up the students: Have one person, in a stationary position, kick the ball to a moving partner using a leading pass. After 3 kicks, they switch roles.
- ★ In a very large, open area, challenge students to keep a ball moving at all times between themselves and a partner. To do this, they should also be moving at all times; thus, they will need to use dribbling and leading passes.

Belka: *Triangle Soccer*

Emphasize

The specific learnable pieces, which can serve as a focus for lesson instruction (lesson outcomes) at the different grade levels, are given here. You will find accompanying Ideas for Lesson Development that complement these learnable pieces.

Ideas for Lesson Development

Kid-tested, ready-to use ideas you can incorporate into lessons are presented under this heading. These ideas may relate to physical skills or (as with the fitness theme) they may be questions for discussion about a specific concept. You will also find helpful hints for making and setting up equipment, as well as cross-references to additional lesson ideas in the AMTP content books. These ideas are intended as suggestions for what to use at various grade levels.

AMTP Content Books Cross-References

Additional ideas for lesson development can be found in the American Master Teacher Program (AMTP) for Children's Physical Education Content Books series. Where applicable, relevant learning experiences (LEs) from these books have been listed to give you a quick, readable source of additional information. You will find the following books, referenced by author, along with the applicable LEs: *Teaching Children Games: Becoming a Master Teacher* by David Belka; *Teaching Children Movement Concepts and Skills: Becoming a Master Teacher* by Craig Buschner; *Teaching Children Dance: Becoming a Master Teacher* by Theresa Purcell; *Teaching Children Fitness: Becoming a Master Teacher* by Tom and Laraine Ratliffe; *Teaching Children Gymnastics: Becoming a Master Teacher* by Peter Werner.

We hope you'll find the information in Part II helpful and of interest. We encourage you to take from it what is useful, adapt it when necessary, and improve it if needed.

CHAPTER 3 Safety and Participation

Sample Overall Unit Outcomes

By the end of elementary school, students should be able to

- apply appropriate safety rules both in and out of physical education class,
- recognize the time, effort, and feelings that are part of participating in activities to improve and maintain physical fitness and skill levels,
- recognize that fun, excitement, and other feelings can be expressed and achieved by participating in physical activities,
- show verbal and physical support of and respect for others while participating in physical activities,
- enjoy the participation and companionship that result from cooperating with a partner or others in physical activities,
- enjoy regular participation in physical activity for its physical, emotional, and social benefits, and
- enjoy the feelings of success, improvement, and meeting challenges resulting from positive experiences in physical activity.

SAFETY AND PARTICIPATION

Concepts and Skills	Learnable Pieces
Rules for safety	
	There are important rules you need to remember in physical education. (K)
	Rules allow everyone to be safe and have fun in physical education. (1-2)
Cooperating with others	
	Cooperating involves working together and helping others. (K, 1-2)
Respecting others	
	Respect involves treating others with a positive attitude, being considerate, and listening to what teachers and others have to say. (1-2, 3-4)
Learning about others	
	Participating in activities with others can be fun and enjoyable for everyone. (5-6)
	Sports and dance are ways to get together and learn about other people. (5-6)
Improving your skills	
	Improving your skills and fitness isn't always easy; it takes time and work. (5-6)

GRADES 5-6

Sample Portfolio Task

Have students reflect, in writing, on an activity or sport that they feel they have improved in. What did they do to improve? Who helped them to improve? How did they feel as a result of improving? Then have them describe an activity or sport in which they would especially like to improve in the future. What do they think they will need to do to improve? Who can help them improve?

RUBRIC CLUES **To what extent do students**

- give responses that show they understand the time and effort it takes to improve?

NASPE BENCHMARKS Recognize that time and effort are prerequisites for skill improvement and fitness benefits. (5-6, #18)

Identify opportunities in the school and community for regular participation in physical activity. (5-6, #20)

Emphasize / Ideas for Lesson Development

Learning about others

Participating in activities with others can be fun and enjoyable for everyone.

★ Have a "[Your School] Friends and Family Plan." Discuss sports and activities that are fun for students to do with a friend or family member. Encourage students to try one of these activities at least once a week. If they do, have them write it down or draw it; put these up weekly on a bulletin board or spotlight one or two examples in the school (or your physical education) newsletter.

Sports and dance are ways to get together and learn about other people.

★ Discuss how people can get together and learn about other cultures through sports and dance. Discuss the role of folk dances in other cultures or how the Olympics bring together people from all over the world. Use excerpts from Olympics or cultural videos to illustrate your discussion.

★ Have the librarian highlight books dealing with the Olympics and other international competitions or with athletes from other countries for children to look through, read, and check out.

★ Ask students to describe examples of how sport and dance events have helped them get to know other people in the community and from other cities, states, or countries.

★ Invite an exchange student at your local high school or in the community to talk with your students about the games, sports, and dances that are popular in his or her native country and even participate with your students in one of these activities.

Improving your skills

Improving your skills and fitness isn't always easy; it takes time and work.

★ In the beginning of the school year ask students to write down something they would like to improve in during the coming year (you can do this in conjunction with the portfolio assessment). Use this as a goal; revisit this goal during the year (e.g., once a quarter), asking students to reflect on the progress they are making toward their goals.

★ Use personal stories from popular athletes—or your own—to explain the concept that getting better at skills or fitness takes time and hard work. Having the librarian feature books or articles telling stories of people's triumphs (not only in physical education) can be helpful.

GRADES 3-4

Sample Portfolio Task

Ask students to reflect, in writing, on an activity they think they are good at in physical education. How does it make them feel about themselves? Why do they feel that way? Do they think everyone is good at this? Why or why not?

RUBRIC CLUES **To what extent do students**

- give responses that show they understand and support others' abilities and feelings?

NASPE BENCHMARKS Identify activities that contribute to personal feelings of joy. (3-4, #22)

Appreciate differences and similarities in others' physical activity. (3-4, #27)

Emphasize

Respecting others

Respect involves treating others with a positive attitude, being considerate, and listening to what teachers and others have to say.

Ideas for Lesson Development

★ Discuss how students can work to solve small problems without involving the teacher. Introduce some common problems; talk about how they can be handled individually. Discuss what kinds of problems students should—and shouldn't—try to solve on their own.

★ To promote a positive, accepting class attitude, first discuss how everyone can do something well, whether in the classroom or physical education. Then give each student in the class a small piece of paper and a pencil. Have each one write his or her name on one side of it and fold it in half. Put all these into a box or hat. Each student takes out one name and writes something good about the person whose name she or he picked. Try to have students identify something good that the person does in physical education class; you may need to give them examples (e.g., cooperates well, runs well, makes up good routines). If necessary, allow them to put anything down (they smile nice, they read well, etc.) if they can't think of something specific to physical education. Have each student hand the paper to the other person; then students read their "positive promoter" aloud.

GRADES 1-2

Sample Portfolio Task

Ask students to draw a picture of a way they can cooperate with others in physical education and to write a short description of what they are doing.

RUBRIC CLUES **To what extent do students**

- show they comprehend the concept of cooperation through their picture and explanation?

NASPE BENCHMARKS Appreciate the benefits that accompany cooperation and sharing. (1-2, #27)

Emphasize	Ideas for Lesson Development
Rules for safety Rules allow everyone to be safe and have fun in physical education.	★ Discuss why rules are important in physical education; ask students for input about what they think are important rules to have for class. Relate their suggestions to rules you have in mind. If they haven't thought of a specific rule, give a common scenario and ask for a rule that might be of help in this instance. ★ Set up situations in the beginning of and during the school year that allow students to practice rules. When needed, bring students together and discuss their use (or nonuse) of the rules. Take a few minutes to discuss why the rules are or aren't working and ask them for suggestions on how to improve this. ★ For working in stations, instead of using a signal, use music. When the music stops, have students stop and point to the next station they will be moving to (this gives you a quick comprehension check); when the music begins, they move on to the next station. ★ For taking care of equipment, this idea works especially well when students work outdoors and have a good distance to get to the activity area: Once students know the protocol for properly choosing equipment, allow them to run to where the equipment is set out and (safely) take a piece, then move to a self-space and begin to manipulate the object any way they wish until you get there and give the signal to stop. As they don't all run at the same speed, this method helps keep them from arriving simultaneously at the equipment, gives them a good warm-up, allows you to walk and talk with students on the way, and is a great way to involve the students in an instant activity. ★ Instead of having students line up in one long line, try having them line up in two lines (boys and girls, for example). This can cut down on pushing and shoving. Two lines can easily move through the hallways as well. Challenge each line to see if it can do a better job of lining up than the other! ★ If the class is walking through the hallway, pick a student to walk backward in front of the line as the "line conductor" instead of you. This child can use only hand signals to direct other students in line to move over, stop, or turn. (First graders may not be ready for this at the beginning of the year.) Try selecting a student conductor who isn't first in line: Perhaps choose someone who did especially well that day or showed good cooperation. This helps to cut down on students who "have to be first" in line, and gives the chance to reward even "problem" students for good work. Plus, students love getting to be in charge. ★ If students have to go quite a distance before they line up, allow them to run until they reach a certain distance away from the line, at which point they must walk to get into line. This also helps alleviate some problems of running to be the first in line. Stress—and expect—students to walk to get in line, once they are past the designated point.

Emphasize	Ideas for Lesson Development
Cooperating with others Cooperating involves working together and helping others.	★ To foster cooperative behaviors between students, you must put them in situations that require cooperation. Early in the semester, take a day to talk about and practice cooperation to set the tone for what you expect of students during the year. Working with the parachute is a good example of a fun, cooperative activity that students enjoy. ★ Give students positive feedback whenever they show cooperative behaviors, especially those who tend to neglect cooperation. When you give feedback remember not to overdo it, but to always be sincere.
Respecting others Respect involves treating others with a positive attitude, being considerate, and listening to what teachers and others have to say.	★ Ask students to discuss helpful behaviors for participating in physical education (e.g., sharing, cooperating, using the rules, taking turns). Ask them to talk about behaviors that hurt others, such as pushing in line, making others feel bad about their abilities, saying no if a person asks you to be a partner, or name-calling. Discuss how both helpful and hurtful behaviors make others feel, and how to respond or take appropriate action (tell the person thank-you; ignore a person; tell the teacher if necessary). ★ Promote helpful behavior by giving positive feedback to students when they demonstrate them, just as you would when they show proper psychomotor skills.

KINDERGARTEN

Emphasize	Ideas for Lesson Development
Rules for safety There are important rules you need to remember in physical education.	★ For a "quiet" signal, have students talk as much as they want; see how fast they can stop when you give the signal (e.g., a drum or tambourine beat, your hand raised up). ★ For a "stop" signal, see how fast students can stop moving their bodies or body parts in their self-space at the signal. ★ Teach that one signal is for "go" and two are for "stop." Have the students move throughout general space and stop at the signal; "trick" them by pretending to give a signal or giving two to go instead of one. ★ Introduce your special "safety alert" signal for use in emergencies. Have students practice responding to it when they are working with equipment or playing on the playground. Bring them back in and discuss how they did; practice responding to the signal if needed. Occasionally revisit this throughout the beginning of the school year, making sure the students know it is a practice run, not a real one. ★ For "self-space" have the students pretend that there is a bubble around them (their self-space), and that they must stay in their own bubbles while they line up, not breaking anyone else's bubble.

Emphasize	Ideas for Lesson Development
	★ For taking care of equipment, set up stations with various pieces of equipment. Have students practice putting the pieces away correctly at your signal.
	★ To stagger the timing when students put away equipment, call for those who have on jeans, blue clothing, high-top tennis shoes, and so forth to put their equipment away when their category is called. Try tricking boys by calling out "girls with shorts on," "boys with shorts on," "girls with dresses on," then "boys with dresses on."
Cooperating with others Cooperating involves working together and helping others.	★ Discuss the concept of cooperation; use activities, such as the parachute, to help demonstrate how everyone must work together.

CHAPTER 4 Movement Concepts

Sample Overall Unit Outcome

By the end of elementary school, students should be able to

- design, refine, and perform dance and gymnastics sequences, either with or without partners, that focus on the use of body shapes and body movements.

BODY AWARENESS

Concepts and Skills	Learnable Pieces
Body parts	
	Arms (K, 1-2)
	Head (K, 1-2)
	Legs (K, 1-2)
	Elbows (K, 1-2)
	Knees (K, 1-2)
	Others (K, 1-2)
Body shapes	
Angular	Make your body bend or point. (K, 1-2)
Curved	Be round like a tire. (K, 1-2)
Twisted	Face part of your body one way, and part of it another way. (K, 1-2)
Narrow	Stretch so you're long and skinny! (K, 1-2)
Wide	Stretch arms and legs out to the side! (K, 1-2)
Symmetrical	If you cut your body in two, each side would look the same. (1-2, 3-4)
Asymmetrical	If you cut your body in two, each side would look different. (1-2, 3-4)
Body movements	
Swing	Make big, free movements of your body parts. (K, 1-2)
Sway	Make small movements side-to-side or front-to-back. (K, 1-2)
Twist	Move part of your body one way, and move part another way. (K, 1-2)
Turn	Spin like a top! (K, 1-2)
Bend—Curl	Close up your body. (K, 1-2)
Stretch	Stretch your body parts away from your middle. (K, 1-2)
Shake	You're shivering! (K, 1-2)
Rise	Move up away from the ground. (1-2)
Sink	Move down slowly toward the ground. (1-2)
Push	Move it [object] away from you. (1-2)
Pull	Move it [object] toward you. (1-2)

GRADES 5-6

Sample Performance Task

Students are asked to design, refine, and perform a movement sequence with two or three other students. The sequence must last at least for 48 counts of music with a 4/4 meter, and it must have a definite beginning and ending. The music can be chosen by the students, with approval by the teacher. In the sequence, students are asked to demonstrate at least three different body movements and three different locomotor movements.

RUBRIC CLUES To what extent do students

- demonstrate the required number of body and locomotor movements in the sequence?
- design the sequence so it lasts for the minimum number of counts?
- smoothly perform (with a minimum of breaks in timing) the sequence to the beat of the music and with the partner?

Sample Portfolio Task

Students are given an assessment sheet (see Figure 4.1) pertaining to the sequence task. Each group is to evaluate another group's routine using the given criteria (e.g., circle which movements are used, how many beats the sequence lasts). The group doing the rating must decide which of its members will be responsible for watching which criterion. After the performance, students collectively decide if the dancing group they watched has met the given criteria. The group then briefly discusses its report with the teacher; afterward, sheets are filed into each of the dancing group members' portfolios.

RUBRIC CLUES To what extent do students

- work as part of their group to determine the roles of each rater?

NASPE BENCHMARKS Detect, analyze, and correct errors in personal movement patterns. (5-6, #24)

Emphasize

The use of specific body shapes and body movements as they pertain to the contexts of games and, especially, dance and gymnastics activities

Ideas for Lesson Development

★ Have students design and refine a sequence with two to four other students, using at least two different kinds of body shapes, of body movements, and of weight transfers. The sequence may include any equipment, including music, that the students wish to use. After giving the criteria for the sequence, help students in the process of choosing shapes, movements, and equipment. The sequence should be written down.

★ Allow students to use such props as scarves, sheets, giant "rubber bands" (made out of stretchable cloth; these can be purchased from sporting equipment companies), and such equipment as balls for the design and performance of their sequences.

★ For additional ideas to teach body awareness concepts, see the themes of effort and relationships later in this chapter, as well as the specific themes under nonlocomotor (chapter 6) and manipulative skills (chapter 7).

Werner: *See What I Can Do*
Purcell: *New Square Dance*

Name ______________________________

Class ______________________________

Others in my group ____________________

We're watching:

____

____

____

____

Circle which locomotor movements you saw.

walk	skip
jog	slide
hop	gallop
jump	leap

Circle the nonlocomotor movements you saw.

swing stretch
sway rise
twist sink
turn push
bend pull
shake

Does the sequence have

a beginning? ☐ an ending? ☐

Did the group you watched

★	Use 3 locomotor movements?	yes	no
★	Use 3 nonlocomotor movements?	yes	no
★	Have a definite beginning and ending?	yes	no
★	Use at least *48* counts of music?	yes	no

Count how many sets of 8 beats of music were used:

1-8 9-16 17-24 25-32
33-40 41-48

Figure 4.1 *Sample body awareness assessment sheet for Grades 5-6.*

GRADES 3-4

Sample Performance Task

Ask students to design, refine, and perform a movement sequence with a partner (with or without music). The use of two different body movements, three body shapes, and two different locomotor movements must be clearly shown in their sequences.

RUBRIC CLUES **To what extent do students**

- incorporate the required number of body movements, shapes, and locomotor movements into their sequences?
- refine the sequence so they move smoothly from one element to another, without hesitation or memory lapses?

Sample Portfolio Task

Students are asked to map out their sequence, showing the starting and stopping points, pathways followed, locomotor movements, and points where they will make the body movements and shapes.

RUBRIC CLUES **To what extent do students**

- clearly show the starting and stopping points?
- clearly mark the places in the sequence where body movements and shapes are made?

NASPE BENCHMARKS Design games, gymnastics, and dance sequences that are personally interesting. (3-4, #26)

Emphasize

Body shapes

Symmetrical
If you cut your body in two, each side would look the same.

Asymmetrical
If you cut your body in two, each side would look different.

Ideas for Lesson Development

★ Ask the students to balance in a symmetrical shape; then ask them to stretch, bend, or twist into an asymmetrical shape.

★ Have students use symmetrical shapes in order to move onto and jump off equipment (boxes, benches, etc.). Then mix up the shapes so students move onto equipment with an asymmetrical shape; move off equipment with a symmetrical shape.

★ Have students, with a partner, pick a symmetrical and asymmetrical shape. Each pair must use these shapes to begin and end a sequence; their sequences must also include two locomotor movements and two body movements. They can decide in what order to arrange these movements and what equipment (if any) to use (gymnastics equipment; ropes, scarves, etc.) for dance props. Sequences should be written down and practiced until they can be performed from memory.

★ Stretch, twist, or bend into a roll.

★ See the theme of nonlocomotor skills (in chapter 6) for additional ideas.

Werner: *Ready for Takeoff; Same, Different; Taking a Spin*
Purcell: *The Homework Machine*
Buschner: *Twisting, Spinning, and Throwing*

GRADES 1-2

Sample Performance Task

Students are asked to make a specific shape that can be found in a sport of their choice. Examples might be angular in football, stretched in gymnastics, twisted in baseball, wide in basketball, narrow in swimming or diving, and curved in gymnastics.

RUBRIC CLUES To what extent do students

- show correct, definite examples of each shape?
- know which sport their shapes are found in?

Sample Portfolio Task

Using magazines from school or home, students are to cut out pictures of people using different shapes in sports or everyday life. Each shape should be labeled.

RUBRIC CLUES To what extent do students

- correctly identify the shape that the picture illustrates?

NASPE BENCHMARKS Balance, demonstrating momentary stillness, in symmetrical and asymmetrical shapes on a variety of body parts. (1-2, #7)

Combine shapes, levels, and pathways into simple sequences. (1-2, #17)

Recognize similar movement concepts in a variety of skills. (1-2, #23)

Emphasize

Body parts

Arms, Head, Legs, Elbows, Knees, Others

Ideas for Lesson Development

★ Travel—have children put specific body parts on their carpet squares or in their hoops at the signal.

★ Ask students to balance on specific body parts or on a specific number of bases of support (e.g., 3 bases, 5 bases).

★ Assign travel using specific body parts (two hands and two feet; one hand and one foot; behind and hands).

★ Make a large cube showing a different body part on each side; have children roll the cube to show the body part they must balance on, touch to a partner, and so forth.

Werner: *Patches and Points*

Emphasize

Body shapes

Angular
Make your body bend or point.

Curved
Be round like a tire.

Ideas for Lesson Development

★ Students travel, then freeze in a specified shape at your signal. They also can travel to music: Stop the music at intervals, and have the students make shapes to interpret the music. Don't ask them to hold the shape too long; vary how long the music plays.

★ A partner "molds" the other child into a symmetrical or asymmetrical shape ("look around you. What do you see that is symmetrical?").

Emphasize	Ideas for Lesson Development
Twisted Face part of your body one way, and part of it another way. *Narrow* Stretch so you're long and skinny! *Wide* Stretch arms and legs out to the side! *Symmetrical* If you cut your body in two, each side would look the same. *Asymmetrical* If you cut your body in two, each side would look different.	★ Students make a jump rope into the shape of a symmetrical or asymmetrical letter or number; then they shape their bodies into the same letter or number (show letters and numbers on a poster or chalkboard). ★ Tell the children to make a specified shape while they somehow touch a hula hoop with some part of the body. Let them make a shape with a partner while they touch a hoop between them. ★ Ask the students to move over, through, around a hoop using different shapes. ★ Vary the activity, having students jump off the ground, a box, or tire while they make a specified shape. ★ Teach that a sequence always starts and ends with a shape. "Make a sequence where you start with a shape, travel, and then end in a different shape." Afterward, ask which shapes the students used. ★ Relate the different shapes to ones made by athletes in sports. Discuss how a batter in baseball makes a twisted shape, a diver curls up and makes a curved shape diving off the board, a wide receiver in football jumps up and makes a stretched shape to catch the ball, and a basketball player uses a wide shape to keep someone from passing the ball. **Purcell:** *April Showers; Streamer Dance; Spaghetti Dance* **Buschner:** *Movement Shapes*

Emphasize	Ideas for Lesson Development
Body movements *Swing* Make big, free movements of your body parts. *Sway* Make small movements side-to-side or front-to-back. *Twist* Move part of your body one way, and move part another way. *Turn* Spin like a top! *Bend—curl* Close up your body. *Stretch* Stretch your body parts away from your middle. *Rise* Move up away from the ground.	★ Perform different body movements to a series of beats in varying tempos (e.g., fast, slow). ★ One or two students use different instruments (commercial or homemade) to make a rhythm, while other students move, using body movements, to match the rhythm and sounds. Let all the students get the chance to make a rhythm with the instruments. For example, students shake to maracas, march to the drum beat, or tiptoe to a triangle. ★ Ask the students to make a sequence, starting with a body shape for 8 counts, moving by any locomotor movement for 8 counts, performing one or more body movements for 8 counts (e.g., sink and rise), traveling for 8 more counts, and finishing with a different body shape for 8 counts. Mark the beat and count out loud for them (i.e., "Make a shape, 2, 3, . . . 8; travel, 2, 3, . . . 8; movement, 2, 3, . . . 8; travel, 2, 3, . . . 8; ending shape, 2, 3, . . . 8.").

Emphasize

Sink
Move down slowly to the ground.

Push
Move it [object] away from you.

Pull
Move it [object] toward you.

Shake
You're shivering!

Werner: *Sit-Spins*
Purcell: *The Playground*

KINDERGARTEN

Sample Performance Task

Students are asked to put whichever body part (hands, feet, knees, behind, back, head, shoulder) you call out on their carpet squares.

RUBRIC CLUES **To what extent do students**

- put the correct body part on the carpet square?

NASPE BENCHMARKS Make both large and small body shapes while traveling. (K, #5)
Form round, narrow, wide, and twisted body shapes alone and with a partner. (K, #14)
Identify selected body parts, skills, and movement concepts. (K, #18)

Emphasize

Body parts

Arms, Head, Legs, Elbows, Knees, Others

Ideas for Lesson Development

★ Have children strike balloons using specific body parts.
★ Ask them to break bubbles using specific body parts.
★ Tell the students to shake (stretch, twist, etc.) specific body parts to a drum signal or other music (alternate fast and slow speeds).
★ Travel—have students find a partner and touch the same specific body part (i.e., elbow to elbow, knee to knee, back to back) at your signal.

Werner: *Bunny Hop; Patches and Points*
Buschner: *Anatomy*

Emphasize	Ideas for Lesson Development
Body shapes *Angular* Make your body bend or point. *Curved* Be round like a tire. *Twisted* Face part of your body one way, and part of it another way. *Narrow* Stretch so you're long and skinny! *Wide* Stretch arms and legs out to the side!	★ At the signal, have youngsters quickly change to the shape that you call out. ★ Students travel, find a partner, and make the same (mirror) shape at the signal. ★ Place different objects (e.g., apple, stapler, rubber band, banana, balloon, piece of paper) in a bag. Take one out at a time, asking the students to shape themselves like that object. Move the object (blow up the balloon, stretch the rubber band, etc.) and have them move just like it, imitating its shape.

Emphasize	Ideas for Lesson Development
Body movements *Swing* Make big, free movements of your body parts. *Sway* Make small movements side-to-side or front-to-back. *Twist* Move part of your body one way, and move part another way. *Turn* Spin like a top! *Bend—Curl* Close up your body. *Stretch* Stretch your body parts away from your middle. *Shake* You're shivering!	★ The students travel using a specified locomotor movement to a popular song; at the chorus, they stop and move the body using a movement you specify, with a partner, and then they continue traveling when the chorus ends. ★ The children shake their bodies while moving from a high to a low level; when you give a loud signal, they rise up quickly, like a jack-in-the box!

Sample Overall Unit Outcome

By the end of elementary school, students should be able to

- design, refine, and perform dance and gymnastics sequences that focus on the use of one or more of the directions, levels, pathways, extensions, and space concepts.

SPACE AWARENESS

Concepts and Skills	Learnable Pieces
Self- or personal space	
	Space right next to you, where you can't touch anyone or anything. (K, 1-2)
General space	
	Empty or open space all around you. (K, 1-2)
Offense	Keep your body between the ball and the defender. (3-4, 5-6)
	Create space by moving to open areas to pass or receive the ball. (5-6)
	Hit the ball to where opponents aren't standing. (5-6)
Defense	Deny space by keeping between the opponent and intended goal. (5-6)
	Be ready to move. (5-6)
	Partners equally cover the area. (5-6)
Directions	
Forward	Your front leads. (K, 1-2)
Backward	Your back leads. (K, 1-2)
Sideways	Your side (right or left) leads. (K, 1-2)
Up	Toward the sky. (K, 1-2)
Down	Toward the ground. (K, 1-2)
Levels	
Low	Below your knees. (K, 1-2)
Medium	Between your shoulders and knees. (K, 1-2)
High	Above your shoulders. (K, 1-2)
Pathways	
Curved	Rounded like a rainbow. (K, 1-2)
Straight	Like a line or pencil. (K, 1-2)
Zigzag	Straight lines connected to make sharp points. (K, 1-2)
Extensions	
Near	When your body parts are close to your body. (1-2)
Far	When your body parts are far from your body. (1-2)

GRADES 5-6

Sample Performance Task

In groups of three, students create three different running or passing plays in football using all three of the pathways. Each play should be drawn on paper and practiced, using a football or other preferred object. After each student is familiar with each play, the groups can rotate the passer, receiver, and defender positions.

RUBRIC CLUES **To what extent do students**

- use all three pathways?
- run each play correctly, so that the pathway they use can be clearly identified?

Sample Portfolio Task

Have students watch an athletic performance on TV, attend a game, or watch a tape of one at school. Have them discuss, in writing, the space awareness concepts athletes used during their performances. What did the athletes do at a high, medium, or low level? What kinds of pathways did they use? directions? What kind of space did they move in? Have them give examples of how athletes use these concepts.

RUBRIC CLUES **To what extent do students**

- show a clear understanding of the different space awareness concepts in their use of examples?

NASPE BENCHMARKS Design and play small-group games that involve cooperating with others to keep an object away from opponents (basic offensive and defensive strategy). (5-6, #8)

Emphasize

General space

Offense

Create space by moving to open areas to pass or receive the ball.

Keep your body between the ball and the defender.

Defense

Deny space by keeping between the opponent and intended goal.

Ideas for Lesson Development

★ Ask students to compare how space is created or denied in invasion, net, and fielding games. Why is space created or denied? How do team members do this?

★ See manipulative skills themes (in chapter 7) for further ideas on the use of space in the context of games play.

Belka: *Advance and Score Soccer; Advance and Score Basketball*

Emphasize	Ideas for Lesson Development
General space *Offense* Hit the ball to where opponents aren't standing. *Defense* Be ready to move. Partners equally cover the area.	★ Discuss with students how, in certain net and volley games (e.g., volleyball, tennis), the objective is to hit to where one's partners are *not*, rather than to where they are. Also, discuss the defensive strategies of being ready to move at all times and covering the area between partners. ★ See volleying in the theme of manipulative skills (chapter 7) for further ideas on the use of space in the context of games play.

Emphasize	Ideas for Lesson Development
Directions, Levels, and Pathways—as they pertain to movement sequences and situations.	★ Have students form small groups to design, set up, and move through an obstacle course. They can choose what to use from equipment selected or approved by the teacher. The course must incorporate the body moving in at least two different directions, levels, and pathways. When they have completed the course themselves, have students teach it to a group of younger students or to a different group in their class.

GRADES 3-4

Sample Performance Task

Students design, refine, and perform a dance or gymnastics sequence with a partner that uses movements in at least two different directions and at two different levels. The sequence must have a definite beginning and ending shape.

RUBRIC CLUES To what extent do students

- use the required number of levels?
- use the required number of directions?
- show a definite beginning and ending?
- refine the sequence so it can be repeated smoothly and without memory lapses?

Sample Portfolio Task

Students are asked to briefly describe and draw how a participant in one activity or sport would use one or more of the different pathways.

RUBRIC CLUES To what extent do students

- show a clear understanding of the different pathways?
- make a clear connection between the activity they choose and the pathway(s) they use?

NASPE BENCHMARKS Identify ways movement concepts can be used to refine movement skills. (3-4, #21).

Emphasize	Ideas for Lesson Development
Pathways—in the contexts of gymnastics and dance	★ Using the floor and their mats, students create an interesting sequence with different pathways. They write it down and teach it to a partner.

Emphasize	Ideas for Lesson Development
Directions—in the contexts of gymnastics and dance	★ Using an appropriate piece of gymnastics equipment (small or large), students find a way to move up to it, on to it, and off it, using the directions of up and down.

Purcell: *Action Words*
Buschner: *Directional Gymnastics*

Emphasize	Ideas for Lesson Development
General space *Offense* Keep your body between the ball and the defender.	★ See more "Ideas for Lesson Development" in the themes of chasing, fleeing, and dodging (in chapter 5).

GRADES 1-2

Sample Performance Task

Provide music, and ask students to move to it throughout a large boundaried area while they use a variety of locomotor and nonlocomotor movements as you call them out, and they avoid bumping into others or leaving the boundaries.

RUBRIC CLUES **To what extent do students**

- keep a self-space as they move throughout the area?
- move to the open areas and throughout the whole area, not only in a circular fashion?

Sample Portfolio Task

Give students a copy of Figure 4.2. Ask them to color in the part of the child's body that is at a low level using a red crayon; the part of the body that is at a medium level using blue crayon, and the part of the body that is at a high level using green.

RUBRIC CLUES **To what extent do students**

- correctly identify, through coloring, the different levels?

NASPE BENCHMARKS Travel in a backward direction and change direction quickly, and safely, without falling. (1-2, #1)

Travel, changing speeds and directions, in response to a variety of rhythms. (1-2, #2)

Name ______________________ Class ______________

What's Your Level?

Directions:

What part of the body is at a low level? Color it red.

What part of the body is at a medium level? Color it blue.

What part of the body is at a high level? Color it green.

Figure 4.2 *Sample space awareness assessment sheet for Grades 1-2.*

Emphasize	Ideas for Lesson Development
Self-space Space right next to you, where you can't touch anyone or anything. **General space** Empty or open space all around you.	★ Have students move through general space. Little by little, move the boundaries of the area in; when students are crowded, move them back out. Discuss what happened. Which was easier, to move in or to move out? Make three different boundaries—one large, one medium, one small—and have children play with a ball in each of them. Which was easier? harder? Why? ★ Trees in the Forest—about six to eight students each have their own hoop inside the boundaries. Other youngsters travel with a specified movement; they try to get as close as possible to the self-space of the "trees" without getting touched. Trees try to reach as far as possible, although one foot (root!) must stay inside the hoop at all times. When students get caught, they trade places with the trees. Discuss the limits to self-space and the difference between self-space and general space.

Buschner: *Staying at Home; Painting Movement Pictures*

Emphasize	Ideas for Lesson Development
Directions *Forward* Your front leads. *Backward* Your back leads. *Sideways* Your side (right or left) leads. *Up* Toward the sky. *Down* Toward the ground.	★ Travel—at your signal, the students move in a different, specified direction (you may also want to specify the locomotor movement). ★ Using one large, or a few small, parachutes, have the students move in different directions to counts of 8 (forward 8, backward 8, sideways 8, down 8, up 8). Call out the beats to a drum or other music. (Just for fun, have students move the parachute up and down together to try to get a beanbag through the hole in the middle of the parachute).

Emphasize	Ideas for Lesson Development
Pathways *Curved* Rounded like a rainbow. *Straight* Like a line or pencil. *Zigzag* Straight lines connected to make sharp points.	★ If available, use a chalking machine that makes lines for football and softball fields to make large pathways on the grass. ★ Give out 5 × 8-in. or 8 × 11-in. cards with pathway maps marked on them. After making the pathway, students trade maps with another student. ★ Treasure Hunt—Use different pathways to connect about 6 stations. Draw these pathways on the chalkboard, a poster board, or directly onto the floor. Ask the students to do something at each station with an object or to enhance fitness. When it is time to change stations, they must follow a partner to the next station, properly following the given pathway.

Ideas for Lesson Development

- ★ Students use chalk to draw a (straight) pathway on the blacktop. They then use other pathways to connect it to another person's pathway and move on the whole pathway. Ask them what kind of pathway they are using—while they are moving—to check their understanding.
- ★ Write letters and numbers on the board. Students copy a letter or number that uses a specific pathway you call out by manipulating a jump rope (beaded ones work best for this). Have two or three students work together to "write" a three-letter word made up of straight, curved, or zigzag pathways.
- ★ Have students draw out a pattern using two or all three of the pathways. Have them draw this pattern on the blacktop and then move on it.
- ★ See if students can dribble a ball or move a wiffle ball with a hockey stick along different pathways.

Purcell: *Spaghetti Dance*
Buschner: *Trails and Roads*

Emphasize

Levels

Low
Below your knees.

Medium
Between your shoulders and knees.

High
Above your shoulders.

Ideas for Lesson Development

- ★ Have a variety of objects to manipulate at different levels: Ask students to catch a yarn ball with a scoop at a high (medium, low) level, dribble a ball at the different levels, roll a ball to a partner, and so forth. Don't tell them the level; after they have performed the action, ask which level they used, as a check for comprehension.
- ★ Have students make up simple sequences, requiring them to use at least two different levels. The sequence should have a definite beginning and ending.

Purcell: *Ocean and Swimmers*

Emphasize

Extensions

Near
When your body parts are close to your body.

Far
When your body parts are far from your body.

Ideas for Lesson Development

- ★ Balloon sequence—Blow up an imaginary or real balloon to show near and far; have body parts get farther away from the middle of the body as the balloon expands. Let the balloon go; this movement becomes the second part of the blowing-up sequence. If you wish, have students add a "run, jump, land (without noise)" sequence to imitate the balloon moving quickly before it lands.

Purcell: *Balloons*

KINDERGARTEN

Sample Performance Task

Students are allowed to choose a piece of equipment (ball, streamer, bean bag, etc.) and are asked to take it to a space inside the boundaries where they can move it safely.

RUBRIC CLUES **To what extent do students**

- find a self-space on their own to move to and in?

NASPE BENCHMARKS Travel, in different ways, in a large group without bumping into others or falling. (K, #1)

Identify selected body parts, skills, and movement concepts. (K, #18)

Emphasize

Self-space

Space right next to you, where you can't touch anyone or anything.

General space

Empty or open space all around you.

Ideas for Lesson Development

- ★ Use hoops or carpet squares to help students define their self-space.
- ★ Have students explore the boundaries or limits to their self-space, or personal space, alone and with equipment, such as streamers and balls. Have them use *all* the space.
- ★ At the signal, tell them to move to and touch the boundary of their areas (you can mark the areas with a cone, or indicate to the children that they should stand on the line that "connects each cone like a dot-to-dot").
- ★ From their hoops or squares, students throw the yarn ball to the space "where nobody is" (general space).
- ★ The children travel to music using whichever locomotor movement you call out; they each find a carpet square or hoop (self-space) when the music stops.
- ★ Students travel to the beat of the drum and freeze when it stops. They check to see how close they are to other people. Or, play music and have students stop when the music stops (use different durations to keep up their interest).

Emphasize

Directions

Forward
Your front leads.

Backward
Your back leads.

Sideways
Your side (right or left) leads.

Up
Toward the sky.

Down
Toward the ground.

Ideas for Lesson Development

- ★ Students travel to music in general space in the direction you call out. (You may also call out a movement, for example, "skip forward.") Periodically call out a new direction and movement. For a "breather" have students stop and pat their heads, slap their knees, clap their hands, etc., to the music. For a variation, call students to get a partner and perform the movement in the specified direction together.

Emphasize	Ideas for Lesson Development
Pathways *Curved* Rounded like a rainbow. *Straight* Like a line or pencil. *Zigzag* Straight lines connected to make sharp points.	★ Put gymnastics chalk on the floor and have the students walk through it, using their bare feet to make a pathway. Provide damp sponges to clean up with. ★ Give students large pieces of chalk; have them draw small straight, curved, and angular pathways on the blacktop (after they've learned about them). ★ Again, use chalk to make large straight, curved, and zigzag pathways on the blacktop area (or have the students draw them), but now have students travel, using different locomotor movements, throughout the (boundaried) area. At the signal, call out a pathway, which they must find and move on. Encourage them to keep moving until they find a pathway that is open.

Buschner: *Trails and Roads*

Emphasize	Ideas for Lesson Development
Levels *Low* Below your knees. *Medium* Between your shoulders and knees. *High* Above your shoulders.	★ On a large body shape posted on a bulletin board, illustrate where the different levels are. ★ For travel, have students listen for when the music stops and put the body part you specify into a particular level (e.g., behind—middle; feet—high; whole body—low). ★ The children put a hula hoop at the different levels in relation to their bodies. Challenge them to move it as you direct them (hand and neck—high, waist—medium; foot—low).

Sample Overall Unit Outcome

By the end of elementary school, students should be able to

- design, refine, and perform dance and gymnastics sequences that focus on the use of one or more of the effort concepts of force, flow, and speed.

EFFORT

Concepts and Skills	Learnable Pieces
Speed	
Fast	Like a rabbit! (K, 1-2)
Slow	Like a turtle! (K, 1-2)
Acceleration	Speed up. (1-2, 3-4)
Deceleration	Slow down. (1-2, 3-4)
Force	
Strong	Make your muscles tight. (1-2, 3-4)
Light	Make your muscles relaxed. (1-2, 3-4)
Flow	
Bound	You can stop yourself quickly and be very controlled. (3-4, 5-6)
Free	It's hard to stop the movement, which is very smooth and fluid. (3-4, 5-6)
	Smooth transitions. (5-6)

GRADES 5-6

Sample Performance Task

In small groups of four to six, students are asked to choose an event of significance in our culture related to the concept of force (e.g., Hurricane Andrew, the Berlin Wall coming down, Los Angeles riots, World Trade Center bombing, the fall of apartheid, humanitarian aid for Somalia). They are asked to choose one of these (or other) topics and then create and refine a folk dance around it: This dance will then be put to music portraying strong force.

RUBRIC CLUES **To what extent do students**

- express the concept of force through their chosen topic?
- refine the sequence so it can be performed smoothly?
- make an important contribution to the group's work?

Sample Portfolio Task

Students should think about an athletic or recreational activity they will participate in the next week and analyze it in terms of one of the concepts of either force, flow, or speed. They should describe the types of force, flow, or speed; why these are important for the overall performance of the activity; and an example, if appropriate.

RUBRIC CLUES **To what extent do students**

- show a complete and accurate understanding of the concepts in their discussion and elaboration?

NASPE BENCHMARKS Design and perform gymnastics and dance sequences that combine traveling, rolling, balancing, and weight transfer into smooth, flowing sequences with intentional changes in direction, speed, and flow. (5-6, #4)

Detect, analyze, and correct errors in personal movement patterns. (5-6, #24)

Describe ways to use the body and movement activities to communicate ideas and feelings. (5-6, #25)

Emphasize	Ideas for Lesson Development
Speed—Fast, Slow, Acceleration, and Deceleration—in the contexts of dance, gymnastics, and games	★ Use folk dances that change in speed and require students to accelerate or decelerate their movements (Seven Jumps, Les Statues). ★ See the themes of locomotor (chapter 5), nonlocomotor (chapter 6), and manipulative skills (chapter 7) for additional uses of effort concepts.

Emphasize	Ideas for Lesson Development
Force—Strong and Light—in the contexts of dance, gymnastics, and games	★ Use various kinds of folk music representing strong or light force. Discuss what kind of flow the students think the dance portrays and why. ★ See the themes of locomotor (chapter 5), nonlocomotor (chapter 6), and manipulative skills (chapter 7) for additional uses of effort concepts.

Emphasize	Ideas for Lesson Development
Flow *Bound* You can stop yourself quickly and be very controlled. *Free* It's hard to stop the movement, which is very smooth and fluid. Smooth transitions.	★ Discuss how various sports and movements use different types of flow, including such examples as a gymnast swinging on the bars who uses free flow, a batter swinging the bat who uses a free-flowing movement, a bunt in baseball as an example of a bound-flow movement, and a gymnast pushing up to a handstand on the balance beam using bound flow. ★ Have the students demonstrate movements from different sports, such as examples of free or bound flow, and then work together to put them into a sequence. Use music that is structural or free flowing to go along with their movements. ★ See the themes of rolling, balancing, and weight transfer in chapter 6 and locomotor skills (chapter 5) for additional uses of effort concepts.

Purcell: *Bubbles*

GRADES 3-4

Sample Performance Task

Students are asked to design, refine, and perform a movement sequence with a partner that uses at least four action words (e.g., melt, punch, angry, pop) (Graham, Holt/Hale, & Parker, 1993) to express their choice of either light or strong force and bound or free flow.

RUBRIC CLUES To what extent do students

- use action words that express the concept they chose?
- refine their sequences and perform them smoothly and without hesitation?

Sample Portfolio Task

Students are asked to choose the effort concept (i.e., bound or free flow, fast or slow speed, light or strong force) that interests them the most and to discuss their choice in writing (see Figure 4.3). They should describe why they like this particular concept, why it is important, and give specific examples from their own movement experiences (in everyday life or in athletic or recreational experiences) to illustrate their choice.

RUBRIC CLUES To what extent do students

- describe and elaborate on the concept?
- accurately describe examples of the concept from their own lives?

NASPE BENCHMARKS Identify ways movement concepts can be used to refine movement skills. (3-4, #21)

Design games, gymnastics, and dance sequences that are personally interesting. (3-4, #26)

Name ______________________________ Class ___________________

Force

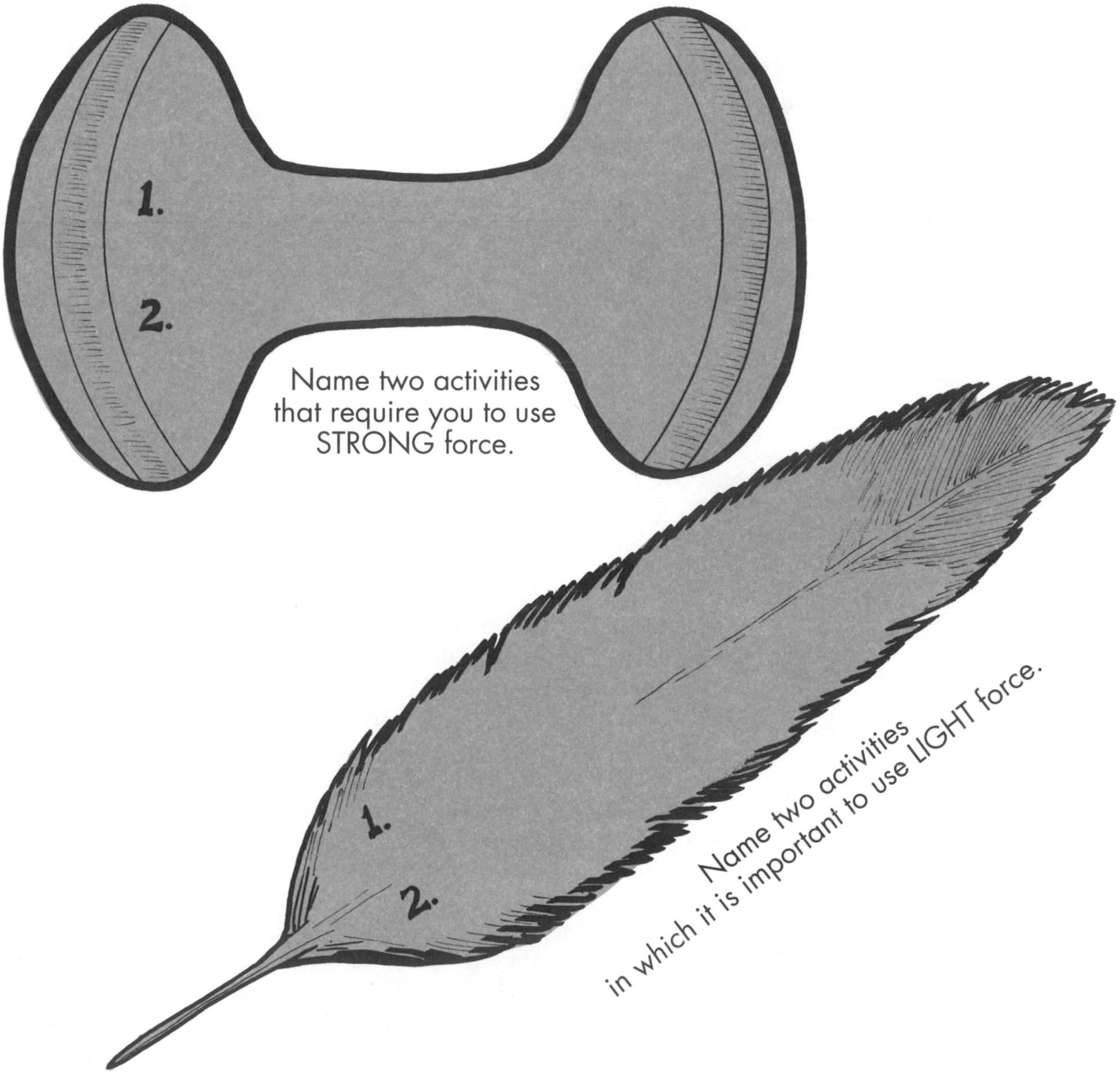
1.
2.
Name two activities
that require you to use
STRONG force.
1.
2.
Name two activities
in which it is important to use LIGHT force.

What kind of force do you like to use most?
Why?

Figure 4.3 *Sample effort assessment sheet for Grades 3-4.*

Emphasize	Ideas for Lesson Development
Speed *Acceleration* Speed up. *Deceleration* Slow down.	★ Students move on mats continuously, alternating between fast and slow movements without stopping to change speed. Have them do one movement (e.g., roll) fast, then slow. ★ They move to a piece of equipment using fast speed, move across or over the equipment using slow speed (or vice versa). ★ The children make three different shapes: the first one is slow and the last one is fast; then they do the opposite—the first one, fast and the last one, slow. (This demonstrates the ability to accelerate or decelerate speed.)

Emphasize	Ideas for Lesson Development
Force *Strong* Make your muscles tight. *Light* Make your muscles relaxed.	★ Put together snippets of music that convey the qualities of strong or light force. Ask the students to move (with or without a prop) to the music, either while it is playing, or after they have listened to the snippet and you have stopped the music. ★ Provide props such as parachutes, rhythm sticks, scarves, and streamers. Students use the props as they work in groups on sequences focusing on speed, force, or flow.

Purcell: *Float and Punch*

Emphasize	Ideas for Lesson Development
Flow *Bound* You can stop yourself quickly and be very controlled. *Free* It's hard to stop the movement, which is very smooth and fluid.	★ Feathers and bubbles are good props to use for free flow. ★ Students can move over their mats in any way that demonstrates free or bound flow. ★ Use music (folk, popular, and classical) suggesting the contrasts between free and bound movements. Give students props to use while they move to the music, and have them show free- or bound-flowing movements. Have groups of two or three students make up a sequence of at least 40 counts. ★ Travel Cards—show a large card with three locomotor movements on it. Use commas in between the movements to designate a "bound" sequence (students must pause after each movement). Omit the commas to designate one movement after the other without stopping, a "free" sequence. First practice a few together as a class and then give each student a card with the sequence notated. Once the students have completed it, they switch cards with someone else. As they work on their sequences, ask students what kind of flow they are using. ★ Discuss how changes in force, flow, and speed are used in dance and gymnastics to add variety to a movement or routine or to express a certain feeling or idea. They are used in games to produce a particular result. Here is an example: In football, the quarterback sometimes wants to throw a fast, deep pass with great force, but at other times a soft touch pass with more control and less force.

Buschner: *Sentence Scrabble*

GRADES 1-2

Sample Performance Task

Number and arrange three to five crates, boxes, or paper bags holding objects of varying weights. Place them at several different stations; set up enough so that there are no more than five students at one station, or use this one station as one of a number of different stations. Such objects as Indian clubs, bowling pins, plastic liter bottles with sand in them, small weights, bean bags, scarves, or frisbees can be placed in the crates and boxes. Other small pieces of equipment, such as hand weights or large PVC pipes, can also be used outside of a container. Make sure that there is a distinct difference between the weights in the containers, especially between the lightest and heaviest ones.

At their stations, students are asked to pick up each container or object, carry it to a designated line, and back to the starting point. They are then asked to rank the containers, by number, along a scale of lightest to heaviest.

RUBRIC CLUES **To what extent do students**

- correctly determine the amount of force needed to lift the different objects?
- use the concept of force to explain and justify their answers?

Sample Portfolio Task

Students are asked to cut out two pictures from magazines showing the use of strong and light force (from athletics or everyday life) and label each with the type of force it requires.

RUBRIC CLUES **To what extent do students**

- show an understanding of the concepts of strong and light force?

NASPE BENCHMARKS Recognize similar movement concepts in a variety of skills. (1-2, #23)

Emphasize

Speed

Fast
Like a rabbit!

Slow
Like a turtle!

Acceleration
Speed up.

Deceleration
Slow down.

Ideas for Lesson Development

- ★ Play different excerpts of music, some in a fast tempo and others in a slow tempo. Ask students to travel or move an object (such as a streamer or scarf) in the speed they think the music portrays.
- ★ Direct the children, "Show me how you can move fast across your mat. Now how you can go slow."
- ★ Have the students travel fast in general space, explaining that when they come to a mat, they are to move slowly across it. Then switch the speeds.
- ★ Students move in self-space using different body movements (twist, rise and fall, etc.) to music or to a signal with varying tempos.
- ★ Play a drum or tambourine to give students either a fast or slow speed they must use to travel through general space. Alternate between fast and slow speeds; at times have the signal accelerate or decelerate.

Emphasize	Ideas for Lesson Development
Force *Strong* Make your muscles tight. *Light* Make your muscles relaxed.	★ Say to students "Show me something in the sport of baseball (gymnastics, football, basketball, ice-skating, etc.) that uses strong force. Show me a light force." Have students perform one or two of these actions together to counts of 8. ★ The children bounce a ball using different amounts of force as you direct them: "Bounce it so it rebounds at a low (medium, high) level. What kind of force did you use?" ★ Ask the students to throw a ball to the wall using strong or light force. Have them discuss which force makes the ball get to the wall faster or slower and why. ★ Use forceful-sounding classical music with big, strong clashes. As they listen, children move and juggle scarves like swords, using strong force. Contrast this with music that sounds light. Have the students use balloons and light running with this music. ★ Gallery Statues—the children stand like statues representing strong or light forces. Their partners guess which kind of force they are using. ★ Ask the children to travel, then freeze in a strong or light pose at the signal or when music stops (use music that illustrates the different force).

Purcell: *April Showers; Percussion Instrument Dance*
Buschner: *Only the Strong and Light Survive*

KINDERGARTEN

Sample Performance Task

Within a large boundaried area, students are asked to travel safely to match both a fast and slow beat.

RUBRIC CLUES **To what extent do students**

- move at a speed appropriate for the given beat?

NASPE BENCHMARKS Demonstrate clear contrasts between slow and fast speeds while traveling. (K, #3)

Identify selected body parts, skills, and movement concepts. (K, #18)

Emphasize

Speed

Fast
Like a rabbit!

Slow
Like a turtle!

Ideas for Lesson Development

★ Put up pictures on a bulletin board or chalkboard depicting places where one moves at a slow or fast speed (e.g., the school hallway, a highway, a play area with lots of equipment, a large open yard). Ask the students which speed they should use at each place.

★ At the signal, have students move either fast or slow to a new carpet square within a large boundaried area. Give them a second signal that tells them they should almost be on a square if they're not already there.

★ Get a slide whistle at a music store (about $3). Move it slowly; have students move their body parts from high to low level slowly. Then move the whistle fast; students move their body parts fast!

★ Have students move their body parts in their self-space, either fast or slow (i.e., hands slow, then fast; head slow; shoulders slow, then fast; feet slow, then fast; body slow, then fast).

Purcell: *The Cat*
Buschner: *Turtles and Rabbits*

Sample Overall Unit Outcome

By the end of elementary school, students should be able to

- design, refine, and perform dance, gymnastics, and small-group games that focus on the use of specific relationships to others and objects.

RELATIONSHIPS

Concepts and Skills	Learnable Pieces
Relationships to objects or others	
	Between/inside/outside (K, 1-2)
	Around/through (K, 1-2)
	In front of/behind/beside (K, 1-2)
	Under/over (K, 1-2)
	On/off (K, 1-2)
	Across (K, 1-2)
	Above/below (K, 1-2)
Relationships to partners	
Leading	Moving ahead of a partner. (1-2)
Following	Moving behind a partner. (1-2)
Meeting	Moving toward a partner. (1-2, 3-4)
Parting	Moving away from a partner. (1-2, 3-4)
Matching	In unison; side by side with a partner. (1-2, 3-4)
Mirroring	In contrast; opposite a partner. (1-2, 3-4)

GRADES 5-6

Sample Performance Task

In groups of three to five, students design, refine, and perform a jump-rope sequence that uses the relationships of meeting, parting, leading, and following. The sequence must last at least 45 seconds and can be performed in either 3/4 or 4/4 meter, to music of their choice (with teacher approval, if necessary).

RUBRIC CLUES **To what extent do students**

- meet the given sequence criteria?
- refine the sequence so it is repeated smoothly and without hesitation by all group members?
- match their movements to the beat of the music?

Sample Portfolio Task

Students are asked to describe a situation in a sport or activity (which they participate in, or watch others play) that uses mirroring (matching, meeting, parting, leading, and following) relationships between players.

RUBRIC CLUES **To what extent do students**

- use examples that correctly illustrate the different relationships?

Emphasize

Relationships to partners and others in the contexts of games, dance, and gymnastics activities.

Ideas for Lesson Development

- ★ Have students mirror the movement of a partner as they both dribble a ball with their hands and move sideways, as they jog and dribble the ball with their feet, and so forth.
- ★ The students dribble and pass a ball back and forth continuously (using the hand or foot) with a partner, so that the person receiving the ball doesn't stop to receive it. Discuss how this relates to a leading relationship.
- ★ Discuss the relationship between an offensive and defensive player. How does one person move in relation to the other? Why do they move this way?
- ★ See other themes for additional activities that use effort concepts.

Werner: *Me and My Shadow*
Purcell: *New Square Dance; Troika; Baseball Dance*

GRADES 3-4

Sample Performance Task

Students are asked to design and perform a movement sequence in small groups that uses matching and mirroring movements. During the sequence (about 30 seconds), they must also use the relationships of meeting and parting. The movements can be taken from a game or sport, dance, gymnastics, or fitness context. They may use their choice of props and music (with teacher approval, if necessary).

RUBRIC CLUES To what extent do students

- mirror and match movements to each other?
- refine the sequence until it is smoothly performed without hesitation by group members?
- use the relationships of meeting and parting?

Sample Portfolio Task

Students are asked to reflect in writing how well they feel their group worked together and how this affected their performance of the sequence. What was easy about working together? difficult? What, if anything, would they change about how they worked together?

RUBRIC CLUES To what extent do students

- put effort into reflecting on the given questions?
- show an understanding of the skills they need to work together with others?

NASPE BENCHMARKS Design games, gymnastics, and dance sequences that are personally interesting. (3-4, #26)

Appreciate differences and similarities in others' physical activity. (3-4, #27)

Emphasize

Relationships to partners

Meeting
Moving toward a partner.

Parting
Moving away from a partner.

Matching
In unison; side by side with a partner.

Mirroring
In contrast; opposite a partner.

Ideas for Lesson Development

★ In a small group (three to four students), students must make up a sequence to music where all members of the group do three matching shapes. Locomotor and nonlocomotor movements can be used in the sequence.

★ Have students form small groups, each having an instrument that makes the same kind of sound. (Instruments can be homemade, such as dried beans inside small plastic containers or plastic cartons and wood blocks—bare or covered in sandpaper. Manufactured instruments might be small tambourines, drum sticks, or triangles. See the school music teacher for help.) The students move to match the sound of one group's instruments, then they put these movements together in a sequence.

Ideas for Lesson Development

★ With partners, students make up a sequence that includes mirroring or matching, meeting, and parting while manipulating an object, such as a streamer, ball, wand, scarf, or jump rope. Specify the duration in counts of the sequence (e.g., five actions to sets of 8 to equal 40 beats). Music may be used. For example, students take a count of 8 to move toward each other while dribbling a ball, dribble in place for another count of 8, mirror a swaying movement while the ball is held over the head for a count of 8, lead and follow while dribbling on a specific pathway for a count of 8, then dribble in place at a low level for a count of 8.

Purcell: *Birthday Celebration*
Buschner: *Moving Scarves; Name That Movement*

GRADES 1-2

Sample Performance Task

Students are asked to find a way, using both the playground equipment and smaller equipment you put out (boxes, hoops, etc.), to demonstrate the relationship (over, under, etc.) that you call out.

RUBRIC CLUES To what extent do students

- correctly demonstrate the different relationships?

Sample Portfolio Task

Ask students to draw a picture of themselves doing an activity that shows them in relation to an object or other person. They should describe, in writing, what they are doing (e.g., jumping over a rope, moving a hula hoop around their arm, climbing over a fence).

RUBRIC CLUES To what extent do students

- use the correct terminology to explain the relationship?
- correctly interpret a possible relationship?

NASPE BENCHMARKS Recognize similar movement concepts in a variety of skills. (1-2, #23)

Emphasize

Relationship to objects or others

Between/inside/outside; Around/through; In front of/behind/beside; Under/over; On/off; Across; Above/below.

Ideas for Lesson Development

★ Vary your methods of working with the relationship words. For example, sometimes call out a word (e.g., over, behind, above) and other times write each word on a large card. (Help students to recognize the words if needed.) Have the students then move accordingly.

★ Call out a specific relationship to an object or person. Have students move to a piece of large playground equipment and demonstrate that relationship (i.e., find a way to go around a piece of equipment; move over or under something; freeze beside something). To add activity, have them return to the area near you at the signal before they move

Ideas for Lesson Development

to complete the next relationship. Make sure you provide plenty of equipment for students to use (tires, crates, and boxes also can be used).

- ★ Have students get partners; one will be the "mover" and the other will be the "freezer." When a relationship word is presented, the mover finds a way to move that way in relationship to the freezer, who must freeze in a shape that allows the mover safe movement. After going through the words, have partners change their roles.
- ★ *A* rolls a hula hoop to a partner, *B*, who holds it. *A* goes over, under, around, through, moving in as many ways as possible. Then *B* rolls it to *A* and has a turn.
- ★ Place a jump rope on the ground and have students jump over it ("stand with the rope in front of you"), going forward and backward; stand beside it, jump over it, walk on it ("now close your eyes"), race around it and so forth.

Werner: *And Away We Go*

Emphasize

Relationships to partners

Leading
Moving ahead of a partner.

Following
Moving behind a partner.

Meeting
Moving toward a partner.

Parting
Moving away from a partner.

Matching
In unison; side by side with a partner.

Mirroring
In contrast; opposite a partner.

Ideas for Lesson Development

- ★ Students lead or follow a partner through general space; the leading partner gets to decide the movement. On the signal, they switch roles.
- ★ Have the follower stand behind the leader; on the signal, leaders start to run away from their followers. After a head start of 5 counts, the follower tries to run and safely tag the leader. At the next signal, they prepare so that the follower becomes the leader.
- ★ While facing their partners, one follower in each pair mirrors simple movements initiated by the leader. At the signal, the roles are reversed.

KINDERGARTEN

Sample Performance Task

Students are asked to move through an obstacle course in which they have to jump over ropes or low jump-rope hurdles, crawl through mat- or large-box "tunnels," crawl under a table covered by a mat, jump on and off a box, and walk across a balance beam (you can use other words as well). Use pictures to help explain each relationship.

RUBRIC CLUES **To what extent do students**

- move using the correct relationship to the object?

NASPE BENCHMARKS Travel, demonstrating a variety of relationships with objects (e.g., over, under, behind, alongside, through). (K, #6)

Identify selected body parts, skills, and movement concepts. (K, #18)

Emphasize

Relationships to objects or others

Between/inside/outside; Around/through; In front of/behind/beside; Under/over; On/off; Across; Above/below

Ideas for Lesson Development

- ★ Have students put a ball in front of them, behind them, above them, or under them (but not sitting on it!), while in their self-space.
- ★ Make up an obstacle course in which students must jump over low rope hurdles, roll across mats, pull themselves under hurdles, walk along jump-rope lines, and crawl through rolled-up mats, standing hula hoops, or foam shapes. Use a variety of equipment and relationships.

Werner: *And Away We Go*
Buschner: *Hoops and Me*

CHAPTER 5 Locomotor Skills

Sample Overall Unit Outcome

By the end of elementary school, students should be able to

- develop, in a small group, repeatable patterns of one or more locomotor skills into a sequence, which is performed to music.

LOCOMOTOR MOVEMENTS

Concepts and Skills	Learnable Pieces
Walk	
	Heels touch ground first. (K) Arms move opposite legs. (K)
Run	
	Ball of foot touches ground first. (K) Arms move opposite legs. (K)
Jump	
	Bend knees. (K, 1-2) Push off, land on balls of feet. (1-2) Use both feet. (K, 1-2)
Hop	
	Bend knees. (K, 1-2) Jump, land on ball of foot. (1-2) Use only one foot. (K, 1-2)
Gallop	
	Toe-to-heel. (K, 1-2) One foot always chases the other. (K, 1-2)
Slide	
	Side—together. (K, 1-2) One foot pushes the other sideways. (K, 1-2)
Skip	
	Step—hop. (K, 1-2) Kick the beach ball. (K, 1-2) Arms move opposite legs. (1-2)
Leap	
	Bend knees. (1-2) One foot to the other. (K, 1-2) Land on balls of feet. (3-4) Stretch legs wide. (5-6)

GRADES 5-6

Sample Performance Task

In groups of four, students should design a sequence of locomotor patterns (e.g., moving 4 steps forward and then 4 steps backward, or sliding to the left 4 times and then right 4 times) and nonlocomotor movements that can be repeated to music in 4/4 meter (provided or approved by the teacher). The sequence should include at least two patterns of locomotor movements and at least two nonlocomotor movements (done in place). It should be repeatable for at least 64 counts.

RUBRIC CLUES To what extent do students

- meet the given sequence criteria?
- refine the sequence so partners can perform it smoothly and without hesitation?
- match their movements to the music's beat?
- repeat the sequence for the desired length?

Sample Portfolio Task

Students are asked to list and describe various sports or activities that involve the use of the different locomotor movements (see Figure 5.1).

RUBRIC CLUES To what extent do students

- show a correct understanding of the locomotor skills used in various sports and activities?

NASPE BENCHMARKS Design and perform gymnastics and dance sequences that combine traveling, rolling, balancing, and weight transfer into smooth, flowing sequences with intentional changes in direction, speed, and flow. (5-6, #4)

Emphasize

The use of locomotor movements in the contexts of gymnastics, dance, and game activities.

Leap

Stretch legs wide.

Ideas for Lesson Development

- ★ Name different emotions and ask students to express each emotion through a locomotor movement. Examples might include happiness or joy as jumping; sadness, happiness, or cheerfulness as walking; joy as leaping. Discuss how folk dances use locomotor movements to help peoples of a culture express their feelings, beliefs, and lifestyles.
- ★ Write one pattern on a card of even or uneven locomotor movements that can be done to counts of 6 or 8 (e.g., walk 3 or 4 steps forward, then 3 or 4 steps backward; step—touch to the right and then to the left 3 or 4 times; jog 6 or 8 steps; skip 6 or 8 steps forward; or slide to the right and then to the left 3 or 4 times). Students each pick one card and perform the pattern to 3/4 or 4/4 music; then they work with a partner and combine their two patterns (one after the other) to make a sequence. Have them combine their paired sequence with two other students' sequence (again, one sequence after the other) to make an even larger sequence! Have them write their sequences down. More advanced students can make up their own patterns.
- ★ Let students design their own small-group sequences, which incorporate different locomotor movements and changes in relationships, effort concepts, and so forth (depending on your choice of criteria).
- ★ See Phyllis Weikart's *Teaching Movement and Dance: Intermediate Folk Dance* (1989), an excellent resource.

Name ______________________ Class ______________

Can you name a sport or game that uses the following locomotor movements?

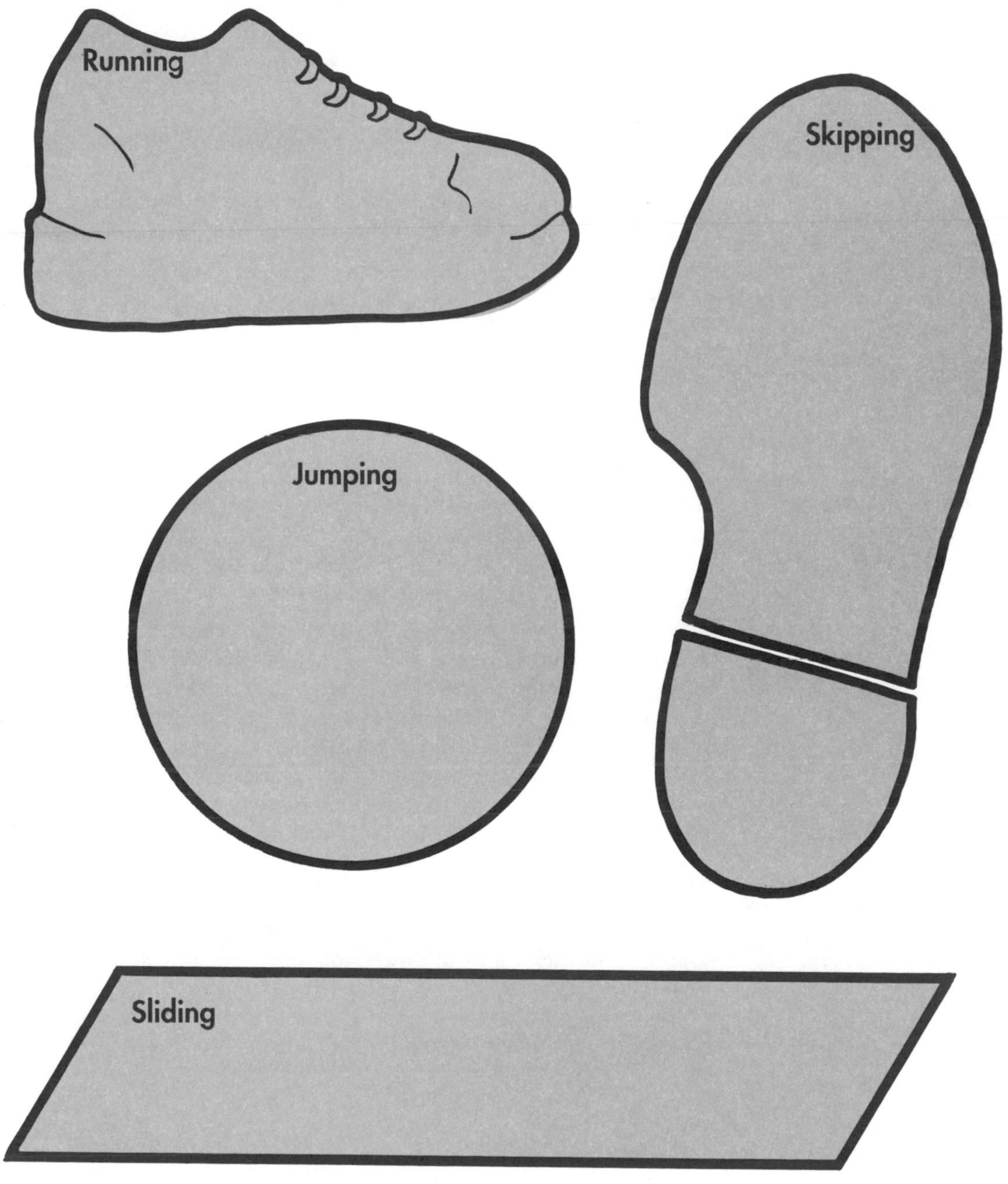

Figure 5.1 *Sample locomotor skills assessment sheet for Grades 5-6.*

GRADES 3-4

Sample Performance Task

Students work with a partner to design a sequence of four different patterns of locomotor movements. Each pattern should last for 8 counts (e.g., slide to the left 4 times, slide to the right 4 times or walk 4 steps forward, walk 4 steps backward). The sequence should be repeatable 4 consecutive times to 4/4 music (provided by the teacher).

RUBRIC CLUES **To what extent do students**

- meet the given sequence criteria?
- refine the sequence so both partners can perform it smoothly and without hesitation?
- match their movements to the music's beat?
- repeat the sequence the required number of times?

Sample Portfolio Task

While watching a music or athletic event video (students' choice) at home or school, or watching an athletic event in person, students try to identify the various locomotor movements they observe. They should include a general description of what the dancer or athlete was doing when performing these movements.

RUBRIC CLUES **To what extent do students**

- identify the different locomotor movements?

NASPE BENCHMARKS Design games, gymnastics, and dance sequences that are personally interesting. (3-4, #26)

Emphasize

The use of locomotor movements in the contexts of gymnastics, dance, and games activities.

Ideas for Lesson Development

- ★ Set up an obstacle course that designates specific locomotor movements to be done in relation to objects—around, over, between, and so forth. Use jump-rope hurdles, cones, crates, and other equipment. Let students also design their obstacle courses.
- ★ Give students gymnastics or dance routines that show several different locomotor movements. Here are a few examples: (a) In a group of 8, start in a position that is far apart; move together using any jumping action; show a symmetrical balance; part by using your choice of movement; end in a low-level position. (b) Start at low level; roll to meet or part; show a movement that requires strong force; travel while meeting or parting; end in a position showing a medium and low level. (c) One person must start in high level; travel, showing changes in directions; roll, showing changes in speed; end with one person at a high level.
- ★ Design a sequence, done to counts of 8 and using a streamer, in which students show changes in directions and locomotor movements.

Buschner: *Name That Movement*

Emphasize

Leap

Land on balls of feet.

Ideas for Lesson Development

★ Provide a variety of equipment for students to leap over and across. For instance, use two tug-of-war ropes to make a large *V*; encourage students to run and leap over whichever part of the rope they feel they can make. Allow them to change from one part of the rope to another.

Buschner: *Leap for Life*

GRADES 1-2

Sample Performance Task

Four Corners—Set up four stations of choice at the four corners of a large boundaried area. Post two large cards at each station: one should describe what to do at the station and the other should designate the locomotor movement of either skip, hop, gallop, or slide.

At the signal, students use the designated locomotor movement to move on to the new station. During this time, observe the skipping (hopping, galloping, or sliding) locomotor patterns of students in one group. (You can also videotape the activity and look at it more closely at a later time.) Emphasize that you are looking for students' best moving, not getting to the next station first. Keep the time at each station minimal in order to fully observe each student's pattern in that group. If possible, observe more than one group during each session.

RUBRIC CLUES **To what extent do students**

- demonstrate the learnable pieces for each locomotor movement?

Sample Portfolio Task

Students are asked to match the movement word with a picture showing that movement (see Figure 5.2).

RUBRIC CLUES **To what extent do students**

- correctly match the movement with the picture?

NASPE BENCHMARKS Skip, hop, gallop, and slide, using mature motor patterns. (1-2, #18)

Participate in a wide variety of activities that involve locomotion, nonlocomotion, and the manipulation of various objects. (1-2, #22)

Name ______________________________ Class ____________________

Draw a line from the locomotor movement in the picture to the word.

Jump

Walk

Run

Hop

Figure 5.2 *Sample locomotor skills assessment sheet for Grades 1-2.*

Emphasize

Jump

Bend knees.

Push off, land on balls of feet.

Use both feet.

Hop

Bend knees.

Jump, land on ball of foot.

Use only one foot.

Gallop

Toe-to-heel.

One foot always chases the other.

Slide

Side—together.

One foot pushes the other sideways.

Skip

Step—hop.

Kick the beach ball.

Arms move opposite legs.

Leap

Bend knees.

One foot to the other.

Ideas for Lesson Development

★ Have students travel through general space using the specified locomotor movement. When they come to a crate, box, hurdle, rope, or cone, they leap over it and keep going.

★ Students practice traveling and leaping over hoops; with a partner, they put hoops together in a pattern and see how many they can do in a row.

★ Put 4 to 6 "child-designed" hurdles (whose bases insert into a cone) or low and high jump-rope hurdles into a row. Students practice running and leaping over them.

★ Ask students to gallop, then slide. Discuss what the differences are between the two movements. Let students walk through each movement if they aren't able to perform it smoothly or rhythmically.

★ Have students make up a sequence using skipping from one place to another. They should make sure the sequence has a beginning and ending shape.

★ Use paper plates on the floor to designate foot placement for different hopscotch jumping patterns. Let students create their own patterns and try other's patterns as well.

★ Rhythm sticks sequence—Instruct the children to tap the ground 3 times with their foot and then slide 3 times in one direction; they do the same in the other direction. Then they get a rhythm stick and tap it 3 times on the ground and then slide; they repeat this in the other direction. Then have them put this to 3/4 music with a strong beat.

★ Play music with a 4/4 meter. Have the students practice counting the beat and clapping their hands, legs, or head while standing or sitting. Then ask them to walk, count, and clap in groups of four, making sure they move only one step per beat. Next play a song with a 3/4 meter; again, have students count and clap along with you to the beat while still. Finally, have them move, count, and clap to the beat.

★ After students have had experience moving with all the different locomotor movements, mark out an even beat with a drum or tambourine. Ask students to move through general space any way they wish, as long as they can take one movement per beat (walk, run, hop, jump, march). Then, mark out an uneven beat and have them move to it (slide, gallop, skip).

★ Have students design an 8-count sequence using locomotor and nonlocomotor movements. Giving a drum beat, have students explore different ways to move to counts of 8 while standing still (count it out "move, 2, 3 . . . 8; switch, 2 . . . 8; etc.). The next step is for them to practice moving for 8 beats, using any locomotor movement. Then, on counts of 8, have them alternate a nonlocomotor movement they performed earlier with a locomotor movement. Once they can smoothly put together 8 counts of nonlocomotor and locomotor movements, progress to using counts of 4.

Werner: *And Away We Go*
Buschner: *Sports Skipping*
Purcell: *Run, Jump, Hop, and Skip*

KINDERGARTEN

Sample Performance Task

Set up a short track around which students can safely move. Ask the students to walk around the track, run around it, and so forth as part of a warm-up or other class activity (using music makes it more enjoyable). Before students begin to move around the track, identify four to six of them to wear a pinnie, crown, flag tucked in their belt, or other sign. Focus on these students' abilities to walk and run around the track. After the assessment, either have these students give their pinnies to someone else or use them on a different day.

RUBRIC CLUES **To what extent do students**

- walk landing on the heel and pushing off the ball of the foot?
- run landing first on and then pushing off of the ball of the foot?
- move the arms in opposition to the legs?

NASPE BENCHMARKS Walk and run using a mature motor pattern. (K, #15)

Emphasize

Walk

Heels touch ground first.

Arms move opposite legs.

Run

Ball of foot touches ground first.

Arms move opposite legs.

Jump

Bend knees.

Use both feet.

Hop

Bend knees.

Use only one foot.

Gallop

Toe-to-heel.

One foot always chases the other.

Slide

Side—together.

One foot pushes the other sideways.

Skip

Step—hop.

Kick the beach ball.

Leap

One foot to the other.

Ideas for Lesson Development

★ Use an instrument, such as a drum or tambourine, as a signal when working with students on locomotor activities. These instruments are loud enough to be heard over music, and the students love getting to hit the drum or shake the tambourine! Using a wireless microphone can also amplify your instructions to help students hear over the music.

★ Have students travel to music using a locomotor movement you call out; at the signal, they stop and prepare to move in the next way you call out. As students develop in listening and motor abilities, call out the locomotor movement without stopping the music. Intersperse the locomotor with nonlocomotor movements (for instance, every time the chorus comes on, students twist, sway, swing, etc.).

★ To counts of 8, students march and clap to the beat of the tambourine, drum, or other 2/4 music. At intervals, they stop and clap the body part you call out (head, tummy, legs, shoulders, etc.) for 8 more counts, then begin marching again. Vary the directions and pathways they march. For variety, give four to six students a tambourine to beat as they march. Have them give it to someone else during the "rest stops."

★ Students walk in different directions through general space. When they come to a jump rope lying on the ground, they jump over it in the direction they are moving and keep going.

★ Have students practice skipping by imagining they are holding a very large beach ball out in front of them. Each time they step, they kick the beach ball with their other knee. This idea—and others—are found in *Teaching Your Wings to Fly* by Anne L. Barlin, 1979.

Sample Overall Unit Outcome

By the end of elementary school, students should be able to

- use locomotor and nonlocomotor skills in order to successfully chase, flee, and dodge others in game situations.

CHASING, FLEEING, AND DODGING

Concepts and Skills	Learnable Pieces
Chase	
	Move quickly! (K, 1-2) Watch their middle (to see direction they move in). (1-2, 3-4) Quick changes (in direction, pathway, speed). (1-2, 3-4)
Flee	
	Move quickly! (K, 1-2) Quick changes. (1-2)
Dodge	
	Quick movements. (1-2) Keep on the balls of your feet—be ready! (1-2) Quick changes (in direction, pathway, speed). (1-2, 3-4, 5-6)
Fake	
	Your head moves one way, your body goes the other. (3-4) Quick movements. (3-4) Watch their middle. (3-4)

GRADES 5-6

Sample Performance Task

Students design and play a small-group (i.e., three or four students) game in which chasing, fleeing, and dodging are combined with either throwing or dribbling in order to move an object or person toward a specified goal area or other person or object. Students may choose boundaries, rules, and objects to be used in the game.

RUBRIC CLUES **To what extent do students**

- consistently attempt to create space on offense by moving to open areas so that they can receive and move the ball toward a goal?
- consistently deny space on defense by keeping their body between the ball and the intended player or goal?
- cooperate in order to design and play their game?

Sample Portfolio Task

Students are asked to give a name to their games and write their rules. They must explain how the skills of either chasing, fleeing, or dodging are used in their games and how they are scored.

RUBRIC CLUES **To what extent do students**

- sufficiently explain the game and its rules?
- include the skills of chasing, fleeing, and dodging in the game?

Emphasize

Dodge

Quick changes (in direction, pathway, speed)

General space (see "Space Awareness," chapter 4)

Offense
Keep your body between the ball and the defender.

Create space by moving to open areas to pass or receive the ball.

Defense
Deny space by keeping between the opponent and intended goal.

Ideas for Lesson Development

- ★ Two students set up a target (goal area, target on a wall, etc.) in a specified area marked by cones, ropes, or other equipment; one tries to get a ball to the target by dribbling or throwing without its being stolen from them by their partner, a defensive player. Discuss how a defensive player denies space and guards a target.
- ★ Set up lanes about 6- to 8-ft wide with a goal area at one end. Two offensive players and one defensive player stay in each lane. The offensive players try to get past the defensive player by dribbling with the hands or feet to get the ball to the goal. Discuss what the role of each player is.
- ★ Line Soccer or Basketball—Set up lanes the length of the playing area. One defensive and one offensive player stay in each lane, only touching the ball when it comes in their lane. Discuss how offensive players must work to get open to receive a ball, no matter which lane they are in; discuss the positioning that the defensive player must take.
- ★ Discuss how players on offense sometimes move away from the goal area to get open to pass or receive a ball and that to create space players do not always stay near the goal area.

Belka: *Runner, Stay Away*

GRADES 3-4

Sample Performance Task

Set up the Trees-in-the-Forest game (see Grades 1-2) in a boundaried area. Instead of moving from one endline to another, however, students travel and move throughout the area while dribbling a ball with either the feet or hands. As they come to a "tree" standing in the hoop (trees can step out of the hoop with one foot), they try to dodge the tree and also not lose the ball—by positioning their body between the ball and the tree. If the ball is stolen or if the students are tagged, they still keep moving until all observations are made by the teacher. (Have four to six students at a time wear pinnies; observe these students only. After their turn the students give the pinnies to six other students.)

RUBRIC CLUES **To what extent do students**

- consistently use the proper dodging strategy—keeping their body between the ball and the opponent—to avoid losing control of the ball or being tagged?

Sample Portfolio Task

Chasing, fleeing, and dodging are used in many game situations. Students are asked to reflect, in writing, about a game they were either involved in or attended in which the participants had to use these skills. Which skills were used in the game—chasing, fleeing, or dodging? Why did the participants use these? Do you think the players had fun playing this game?

RUBRIC CLUES **To what extent do students**

- describe and give examples in writing that accurately reflect knowledge of the different skills of chasing, fleeing, and dodging?

NASPE BENCHMARKS While traveling, avoid or catch an individual or object. (3-4, #1)

Emphasize

Fake

Your head moves one way, your body goes the other.

Quick movements.

Watch their middle.

Chase

Quick changes (in direction, pathway, speed).

Watch their middle (to see direction they move in).

Ideas for Lesson Development

- ★ Discuss why faking is used: in order to trick a defender into thinking he or she will move one way, when the intention is to move the other.
- ★ With a partner, students start apart and move toward each other in a large boundaried area. When they get close, one partner (the faker) moves first and tries to fake the direction to throw the other person off and avoid being tagged. After three tries, roles are reversed.

Belka: *Partner Tag; Fake and Take*
Buschner: *Dodge and Freeze Tag*

Emphasize

Dodge
Quick changes (in direction, pathway, speed).

General space (see "Space Awareness," chapter 4)

Offense
Keep your body between the ball and the defender.

Ideas for Lesson Development

★ Set up a Trees-in-the-Forest game similar to the assessment task given earlier. For a variation, let students move from one endline to the other. Students can also dribble with the feet instead of the hands.

Belka: *Merry-Go-Round*

GRADES 1-2

Sample Performance Task

Students organize a 2-on-2 Monkey-in-the-Middle dodging game: Two carpet squares about 10 feet apart are used to designate where the two throwers need to stay at or behind, and a soft (yarn, foam) ball is used for throwing. During the game, the "monkey" uses a variety of dodging skills to avoid being thrown out. Care should be taken that the throwers aim at a low or medium level. Each student gets three chances to be the "monkey"; at the third hit, they switch places with a thrower." (Encourage students who stay in the middle for an extended period of time to switch even before they are hit three times.)

RUBRIC CLUES To what extent do students

- consistently use a dodging skill appropriate to the throw?

Sample Portfolio Task

Students are asked to demonstrate their knowledge in writing of chasing, fleeing, and dodging skills (see Figure 5.3).

RUBRIC CLUES To what extent do students

- correctly identify the skills involved?

NASPE BENCHMARKS Demonstrate skills of chasing, fleeing, and dodging to avoid or catch others. (1-2, #5)

Name ____________________ Class ____________

Catch Me If You Can!

Which of these pictures show skills you use when you chase, flee, or dodge? Circle them. Then, put an *X* on the skills you *don't* use.

Name one game that uses chasing, fleeing, or dodging. ____________

Figure 5.3 *Sample chasing, fleeing, and dodging assessment sheet for Grades 1-2.*

Emphasize	Ideas for Lesson Development
Dodge Quick movements. Keep on the balls of your feet—be ready!	★ At the signal, students perform the dodging movement that is called out (duck, twist, collapse, roll, stretch, pivot, jump). They should get ready for the next call as quickly as possible. ★ Students travel through general space; at the signal, they perform a dodging movement that is called out and then continue traveling. Discuss the situations in which each movement would be used.

Belka: *This Way and That Way*

Emphasize	Ideas for Lesson Development
Chase Move quickly! Watch their middle (to see direction they move in). **Flee** Move quickly! Quick changes. **Dodge** Quick movements	★ Students travel through general space; at the signal, they quickly change the direction or pathway they are moving in (specify which of the two they are to focus on). Vary the interval between changes. ★ Students travel through general space and try to get as close as possible to someone, but quickly change directions and pathways in order to dodge the other child. ★ Have students find partners. One partner is the first tagger. All students begin to travel throughout a large boundaried area, and each child tries to avoid being tagged by their "tagger" partner. When one is tagged (or at the signal), they switch roles. If needed, limit students to using a specific locomotor movement, such as walking. ★ Trees in the Forest—start with about 6 hoops spread throughout a boundaried area. At the signal, students travel (locomotor movement only) from one end of the area to the other, trying not to get caught by the "tree" in the hoop. If caught, the student gets a hoop and puts it in the area as well. Start new games often (when about 8 or so students are left) to allow all students the chance to be active. ★ In pairs, at a signal one partner begins to travel quickly away from the stationary partner. At the next signal (or a count of 5) the stationary partner follows and tries to tag the first gently. ★ Flag Tag—all students have a flag belt with one or two flags or a flag stuck in their waistband. Using a very large boundaried area, students try to take flags away from all other students while avoiding loss of their own. If a flag is caught, it can be deposited in a specified area; if both flags are caught, the student can still try to capture others' flags. Start the game over when eight or fewer students still have flags. In a variation to make the game more continuous, students can come to the "safe area" to put a flag back on their belt, if both have been taken.

KINDERGARTEN

Emphasize	Ideas for Lesson Development
Chase Move quickly! **Flee** Move quickly!	★ Have students travel throughout the boundaried area using the specific pathway you call out. ★ Using chalk, make large pathways on a blacktop area or make them on grass using spray paint or line chalk. Students move throughout the area; at the signal, they find the pathway you specify and move on it. Encourage them to keep moving if needed until they find a pathway open. At the next signal, they again travel, waiting until the following signal to find a pathway to move on. Vary the locomotor movements they use. ★ Set up cones, boxes, and crates throughout the boundaried area. As students move throughout general space, encourage them to move as close to the objects as possible and move away quickly, without touching them. ★ Students get a partner; at the signal, one of them runs as quickly as possible toward a long designated line or large area. After the count of 3-alligators, the partner runs and tries to catch up with the first child. If the partners meet, they both run together to the line or area; the second child gets to run first, after a short rest.

Sample Overall Unit Outcome

By the end of elementary school, students should be able to

- as part of a small group, use different jumping patterns to design, refine, and perform a jump-rope routine to music.

JUMPING AND LANDING

Concepts and Skills	Learnable Pieces
Height	
	Feet (shoulder-width) apart. (1-2)
	Bend hips and knees. (1-2)
	(Push off) balls of feet. (1-2)
	Arms (swing) back to up. (1-2)
	Stretch up high. (3-4)
Distance	
	Feet (shoulder-width) apart. (1-2)
	Bend hips and knees. (1-2)
	(Push off) balls of feet. (1-2)
	Arms (swing) back to front. (1-2)
	Heels land first. (3-4)
Short jump rope	
	Bend knees (when pushing off or landing). (1-2)
	Elbows close to body. (1-2)
	Hands down (below the shoulders). (1-2)
	(Push off, land on) balls of feet. (1-2)
	Slow jumps (yield on landing). (1-2)
	Fast jumps (buoyant landing). (1-2, 3-4)
	Jump barely off the ground. (3-4)
	Turn the wrist only (to turn rope). (3-4)
Long jump rope	
	Bend knees. (K, 1-2)
	(Push off, land on) balls of feet. (1-2)
	Slow jumps (yield on landing). (1-2)
	Jump barely off the ground. (1-2)
	Stay in the middle. (1-2)
	Jump when rope is past both shoulders. (1-2)
	Make big circles with your arms (to turn the rope). (K, 1-2)
	Start near turner (to jump in). (3-4)
	Jump in when rope is on its way up. (3-4)

GRADES 5-6

Sample Performance Task

In groups of three to five, the students design, refine, and perform a jump-rope routine to music of their choice. The routine must contain at least five different types of jumps, two different directions, two changes in relationships among group members, and beginning and ending shapes that vary in level. Once refined, the routine must last for at least 30 seconds. It can be performed to music of the teacher's or students' choice.

RUBRIC CLUES **To what extent do students**

- perform a routine that reflects all the criteria?
- refine the routine so all partners can perform it without hesitation and with a minimum of errors?
- perform the routine in time with the music?

Sample Portfolio Task

Students are asked to jump rope at least three different times in 1 week. Each time, they are to record the highest number of jumps they can perform in a row without stopping. At the end of the week, they are asked to reflect in writing on such questions as "Did you increase the number of jumps you could do? Why do you think this did or didn't happen? What fitness components do you think jumping rope helps? What makes you think this?"

RUBRIC CLUES **To what extent do students**

- show they understand how to improve performance of a skill?
- show they understand how rope jumping can develop cardiorespiratory fitness, muscular strength, and endurance?
- complete the assignment three times during the week?

NASPE BENCHMARKS Design and refine a routine, combining various jump-rope movements to music, so that it can be repeated without error. (5-6, #9)

Identify benefits resulting from participation in different forms of physical activities. (5-6, #23)

Emphasize

The use of jumping in the contexts of dance, gymnastics, and games activities

Ideas for Lesson Development

★ Have students practice jumping with tinikling sticks. Discuss the cultural and dance heritage of the activity. Allow students in groups to make up different steps to 3/4 and 4/4 music.

GRADES 3-4

Sample Performance Task

With partners, students make up a short (40 beat), repeatable jump-rope sequence using at least five different jumps of their choice. The sequence should be performed to 4/4 music.

RUBRIC CLUES **To what extent do students**

- perform at least five different jumps?
- perform the sequence smoothly and without hesitation?
- perform the sequence for the required number (40) of counts?
- perform the sequence so both partners' actions match?

Sample Portfolio Task

In groups of three, students are asked to write a rhyme that they can jump to with a long jump rope. The rhyme should last for at least 12 jumps. Each group gets a chance to recite its rhyme while the others in the class jump, if teacher desires.

RUBRIC CLUES **To what extent do students**

- write a rhyme suitable for jumping to?
- write a rhyme at least 12 jumps long?

NASPE BENCHMARKS Develop patterns and combinations of movements into repeatable sequences. (3-4, #8)

Emphasize

Short jump rope

Jump barely off the ground.

Turn the wrists only (to turn rope).

Fast jumps (buoyant landing).

Ideas for Lesson Development

★ Set up stations that focus on different types of jumps (two-foot yielding jumps, skip-step jumps, backward jumps, two-person jumps, etc.). If you wish, intersperse the stations with fitness stations (e.g., situps, jogging around the boundary of the area). Play music; when the music stops, students stop and prepare to move to the next station. Use the music to signal the move.

Emphasize

Long jump rope

Start near turner (to jump in).

Jump in when rope is on its way up.

Ideas for Lesson Development

★ In groups of three or four, students practice jumping into and out of a long jump rope. This can be done as one of many jumping stations or as a separate activity.

Emphasize	Ideas for Lesson Development
Height Stretch up high. **Distance** Heels land first.	★ Set up stations to focus on jumping for distance or height: (1) Students measure their vertical jump against a tape measure. (2) Students run up to a jump-rope line, take off from one foot, and land on two; a partner marks the best of three jumps (running long jump). (3) Students jump for distance from a standing position; partner marks the best jump, and the students measure the distance (standing broad jump). (4) High water, low water: In groups of four with two students holding a long jump rope the other two students jump, from a standing position, over the rope at a height they instruct the holders to use. If they miss the jump, their next height has to be lower. After five jumps, they become the holders. (5) High jump: Using a line or rope weighted at each end and supported on two standards or a rope held by two holders, the students have the chance to run up to and jump over the rope onto a crash pad.

GRADES 1-2

Sample Performance Task

Students are asked to jump forward over a self-turned, short jump rope while keeping in their self-space.

RUBRIC CLUES **To what extent do students**

- jump repeatedly over the rope without stopping?
- bend the knees when jumping and landing?
- push off of and land on the balls of the foot (rather than the whole, flat foot)?

Sample Portfolio Task

Students are asked to write to their friend Murgatroid, who is from another planet and has never jumped rope before (Graham, 1992). What are some hints that they can give Murgatroid to improve jump-rope skills?

RUBRIC CLUES **To what extent do students**

- answer accurately using hints learned in class?
- correctly justify their answers if cues from class are not used?

NASPE BENCHMARKS Jump and land using a combination of one- and two-foot takeoffs and landings. (1-2, #4)

Repeatedly jump a self-turned rope. (1-2, #16)

Emphasize	Ideas for Lesson Development
Jump (see "Locomotor Movements," this chapter) Bend knees. Push off, land on balls of feet.	★ Spread a variety of low rope hurdles, foam shapes, carpet squares, boxes, and hoops in general space. Students travel throughout the area; at the signal, they find an object to jump over and keep on traveling. If you wish, specify a jumping pattern for them to use.

Ideas for Lesson Development

- ★ Make jumping boxes by putting empty vegetable cans (large ones from the cafeteria) bottoms-up back in the original carton. Tape around each box well. Students practice jumping off the box, over the box, and so forth.
- ★ Have students (with or without a partner) create different jumps, give them a name (e.g., Michael Jordan jump, Ninja Turtles jump, helicopter jump, Barbie jump), and then perform them for the class.

Emphasize

Height

Feet (shoulder-width) apart.

Bend hips and knees.

(Push off) balls of feet.

Arms (swing) back to up.

Distance

Feet (shoulder-width) apart.

Bend hips and knees.

(Push off) balls of feet.

Arms (swing) back to front.

Ideas for Lesson Development

- ★ Hang objects (streamer strips, etc.) from ropes at different heights. Have students practice jumping to reach them.
- ★ Students jump three times for distance from behind a jump rope on the ground. A partner marks the longest distance landed, with an object such as a beanbag or cone. Students switch roles. If you wish, have students measure their longest jumps using a yardstick or ruler.

Emphasize

Long jump rope

Bend knees.

(Push off, land on) balls of feet.

Slow jumps (yield on landing).

Stay in the middle.

Jump barely off the ground.

Jump when rope is past both shoulders.

Make big circles with your arms (to turn the rope).

Ideas for Lesson Development

- ★ Draw a box on the ground to show where students should stand as they jump over a long rope. Have them practice jumping forward and backward, side to side over a swinging rope.
- ★ Use a drum signal to show the difference between buoyant (fast jumps) and yielding (slow jumps) landings (buoyant—loud, loud, loud beat; yielding—loud and soft, loud and soft, loud and soft beat). See if they can jump to each beat without using a rope and then transfer the yielding for landing when they jump over the long rope.

Emphasize

Short jump rope

Bend knees (when pushing off or landing).

Elbows close to body.

Hands down (below the shoulders).

(Push off, land on) balls of feet.

Slow jumps (yield on landing).

Fast jumps (buoyant landing).

Ideas for Lesson Development

★ Again, have students first practice jumping without a rope, or over a jump rope lying on the ground, to a "buoyant" or "yielding" beat.

Buschner: *Knees and Ropes*

KINDERGARTEN

Sample Performance Task

In groups of three (two holders and one jumper), students practice jumping over a slowly swinging long rope. Students are asked to practice jumping over the rope using a two-footed jumping and landing pattern (jump off two feet, land on two feet) as many times as possible (at least three times). (If you wish, set up a group of stations; you might have two older students as "turners").

RUBRIC CLUES **To what extent do students**

- bend the knees when jumping over the rope?
- push off of and land on two feet?
- jump over the rope at least three times without losing their balance?

NASPE BENCHMARKS Continuously jump a swinging rope held by others. (K, #13)

Emphasize

Jump (see "Locomotor Movements," this chapter)

Bend knees.

Ideas for Lesson Development

★ Each student practices jumping and landing with a variety of takeoff and landing patterns (two feet-two feet; 2-1; 1-2; 1-1) for jumping over individual low jump-rope hurdles (jump ropes put in cones), hoop, rope on the ground, and so forth.

★ Set up low jump-rope hurdles in a row; students travel up to each hurdle and jump over it with two feet, one foot, or whatever you call out.

Emphasize	Ideas for Lesson Development
Long jump rope Bend knees. Make big circles with your arms (to turn the rope).	★ Set up students in groups of three; two turners and one jumper. Have students practice jumping over a swinging (back-and-forth) and twirling (overhead) rope. Students should start by standing in the middle; have the turners count and then "hit" the rope against the jumper's foot three times, so jumper starts jumping on the count of three. After five tries, students switch roles.

CHAPTER 6 Nonlocomotor Skills

Sample Overall Unit Outcome

By the end of elementary school, students should be able to

- with a partner or small group, combine the skills of rolling, balancing, and weight transfer, along with locomotor skills, in order to design, refine, and perform a gymnastics or dance sequence.

ROLLING

Concepts and Skills	Learnable Pieces
Rocking	
	Chin to chest. (1-2) Head to knees. (1-2) Curved shape—no flat tires! (K, 1-2)
Sideways	
	Like a pencil (head between arms)! (K, 1-2) Tight muscles. (1-2) (Begin to) turn from your tummy. (1-2)
Forward	
	Curved shape—no flat tires! (K, 1-2) Chin to chest. (K, 1-2) Behind up. (K, 1-2) Push with your hands. (1-2) Finish on your feet. (3-4, 5-6) Soft rolls. (3-4, 5-6) Give with your arms. (3-4, 5-6)
Backward	
	Curved shape. (1-2) Head to knees. (1-2) Hands by your ears. (1-2, 3-4) Push up. (3-4) Finish on your feet. (5-6) Soft rolls. (5-6)
Aerial roll	
	Tuck chin to chest. (5-6) Give with your arms. (3-4, 5-6) Soft rolls. (5-6)
Rolling on equipment	
	Tight muscles. (5-6) Shoulders and body over the equipment. (5-6)

GRADES 5-6

Sample Performance Task

In groups of three or four, students design, refine, and perform a sequence that incorporates rolls of at least two different shapes with balances and transfers of weight. The sequence should incorporate a change in the pathways, at least two different relationships between partners, and an example of movements showing both free and bound flow.

RUBRIC CLUES To what extent do students

- meet all given sequence criteria?
- refine the sequence so all group members can perform it smoothly and without hesitation?

Sample Portfolio Task

Rolling skills are used in many different sports and activities. Have students describe two different sports or activities that use rolling movements. If possible, they should include pictures showing the rolling movement in the sports they describe. Students should specifically describe why and how the sport or activity uses rolling. Possible examples include football, rhythmic gymnastics, diving, dance, artistic gymnastics (floor or equipment), trampoline, surfing, skateboarding, and swimming (flip turns).

RUBRIC CLUES To what extent do students

- use knowledge and examples correctly and accurately to explain their answers?

NASPE BENCHMARKS Design and perform gymnastics and dance sequences that combine traveling, rolling, balancing, and weight transfer into smooth, flowing sequences with intentional changes in direction, speed, and flow. (5-6, #4)

Emphasize

Forward [or] Backward

Finish on your feet.

Soft rolls.

Give with your arms.

Ideas for Lesson Development

- ★ Encourage students to use different positions (e.g., legs and arms wide, starting from a medium level) to begin and end both forward and backward rolls. Have them connect these shapes into a sequence.
- ★ Students can practice moving from a balanced position, in either an upright or inverted position, to a roll and back to a different balanced position.
- ★ Make up cards giving different sequences (e.g., handstand, forward roll, and balance on one foot). Make the cards of different levels of difficulty (code by color, for example); let students choose which level they will practice.
- ★ Encourage students to travel to a piece of equipment (box, crate, hurdle, etc.), use a two-footed or spring takeoff to jump over it, land, and roll in any desired direction.
- ★ Working with a partner or a group, students take turns throwing a ball (students choose size and weight) to a student who jumps off the ground or low equipment to catch it, lands, and rolls.

Emphasize	Ideas for Lesson Development
Aerial roll Tuck chin to chest. Give with your arms. Soft rolls.	★ Encourage students to travel to a piece of low equipment, jump and land in front of it, and roll over it. They may start the roll with or without their hands on the floor.

Emphasize	Ideas for Lesson Development
Rolling on equipment Tight muscles. Shoulders and body over the equipment. **Flow** (see "Effort," chapter 4) *Free* Smooth transitions.	★ Encourage students to roll forward and backward on low equipment, such as a bench, beam, or table. ★ Students can make a sequence of moving to the piece of equipment, transferring their weight onto it, rolling on it, and moving off the equipment. ★ Discuss how it is necessary to keep the bases of support (hips and shoulders) directly over the equipment in order to not fall off it, and how this requires very tight muscles and control of speed.

GRADES 3-4

Sample Performance Task

With partners, students design, refine, and perform a sequence that includes at least two different rolls, balanced beginning and ending shapes, at least one weight transfer, and a change of pathway.

RUBRIC CLUES **To what extent do students**

- meet the sequence criteria?
- refine the sequence to perform it smoothly and without hesitations or memory lapses?
- match the movements of their partners?

Sample Portfolio Task

Students are asked to hypothesize about two objects from home or school that might roll in either a forward, backward, or sideways direction and two that cannot roll at all. They are then asked to verify whether their hypotheses were correct.

RUBRIC CLUES **To what extent do students**

- correctly verify that the objects can or cannot roll?

Emphasize	Ideas for Lesson Development
Backward Hands by your ears. Push up.	★ Students are encouraged to roll backward. An incline mat can be a useful teaching aid for learning to roll—especially in a backward direction: A mat with a slight (not severe) incline may be less threatening to beginning students. Hold to high expectations for student behavior with this, and any, equipment used in gymnastics.

Werner: *Roll, Roll, Roll Your Body*

Emphasize	Ideas for Lesson Development
Forward Finish on your feet.	★ Encourage students to roll forward using different beginning and ending positions (e.g., legs wide, body piked). ★ Discuss how different positions affect a roll. Why is more force needed for some rolls than others? Relate force to the length of the body extension: The longer the extension around which the roll is done, the more force is needed for the roll. ★ Have students roll forward at a fast and a slow speed. Discuss why one is easier than the other.

Emphasize	Ideas for Lesson Development
Forward Soft rolls. Give with your arms.	★ Encourage students to jump off low equipment (e.g., boxes, tires, crates), land, and roll. Some students may try landing and then rolling over a jump-rope hurdle. Emphasize that landings should be "soft." ★ Have students in pairs design and refine sequences that include rolls, balances, and transfers of weight. Require changes in relationships, speeds, pathways, directions, or levels (focus on only one or two of these, depending on how many other criteria you give).

Werner: *Same, Different*

Emphasize	Ideas for Lesson Development
Aerial roll Give with your arms.	★ Arrange jump ropes on the ground and low jump-rope hurdles for students to practice rolling over. They can start with the hands on the floor on the far side of the hurdle or hands off the floor. ★ Discuss how giving with one's arms is important to absorb force, especially for starting with hands off the floor.

GRADES 1-2

Sample Performance Task

Students are asked to design, refine, and perform a simple sequence that starts with a definite beginning (balanced) shape, ends with a different shape, and has a roll or rolls (in any direction) in the middle.

RUBRIC CLUES **To what extent do students**

- show a definite beginning and ending shape in their sequences?
- move smoothly from the beginning shape to a roll (or rolls) to the ending shape?

Sample Portfolio Task

Give the students a list of pictured objects: an egg, pencil, ball, box, tire, and toaster. (See Figure 6.1.) Ask them to circle the objects they think can rock or roll if pushed and to cross ("x") out the ones they think cannot rock or roll.

RUBRIC CLUES **To what extent do students**

- show an understanding of the concept of rocking or rolling by accurately circling and crossing out the objects?

NASPE BENCHMARKS Roll smoothly in a forward direction without stopping or hesitating. (1-2, #6)

Emphasize	Ideas for Lesson Development
Sideways Like a pencil (head between arms)! Tight muscles. (Begin to) turn from your tummy.	★ Students practice rolling sideways in self-space the length of a mat and rolling first in one direction, and then in the other. Werner: *Balls, Eggs, and Pencils*

Emphasize	Ideas for Lesson Development
Rocking Chin to chest. Head to knees. Curved shape—no flat tires!	★ Students practice rocking back and forth on their backs and from side to side, while staying in self-space. Encourage them to try rocking hard enough to touch their feet to the ground. ★ Encourage students to transfer their weight from a squatting position onto their backs, then rock back and forth on their backs. ★ From a stand, students move to a low level and rock onto their backs. Encourage them to try to come back up to a squat or stand. Werner: *Break Dance in Slow Motion*

Emphasize	Ideas for Lesson Development
Forward Curved shape—no flat tires! Chin to chest. Behind up. Push with your hands.	★ Encourage students to practice rolling forward at their spaces on the mats, down the mats, and so forth. ★ Students practice jumping into the air, landing, and rolling. You should emphasize soft landings, if needed!

Name ______________________ Class ______________

Roll, Roll, Roll . . .

Circle the objects that will easily roll. Put an *X* on the ones that don't roll very easily.

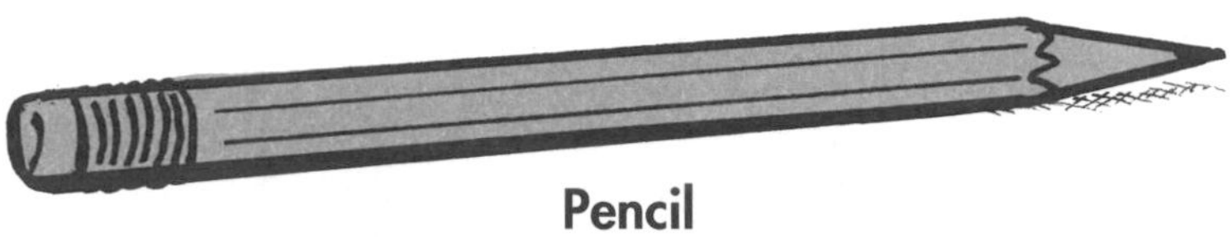

Pencil

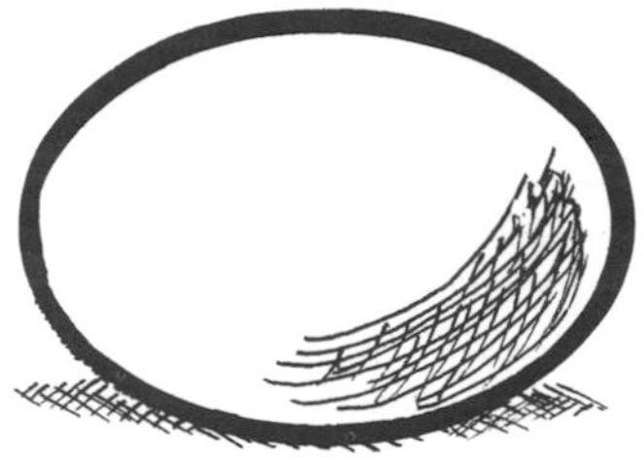

Egg

Ball

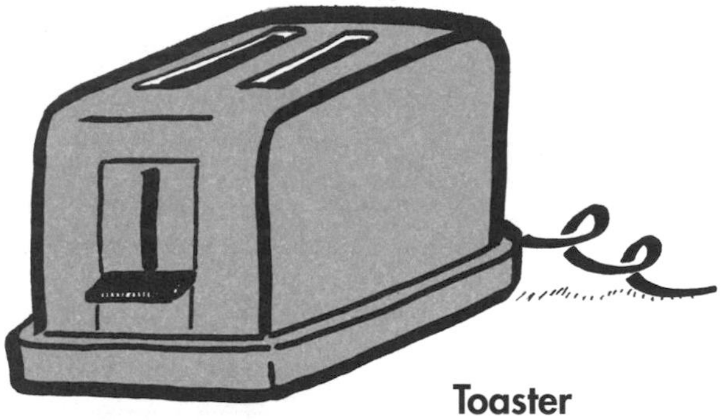

Toaster

Box

Tire

Which shape is best for rolling? **Curved** **Angular**

Figure 6.1 *Sample rolling assessment sheet for Grades 1-2.*

Emphasize	Ideas for Lesson Development
Backward Curved shape. Head to knees. Hands by your ears.	★ Students can practice moving onto their backs and rocking. ★ Write simple sequences on large task cards. Let students pick one from the "deck" and work on it. Here are some examples: starting shape, roll, balance, roll, ending shape; starting shape, roll, travel, roll, ending shape; and starting shape, roll, transfer weight, roll, ending shape. Let students trade cards with another student or group. Be sure to discuss the terms with students when you first use them.

Werner: *You've Got It All Backward*

KINDERGARTEN

Emphasize	Ideas for Lesson Development
Sideways Like a pencil (head between arms)!	★ Students practice rolling sideways (log roll) to the right and left in their self-spaces and across mats.

Werner: *Balls, Eggs, and Pencils*

Emphasize	Ideas for Lesson Development
Rocking Curved shape—no flat tires!	★ In self-space, students practice rocking back and forth and side to side. Encourage them to hold their legs with their arms as they rock.

Emphasize	Ideas for Lesson Development
Forward Curved shape—no flat tires! Chin to chest. Behind up.	★ Set up very low (barely off the ground) jump-rope hurdles; encourage students to practice rolling over a hurdle, starting with their hands on one side of the hurdle and their feet on the other side.

Sample Overall Unit Outcome

By the end of elementary school, students should be able to

- with a partner or a small group, combine the skills of balancing, rolling, and weight transfer, along with locomotor skills, to design, refine, and perform a gymnastics or dance sequence.

BALANCING

Concepts and Skills	Learnable Pieces
Base of support	
	Your bases of support are the body parts that hold you up. (1-2)
	A wide base of support is more stable (or better) than a narrow base of support. (1-2)
	It is harder to balance when your bases of support are far away from or outside your center of gravity. (3-4)
	The higher your center of gravity from the ground or equipment, the more difficult it is to balance. (3-4)
	Counterbalance involves a wide base of support and pushing against each other. (5-6)
	Counter-tension involves a narrow base of support and pulling away from each other. (5-6)
Static	
	Tight muscles. (K, 1-2, 3-4, 5-6)
	Count to 3. (K, 1-2)
	(Eyes) pick a spot. (1-2)
	(Keep the) center of gravity over bases of support. (3-4)
Dynamic	
	(Keep the) center of gravity over bases of support. (3-4)
Inverted	
	Tight muscles. (3-4)
	(Keep the) center of gravity over bases of support. (3-4)
	Behind up. (3-4)

GRADES 5-6

Sample Performance Task

Ask students in groups of three or four to design, refine, and perform a sequence with smooth transitions between balanced, held positions and different weight transfers. The sequence should also incorporate a change in the pathways and at least two different relationships between partners. Using equipment is optional.

RUBRIC CLUES **To what extent do students**

- move smoothly from balanced positions to other elements in the sequence?
- meet all the sequence criteria?
- refine the sequence so all group members perform it smoothly and without hesitations or major breaks?

Sample Portfolio Task

Ask students to describe one situation, not necessarily involving sports or even people, using the principle of counterbalance and one using the principle of counter-tension. They should be able to explain how and why the principle is used in each of these situations. (One example of counterbalance is the structure of an Indian teepee.)

RUBRIC CLUES **To what extent do students**

- understand the concepts of counterbalance and counter-tension?
- fully explain the reasons why a specific concept was used?

NASPE BENCHMARKS Design and perform gymnastics and dance sequences that combine traveling, rolling, balancing, and weight transfer into smooth, flowing sequences with intentional changes in direction, speed, and flow. (5-6, #4)

Emphasize

Base of support

Counterbalance involves a wide base of support and pushing against each other.

Counter-tension involves a narrow base of support and pulling away from each other.

Static

Tight muscles.

Ideas for Lesson Development

★ Discuss the principles of counterbalance (pushing against another person or object and with a wide base of support) and counter-tension (pulling against each other or an object and with a narrow base of support). Discuss and give examples of how each is used.

★ Have students balance first in pairs, using the given examples of counterbalance and counter-tension. Can they move while pushing or pulling against each other? Then ask them to try these in groups of three or four. These examples are some of the ways they can try to move: (1) Sitting back-to-back with the elbows joined, stand up and sit down without moving the feet. (2) Facing their partner, palms against each other at shoulder level, inch the feet away from the center. How far can they get without falling? This can also be done in a group. (3) Partners holding each other's wrists, with the feet close together, can they shuffle the feet sideways and move in a circle?

Werner: *Lean on Me; A Roll by Any Other Name . . .*

Emphasize	Ideas for Lesson Development
Flow (see "Effort," chapter 4) *Free* Smooth transitions.	★ Challenge students to select their three favorite balances. By the time you count to 10, they must do each one, making a smooth transition from one to the other. ★ Have students hold a balanced shape, move smoothly into a roll or transfer-of-weight, and move into a different balance. They can then progress to repeating the sequence with a partner or small group. ★ Students design sequences in which they move onto a piece of large equipment (climbing apparatus, beam, etc.), travel and balance, and move off the piece, ending in a balanced position.

Werner: *Just Hanging Around*

GRADES 3-4

Sample Performance Task

Students cooperatively balance in groups of two to four, so that each person is connected with or partially supported by another group member's body weight.

RUBRIC CLUES To what extent do students

- clearly exhibit held, balanced positions?
- meet the criteria?

Sample Portfolio Task

Ask students to describe a sport or recreational activity requiring great balance from the player. If possible, the students should find or draw a picture of this activity. Why do they think the activity requires so much balance? What should the player remember to help keep better balance?

RUBRIC CLUES To what extent do students

- understand the concept of balance?

Emphasize	Ideas for Lesson Development
Static (Keep the) center of gravity over bases of support. Tight muscles. **Base of support** It is harder to balance when your bases of support are far away from or outside your center of gravity. The higher your center of gravity from the ground or equipment, the more difficult it is to balance.	★ Challenge students to balance with a partner by connecting body parts or supporting each other's body weight. ★ Within their small groups (three to five), ask students to perform a balance in which each child is connected to and/or supporting another child's body weight. ★ Challenge students to balance in a variety of body shapes while they hang from large equipment (bars, climbing apparatus, etc.), with different (combinations of) body parts (hands, knees, ankles). ★ Have the students balance a spoon on one finger to experience the concept of center-of-weight (gravity). Discuss why it did or did not fall off, why the spoon could not be balanced in the middle, and so forth. ★ Challenge students to balance on a variety of large pieces of equipment (beams, tables, benches, horses) in symmetrical and asymmetrical shapes.

Ideas for Lesson Development

- ★ Challenge students to balance on large pieces of equipment using different bases of support.
- ★ Encourage students to change direction, level, and base of support while they move and balance on equipment, such as on a balance beam. Give suggestions on task cards for balances and traveling movements that demonstrate these changes, and allow students to make up others.
- ★ On the ground or on appropriate pieces of equipment, students try moving from one balanced position to another without losing balance. Can they move from a symmetrical to asymmetrical balance? Inverted to upright balance?
- ★ If you can, take photos of the students' balances and display them on a bulletin board. Seeing the results can be great motivation and fun!

Werner: *Just Hanging Around; Same, Different; Shoulder Stand*

Emphasize

Dynamic

(Keep the) center of gravity over bases of support.

Ideas for Lesson Development

- ★ Allow students to experiment with the concept of dynamic (moving) balance by balancing on such objects as balancing boards, stilts, skateboards, and roller skates.

Emphasize

Inverted

Tight muscles.

(Keep the) center of gravity over bases of support.

Behind up.

Ideas for Lesson Development

- ★ Challenge students to balance in inverted (hips up) positions on the ground or on equipment, using bases of support appropriate to their skill level. Here are examples of how they might do these balances: head, both hands, one foot; both hands, one or both feet; both forearms, one or both feet; head, both hands; hands only; and forearms only.
- ★ Additional cues can be used for balancing in a handstand position (introduce these to students as appropriate to their skill level): kick feet up high; hips, shoulders, hands in line; and control balance with fingertips.

Werner: *Bottoms Up*

GRADES 1-2

Sample Performance Task

Ask students to design, refine, and perform a simple sequence starting with a balanced symmetrical shape, ending with an asymmetrical shape, and incorporating either a roll (any direction) or a transfer of weight in the middle.

RUBRIC CLUES **To what extent do students**

- meet the sequence criteria?
- hold the beginning and ending shapes long enough to clearly be in a balanced position?
- choose skills they can complete with moderate success?

Sample Portfolio Task

Ask students to draw pictures of themselves holding a balanced shape. They should specify the base(s) of support their balances use.

RUBRIC CLUES **To what extent do students**

- accurately describe the bases of support in their drawings?

NASPE BENCHMARKS Balance, demonstrating momentary stillness, in symmetrical and asymmetrical shapes on a variety of body parts. (1-2, #7)

Emphasize

Base of support

Your bases of support are the body parts that hold you up.

A wide base of support is more stable (or better) than a narrow base of support.

Ideas for Lesson Development

★ Discuss how shapes that are wider or have a wider base of support are more stable for balancing. Encourage pairs of students to make a balanced shape and to see if their partners can make them lose their balance by *gently* pressing against them with a hand. Challenge them to make a balance that is not quite as well-balanced: Can they hold it?

Werner: *Push and Pull*

Emphasize

Static

Tight muscles.

Count to 3.

Ideas for Lesson Development

★ Have students travel throughout the boundaried area; at the signal, they each find a carpet square and balance on the number of bases of support that you call out. For more fun, make a large cardboard die and roll it (or let students roll it) to come up with the number.

★ See if students can balance a rhythm stick on different body parts while making wild shapes. Challenge them to change their shapes without the sticks falling off.

Emphasize	Ideas for Lesson Development
Static (Eyes) pick a spot. **Body shapes** (see "Body Awareness," chapter 4) *Symmetrical* If you cut your body in two, each side would look the same. *Asymmetrical* If you cut your body in two, each side would look different.	★ Discuss the difference between symmetrical and asymmetrical shapes; have students use different bases of support to make them. Challenge them to make inverted symmetrical and asymmetrical balances as well. ★ Put out various pieces of low equipment (boxes, crates, low balance beams, tires, benches, sturdy sawhorses). Challenge students to balance on them using various bases of support. ★ Challenge students to travel in different directions while on low- or medium-level equipment, such as beams. Encourage them to also change the level they travel in. Werner: *Same, Different*

KINDERGARTEN

Sample Performance Task

Students are asked to perform various simple balances (e.g., on one foot, one foot and two hands, two feet and one hand) on their carpet squares, holding them for a count of 3.

RUBRIC CLUES **To what extent do students**

- hold the balance without falling?

Emphasize	Ideas for Lesson Development
Static Tight muscles. Count to 3.	★ Students travel throughout general space; at the signal, they each find a carpet square and use the specific body part you call out to balance on the square. ★ While in self-space, students balance a beanbag on different body parts that you call out. Challenge them to make wild shapes while balancing the beanbag on that body part. ★ Students travel throughout the boundaried area; challenge them, at the signal, to freeze in a balanced position as quickly as possible. ★ Make large chalk pathways on the blacktop or ground; have students travel on them forward and backward without falling off. Werner: *Patches and Points*

Sample Overall Unit Outcome

By the end of elementary school, students should be able to

- with a partner or small group, combine the skills of weight transfer, rolling, and balancing, along with nonlocomotor skills, to design, refine, and perform a gymnastics or dance sequence.

WEIGHT TRANSFER

Concepts and Skills	Learnable Pieces
Rocking, rolling (from one body part to another)	
	(see "Rolling," this chapter) (K, 1-2)
Feet only (step-like actions with feet)	
	(see "Locomotor Movements," chapter 5)
Feet-to-hands (step-like actions using hands and feet)	
	Kick feet up high (for far extensions). (K, 1-2) Soft landings. (1-2, 3-4) Behind up. (3-4) Strong arms. (or) Tight muscles. (K, 1-2, 3-4, 5-6) Head up (when moving onto equipment). (3-4, 5-6) Arms take weight first. (3-4, 5-6)
Spring takeoffs (flight)	
	Jump from one foot to two feet. (1-2) (Push off) balls of feet. (1-2) Soft landings. (1-2)

GRADES 5-6

Sample Performance Task

Ask students in groups of three or four to design, refine, and perform a sequence incorporating rolls of at least two different shapes with balances and two or more kinds of weight transfers. Their sequences also should include a change in the pathways, at least two different relationships between partners, and examples of movements showing both free and bound flow. Using equipment is optional.

RUBRIC CLUES To what extent do students

- meet all sequence criteria?
- refine the sequence so all members can perform it smoothly and without hesitations or major breaks?

Sample Portfolio Task

Ask students to diagram their sequence. Where will they start? finish? What pathways will they use? What roll, balance, and transfer of weight will they do and where? After they have performed the sequence, ask them to rate and justify their performances on a scale of 1 to 5, 5 being the best, according to the criteria they diagrammed.

RUBRIC CLUES To what extent do students

- correctly diagram their sequences?
- show all of the sequence criteria (e.g., two transfers of weight)?

NASPE BENCHMARKS Design and perform gymnastics and dance sequences that combine traveling, rolling, balancing, and weight transfer into smooth, flowing sequences with intentional changes in direction, speed, and flow. (5-6, #4)

Emphasize

Flow (see "Effort," chapter 4)

Free

Smooth transitions.

Ideas for Lesson Development

★ Challenge students to transfer weight from their feet to hands in a variety of ways on the ground. If a student is advanced enough, add cues for other actions, which might include these: (1) Cartwheel—stretch arms and feet wide; one body part touches ground at a time; hand, hand, foot, foot sequence. (2) Roundoff—snap legs together (at top); twist hips; feet land at same time. (3) Handstand—hips, shoulders, hands in line. (4) Walkover—step into the action (for front walkover); kick leading leg over with force; "split" legs in air. The students must travel smoothly into and out of these weight transfers.

★ Encourage students to transfer their weight along low to medium level equipment (beam, bench, table, etc.) in a variety of ways. You might require changes in levels, speeds, directions, and body shapes.

★ Ask students to design sequences alone or in pairs in which they transfer their weight in order to move *up to, onto, along,* and *off* a piece of equipment.

Werner: *Clock Face; Beam Me Up; Me and My Shadow; A Roll by Any Other Name . . . ; Hip Circles*

Emphasize	Ideas for Lesson Development
Feet-to-hands Strong arms. Tight muscles. Head up (when moving onto equipment). Arms take weight first.	★ Challenge students to transfer their weight *onto* large equipment (beams, bars, climbing apparatus, vault box) in a variety of ways by springing off from two feet. How many different ways can they find to transfer their weight onto a particular piece of equipment? ★ Challenge students, starting with their hands and feet on a chosen piece of equipment, to transfer their weight *off* it. A variety of body actions, such as twisting, stretching, and turning, can be used to move off. ★ Challenge students to move up to and transfer their weight *over* and *off* specific equipment of a chosen size and height.

Werner: *Fantasy Flight*

GRADES 3-4

Sample Performance Task

Students in pairs design, refine, and perform a sequence that includes at least two different rolls, balanced beginning and ending shapes, at least one weight transfer that is *not* a roll, and a change of pathways.

RUBRIC CLUES **To what extent do students**

- meet the sequence criteria?
- refine the sequence to perform it smoothly and with a minimum of hesitations or breaks?

Sample Portfolio Task

At the end of the learning experiences in weight transfer, ask students to reflect, in writing, on where they feel they improved the most. What helped them to do better? What else do they want to improve?

RUBRIC CLUES **To what extent do students**

- complete the assignment?

NASPE BENCHMARKS Transfer weight, from feet to hands, at fast and slow speeds, using large extensions (e.g., mulekick, handstand, cartwheel). (3-4, #4)

Support, lift, and control body weight in a variety of activities. (3-4, #16)

Design games, gymnastics, and dance sequences that are personally interesting. (3-4, #26)

Celebrate personal successes and achievements and those of others. (3-4, #30)

Emphasize	Ideas for Lesson Development
Feet-to-hands Tight muscles. **Flow** (see "Effort," chapter 4) *Free* Smooth transitions.	★ Challenge students to transfer their weight from one body part to another when they are on large equipment (e.g., climbing apparatus, bars, beam). Encourage them to use the hands, knees, and feet to move from one part of the apparatus to another. ★ Have students demonstrate a balance that allows them to move smoothly into and out of a chosen transfer of weight. Have them practice to be able to do it smoothly. ★ Discuss how weight transfers using large extensions (cartwheels, handstands, etc.) require more force and speed to complete the movement than do movements with small extensions.

Werner: *Break Dance in Slow Motion; The String Challenge; Clock Face; A Roll By Any Other Name . . .*

Emphasize	Ideas for Lesson Development
Feet-to-hands Behind up. Tight muscles. Head up (when moving onto equipment). Arms take weight first.	★ Challenge students to step *into* weight transfers, then move *over* low equipment (e.g., box, crate, beam) by placing their hands on the equipment. If you wish, have them begin by starting on the ground, making a circle on the mat or ground in which they can place their hands. Once they are comfortable with this, they can progress to moving over equipment that is higher off the ground. ★ Have students practice transferring their weight *onto* low- and medium-level equipment by first placing their hands on the equipment, then springing off both feet to land on it. Encourage them to land on either their knees and feet or feet only. ★ Encourage students to travel into a spring takeoff, then transfer their weight *onto* low- and medium-level equipment (e.g., beam, bench, table, bar, large tire set in ground).

Werner: *Ready for Takeoff*

Emphasize	Ideas for Lesson Development
Feet-to-hands Tight muscles. Soft landings	★ After transferring their weight onto low- to medium-level equipment, such as boxes, tires, beams, and mats, ask students to transfer their weight *off* the equipment in a variety of ways, starting with their hands on the floor. They can use such actions as rolling and pushing their feet off the equipment.

GRADES 1-2

Sample Performance Task

Students are asked to design, refine, and perform a simple sequence that starts with a balanced beginning shape, ends with a balanced shape, and incorporates at least one example of a transfer of weight.

RUBRIC CLUES **To what extent do students**

- meet sequence criteria?
- choose skills they can perform with moderate success?
- refine the sequence to perform it with a moderate degree of control and continuity?

Sample Portfolio Task

Discuss with students the many ways they can transfer their weight; then ask them to draw a picture of their favorite way to transfer their weight.

RUBRIC CLUES **To what extent do students**

- show an example of weight transfer?

NASPE BENCHMARKS Move feet into a high level by placing the weight on the hands and landing with control. (1-2, #8)

Emphasize

Rocking, rolling (see "Rolling," this chapter)

Curved shape—no flat tires!

Feet-to-hands

Strong arms.

Tight muscles.

Ideas for Lesson Development

★ Ask students to show you how many different ways, using low-rope hurdles, hoops, mats, and so forth, they can transfer their weight over the equipment.

★ Challenge students to move their feet, with their hands on a hoop, to other parts of the hoop.

★ Set up mats at stations, each with a picture and description of the weight transfer students should use to move across that mat. Examples can include the crab walk, bear walk (hand and foot on the same side of the body move forward at same time), inchworm (feet stay in place, hands "walk" forward; hands stay anchored, feet "walk" forward), and wheelbarrow (with a partner). Have one mat and station where students can choose a movement (caterpillar, cartwheel, etc.). Use the stations alone or as part of gymnastics stations, which include rolls and balances as well.

★ Using jumping boxes, tires, bars, and so forth, challenge students to transfer their weight onto and off the equipment, beginning with their hands on the equipment.

Werner: *Bunny Hop; Break Dance in Slow Motion*

Emphasize	Ideas for Lesson Development
Feet-to-hands Strong arms. Soft landings. Kick feet up high (for far extensions).	★ Challenge students in self-space to take as much of their weight as possible on their hands. ★ Have students see if they can make their legs land in different places than they originally were around their body.

Emphasize	Ideas for Lesson Development
Spring takeoffs (flight) Jump from one foot to two feet. (Push off) balls of feet. Soft landings.	★ Have students practice transferring their weight by traveling into a spring takeoff (taking off one foot, landing on two feet). Stress the landings; have different equipment available, which students can travel up and spring onto (jumping boxes, mats, large tires set in the ground). Have them jump off the object, making different shapes.

Werner: *Ready for Takeoff*

KINDERGARTEN

Emphasize	Ideas for Lesson Development
Rocking, rolling (see "Rolling," this chapter) Curved shape—no flat tires!	★ Have students, in self-space, practice transferring their weight from one body part to another by rocking back and forth on their backs and their fronts.

Emphasize	Ideas for Lesson Development
Feet-to-hands Strong arms. Tight muscles. Kick feet up high (for far extensions).	★ Students can practice various transfers of weight, such as the crab walk, bear walk, and leap frog. ★ Encourage students to take their weight onto their hands by transferring it from the feet. Challenge them to kick the feet high! ★ Have a very low jump-rope hurdle or rope on the ground for each student. Challenge them to put their hands on one side of the rope and jump their feet up and over to the other side of the line. They can also start with one hand on each side of the rope and try to move their feet from one side to the other.

CHAPTER 7 *Manipulative Skills*

Sample Overall Unit Outcomes

By the end of elementary school, students should be able to

- design and play a small-group game that incorporates the skills of dribbling with the hands, passing, and shooting to keep a ball away from defenders and move it toward a goal area, and
- use the basic offensive and defensive strategies for keep-away games (i.e., creating and denying space) when playing in small groups.

DRIBBLING WITH THE HANDS

Concepts and Skills	Learnable Pieces
Dribbling	
	Waist high. (K, 1-2) Fingerpads. (1-2) Firm, flexible wrists. (3-4) Ball in front, out to side. (3-4) Look up. (5-6)
Passing (throwing skill specific to basketball)	
	Hands to side, behind ball. (3-4)
Bounce pass	Push the ball out and down. (3-4)
Chest pass	Push the ball away from your chest. (3-4) Step toward your partner or target. (5-6)
Shooting (throwing skill specific to basketball)	
	Pushing hand is behind, toward bottom of the ball. (5-6) Your other hand supports the ball at the side. (5-6) Extend arms up and out. (5-6)

GRADES 5-6

Sample Performance Task

In a small group (2-on-2), students are asked to design and play a keep-away game using dribbling, passing, and shooting to keep a ball away from defenders and move it (if desired) toward a goal area. They may determine their own boundaries and rules except that double dribbling and traveling with the ball are not allowed.

RUBRIC CLUES **To what extent do students**

- try to create space on offense by moving to open areas where they can receive the ball?
- try to deny space on defense by keeping their bodies between the ball and intended player or goal area?
- consistently dribble legally?
- cooperate to play their game?

Sample Portfolio Task

Students view a basketball game on TV or in person. They are asked to respond to these written questions: (a) What does the person with the ball (offensive player) do when dribbling to keep the ball away from the defensive person? (b) What is one thing a player on offense, without the ball, can do to create space to receive the ball?
(c) Name two things a defensive person does to deny space and keep an offensive player from passing the ball to a teammate.

RUBRIC CLUES **To what extent do students**

- show they understand the concepts of creating and denying space through their accurate answers and citation of examples?

NASPE BENCHMARKS Hand dribble and foot dribble while preventing an opponent from stealing the ball. (5-6, #5)

Design and play small-group games that involve cooperating with others to keep an object away from opponents (basic offensive and defensive strategy) (e.g., by throwing, kicking, or dribbling a ball). (5-6, #8)

Accept and respect the decisions made by game officials, whether they are students, teachers, or officials outside of school (5-6, #26)

Emphasize	Ideas for Lesson Development
Dribbling Look up.	★ Have students dribble while traveling in a group (in a large boundaried area) without touching others or stationary objects. Challenge them to go at the fastest speed at which they can control dribbling. ★ Challenge students to travel through general space, moving as close as possible to others without touching them. See how quickly they can move away from the others. ★ Call out different directions as students move through general space; challenge students to dribble, changing direction smoothly without stopping. ★ Use a tambourine or drum to mark different speeds for the students; challenge them to change speed smoothly. Vary the time intervals between changing the speeds.

Ideas for Lesson Development

- ★ Students dribble while they travel through general space and, at the signal, stop traveling but continue dribbling. At the next signal, they begin traveling again.
- ★ Discuss how pivoting means one foot is "glued" to the floor. Have students dribble in any direction and, at the signal, pivot on one foot before dribbling in another direction.

Emphasize

Passing

Bounce pass [or] *chest pass*
Step toward your partner or target.

Ideas for Lesson Development

- ★ Have students practice dribbling, stopping, pivoting, and passing the ball to a partner or target on the wall. Post targets of varying sizes at different heights around the gym for practicing against the wall.
- ★ Have students practice dribbling and throwing a leading pass to a moving partner using a chest or bounce pass. Discuss how a leading pass is thrown where a person will be, not where they are, in order for the receiver not to have to stop for it.

Emphasize

Shooting

Pushing hand is behind, toward bottom of the ball.

Your other hand supports the ball at the side.

Extend arms up and out.

Ideas for Lesson Development

- ★ Put up different-sized targets on the wall; have students shoot toward one of them at an appropriate height from different distances.
- ★ Set carpet squares in various locations and have students shoot toward wall targets from each one (or choose several they want to shoot from). Discuss how distance affects how they must shoot the ball.

Emphasize

General space (see "Space Awareness," chapter 4)

Offense
Create space by moving to open areas to pass or receive the ball.

Keep your body between the ball and the defender.

Defense
Deny space by keeping between the opponent and intended goal.

Ideas for Lesson Development

- ★ Dribble Tag—students dribble anywhere within the boundaries, which are the size of half a basketball court or smaller (if students are highly skilled). They try to avoid being tagged by "it," who also may dribble while moving. If tagged, a student stands and dribbles with the nondominant hand 25 times.
- ★ Students partner up and set up boundaries. The partner on offense dribbles, trying to keep the ball from the defender; the defender tries to maneuver the offense into a position where the person would lose the ball. Allow students to make up additional rules.
- ★ In small groups (2-on-2, 3-on-2, 2-on-1), students on offense use dribbling and passing to keep the ball away from defenders. Allow the players to make up their own rules. When it is appropriate, discuss the offensive and defensive strategies of creating and denying space, and why these are important.
- ★ In small groups, students dribble, pass, receive, and shoot toward a goal of appropriate height or some other target.

Belka: *Advance and Score Basketball*

GRADES 3-4

Sample Performance Task

Ask students to dribble and move at a comfortable speed throughout a large boundaried area while avoiding others and keeping control of the ball.

RUBRIC CLUES **To what extent do students**

- change the direction and pathway of their dribbling to avoid crashing into others?
- control the ball as they move throughout the area?

Sample Portfolio Task

Students are asked to write a letter to Michael Jordan, or to a current basketball player of their choice, as if the player is in a slump and having trouble controlling the ball when dribbling. In the letter, they give the player some hints to help him or her get back to great dribbling.

RUBRIC CLUES **To what extent do students**

- show they understand how to dribble by using cues they learned during instruction?
- accurately justify their suggestions?

NASPE BENCHMARKS Hand dribble and foot dribble a ball and maintain control while traveling within a group. (3-4, #5)

Describe essential elements of mature movement patterns. (3-4, #23)

Emphasize

Dribbling

Firm, flexible wrists.

Ball in front, out to side.

Ideas for Lesson Development

★ Have third and fourth graders teach *you* to dribble; do exactly as they say. They'll learn (and remember) the cues much better!

★ At the signal, have students change the directions they are moving in to the one you call out.

★ See if students can dribble at the speed you mark by tambourine or drum.

★ At the signal, have students change from the pathway they are moving on to the one you call out.

★ Challenge students to dribble while moving to the right and left, each making sure to dribble with the hand opposite the direction she or he is moving in.

★ Have students face you; use hand or verbal signals to indicate the direction they should dribble in (forward, backward, right, left). Then have them get in groups of two or three, with one partner directing the others in the group; rotate so each child gets to be leader.

Emphasize

General space (see "Space Awareness," chapter 4)

Offense

Keep your body between the ball and the defender.

Ideas for Lesson Development

- ★ Variation of Trees in the Forest—have students dribble from one end of the space to the other end, trying to avoid getting touched by students who are standing in hoops scattered throughout general space. If touched, they dribble in their self-space for a count of 10 before moving on toward the end line.
- ★ Set up a zigzag obstacle course using hoops or tires. Students standing in these hoops try to steal the ball away from one student, who moves from one end of the course to the other. Set up enough courses to have about four to five students per course. After the one student dribbles back to the beginning line he or she rotates into a hoop, and the student in the last hoop becomes the dribbler. Have students also try this dribbling with the nondominant hand.

Buschner: *Dribble Tag*

Emphasize

Passing

Hands to side, behind ball.

Bounce pass

Push the ball out and down.

Chest pass

Push the ball away from your chest.

Ideas for Lesson Development

- ★ Have students dribble toward a stationary partner, then chest- or bounce-pass the ball to her or him.
- ★ Have students pair up; one partner dribbles in general space, while the other partner travels away through general space. At the signal, nondribblers freeze, while dribblers move toward their partners. When they are about 10 feet away, the dribblers pass the ball to their partners and they all move again until the next signal.

GRADES 1-2

Sample Performance Task

Students continuously dribble the ball, alternating hands, remaining (stationary) in self-space.

RUBRIC CLUES **To what extent do students**

- keep the ball under control in self-space when dribbling?
- dribble continuously using both preferred and nonpreferred hands?
- dribble using the fingerpads, rather than slapping the ball with their palms?

Sample Portfolio Task

Ask students each to draw an outline of his or her hand on a piece of paper and color in the part of the hand that should touch the ball while dribbling.

RUBRIC CLUES **To what extent do students**

- show they understand which part of the hand to dribble with by coloring in the fingerpads (top third of each finger)?

NASPE BENCHMARKS Continuously dribble a ball, using the hands or feet, without losing control. (1-2, #12)

Emphasize	Ideas for Lesson Development
Dribbling Fingerpads. Waist high.	★ Provide a variety of balls for students to dribble: oversize training volleyballs, regular volleyballs, playground balls, junior basketballs. ★ As motivation, have students trade balls with another student while working on continuously dribbling in self-space. ★ Have students dribble in as many different places around their bodies as possible. ★ Have students dribble a ball in self-space, practicing first one hand and then the other. ★ Challenge students to dribble a ball in self-space while alternating hands. ★ Have students dribble a ball in self-space at low, medium, and high levels. ★ Challenge students to dribble while traveling forward and backward, keeping the ball under control. Have them change the direction they are moving in when you signal. ★ Mark some pathways on the ground; ask students to dribble while following the pathways. Encourage them to go at a speed that is challenging, yet allows them to keep control of the ball.

KINDERGARTEN

Emphasize	Ideas for Lesson Development
Dribbling Waist high.	★ Have students use two hands to bounce and catch a large playground ball while they stand in self-space. Challenge them to try it using only one hand. ★ Have students use two hands to bounce and catch a ball while they slowly travel forward. ★ Challenge students to bounce the ball, clap, then catch the ball, as well as to continuously bounce the ball using two hands.

Sample Overall Unit Outcomes

By the end of elementary school, students should be able to

- design and play a small-group game that incorporates the skills of kicking, passing, receiving, collecting, and punting to keep a ball away from defenders and move it toward a goal area, and
- use the basic offensive and defensive strategies for keep-away games (i.e., creating and denying space) when playing in small groups.

KICKING AND PUNTING

Concepts and Skills	Learnable Pieces
Instep kick	
	Eyes (focus) on the ball. (K)
	Stand a little behind, to one side (of the ball). (1-2)
	(Kick with the) shoelaces (the top part of instep). (1-2)
	Kick hard. (1-2)
	Kick underneath the ball. (3-4)
	Toes (follow through) to target. (3-4)
Inside kick	
	Eyes (focus) on the ball. (K)
	Stand a little behind, to one side (of the ball). (1-2)
	Toes and knee out, like a duck. (1-2)
	Kick through the middle (of the ball). (3-4)
	Inside of foot (points) to the target. (3-4, 5-6)
	Kick to where your partner will be. (5-6)
Dribbling	
	Little pushes. (K)
	Push, don't kick (the ball). (1-2)
	Keep it close (to you). (1-2)
	(Use) insides (of the feet). (K, 1-2, 3-4)
	(Use) outsides (of the feet). (1-2, 3-4)
	Look ahead. (5-6)
Punting	
	Hold (the ball shoulder-level). (1-2)
	Step (with the nonkicking leg). (1-2)
	Drop (the ball). (1-2)
	Kick (with the shoelaces—use the top portion of the foot). (1-2)
	Kick hard. (3-4)
	Foot to target. (5-6)
Collecting	
Inside of foot	Inside of the foot faces the ball. (3-4)
	Contact the middle of the ball. (3-4)
	Give with the foot—trap an egg! (3-4)
With body parts	Move under the ball. (5-6)
	Give with the body—trap an egg! (5-6)

GRADES 5-6

Sample Performance Task

Students form small groups to design and play a keep-away game using dribbling, passing, receiving, collecting, and punting to keep a ball away from defenders and move it toward a goal area. Students can determine their own boundaries, rules, and goal area.

RUBRIC CLUES **To what extent do students**

- try to create space when on offense by moving to open areas to pass and receive the ball?
- try to deny space when on defense by keeping their body between the ball and the intended player or goal?
- cooperate to play their game?

Sample Portfolio Task

Students are asked to show their knowledge related to the skill of kicking by completing Figure 7.1.

RUBRIC CLUES **To what extent do students**

- give appropriate examples of sports involving kicking?
- show a clear understanding of the kicking cues?

NASPE BENCHMARKS Hand dribble and foot dribble while preventing an opponent from stealing the ball. (5-6, #5)

Design and play small-group games that involve cooperating with others to keep an object away from opponents (basic offensive and defensive strategy) (e.g., by throwing, kicking, or dribbling a ball). (5-6, #8)

Emphasize

Inside kick

Inside of foot (points) to the target.

Kick to where your partner will be.

Ideas for Lesson Development

★ In a small-group game situation, students pass to each other and toward a goal area using the instep of the foot. Allow them to set up their own boundaries, determine their rules, and use a goalie, if they wish.

★ Discuss how a leading pass is kicked to where a person will be, so the person doesn't have to stop moving in order to receive the ball. Pair up the students: Have one person, in a stationary position, kick the ball to a moving partner using a leading pass. After 3 kicks, they switch roles.

★ In a very large, open area, challenge students to keep a ball moving at all times between themselves and a partner. To do this, they should also be moving at all times; thus, they will need to use dribbling and leading passes.

Belka: *Triangle Soccer*

Name ______________________ Class ______________

Kicking—What Do You Know?

Name one hint to be a good kicker:

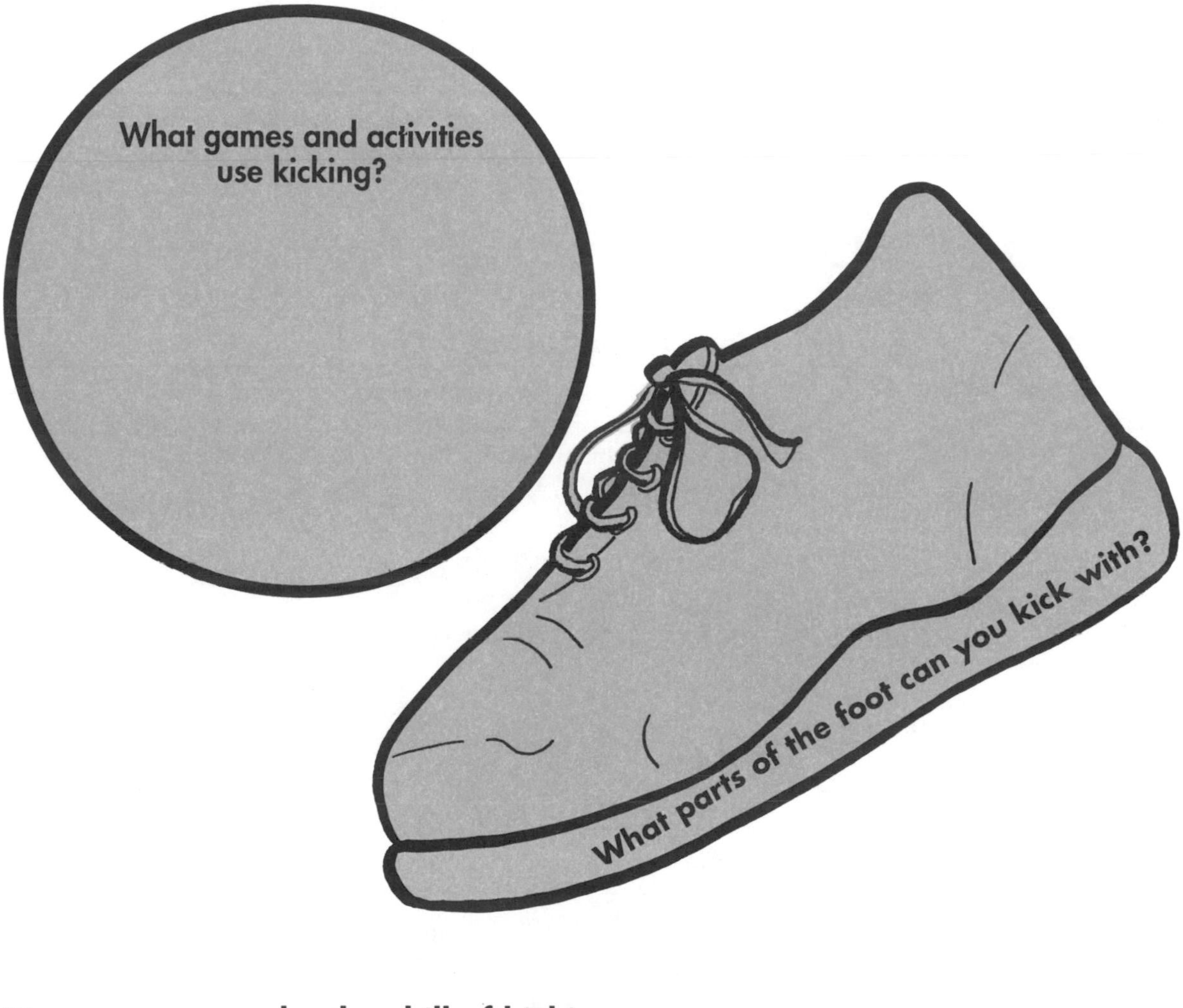
What games and activities use kicking?
What parts of the foot can you kick with?

How can you make the skill of kicking

easy? ______________________

hard? ______________________

Figure 7.1 *Sample kicking and punting assessment sheet for Grades 5-6.* From Schiemer (1993).

Note. *From "Beyond the Traditional Skills Test" by S. Schiemer, 1993,* Teaching Elementary Physical Education, ***4****(2), p. 11.*

Emphasize	Ideas for Lesson Development
Dribbling Look ahead.	★ In a large boundaried area, students dribble to the tempo you mark by tambourine or drum. See if students can keep up with the speed without losing control of the ball.

Emphasize	Ideas for Lesson Development
Punting Foot to target.	★ Encourage students to use a two- or three-step approach for punting. ★ Put up a net or rope for students to punt a ball over; their partners can catch or retrieve it and punt it back. "Slant" the rope, so students can choose the height at which they punt. ★ Pair up the students: One partner hikes the ball to the other, who punts it to targets or zones at various distances.

Emphasize	Ideas for Lesson Development
Collecting *With body parts* Move under the ball. Give with the body—trap an egg!	★ Have one partner toss or gently kick a ball to the other partner at a high level. The receiving partner tries to collect the ball using the chest, thigh, and so forth.

Emphasize	Ideas for Lesson Development
General space (see "Space Awareness," chapter 4) *Offense* Keep your body between the ball and the defender. Create space by moving to open areas to pass or receive the ball. *Defense* Deny space by keeping between the opponent and intended goal.	★ Allow students to set up a small-group game (2-on-2, 3-on-3, 4-on-4, 3-on-2) and use kicking skills to move a ball toward a goal area. Provide a variety of equipment they can use to set up goals; allow the use of a goalie, if they wish.

Belka: *Advance and Score Soccer; Defend the Shot*

GRADES 3-4

Sample Performance Task

Students dribble inside a large boundaried area, keeping the ball away from stationary opponents. There should be enough stationary students in the area to challenge the dribblers. If control of the ball is lost, the student retrieves it and continues dribbling.

RUBRIC CLUES **To what extent do students**

- continuously keep (or lose) control of the ball?
- keep their bodies between the ball and defender?
- change pathways to elude opponents?

Sample Portfolio Task

After students have had learning experiences with kicking, ask them to reflect on what they have learned (see Figure 7.2).

RUBRIC CLUES **To what extent do students**

- demonstrate, by using cues from the instruction phase, they understand how to correctly kick a ball?

NASPE BENCHMARKS Hand dribble and foot dribble a ball and maintain control while traveling within a group. (3-4, #5)

Describe essential elements of mature movement patterns. (3-4, #23)

Emphasize

Instep kick

Kick underneath the ball.

Toes (follow through) to target.

Inside kick

Kick through the middle (of the ball).

Inside of foot (points) to the target.

Ideas for Lesson Development

- ★ Make large goals for kicking. Crisscross masking tape on a large piece of canvas, spray paint over it, and remove the tape. Hang this canvas over a rope for a great target students can kick a ball to.
- ★ Set up different target zones or areas and pair up the students. One partner runs up to and kicks a ball using the instep; the other marks the spot where it lands with a cone. After five kicks, they switch roles. Challenge students to kick to the farthest zone they can.
- ★ Place a soccer or playground ball in a ball net suspended from a rope strung between two standards. Students can practice kicking the ball without it going anywhere!
- ★ Put up targets and challenge students to kick above them, then below them. Discuss what they had to do differently for each kick (for above, use the instep; for below, use the inside).
- ★ Allow students to dribble throughout general space and kick to a goal area or target from a distance of their choice. Discuss how distance from the goal affects the type of kick they choose (instep or inside). After many successful trials, have some students play goalies and defend the target. After a short time, goalies should switch roles with dribblers.

Name ______________________ Class ______________

Kicking the Ball Around

★ **What is a hint to remember when you are dribbling with your feet?**

★ **What is a hint to remember when you kick the ball with either foot?**

★ **What is a game or activity that uses *punting* the ball?**

Figure 7.2 *Sample kicking and punting assessment sheet for Grades 3-4.*

Emphasize	Ideas for Lesson Development
Dribbling (Use) insides [or] outsides (of the feet). **General space** (see "Space Awareness," chapter 4) *Offense* Keep your body between the ball and the defender.	★ Students dribble throughout general space; at the signal, they change pathways or directions (which you specify) as quickly as possible. ★ Set up a large boundaried area as for Trees in the Forest. Have some students stand in hoops scattered throughout the area; others dribble from one endline to the other, trying not to lose control of their ball to a "tree." Trees get 1 point each time they cause someone to lose control of the ball, 2 points if they trap a ball. If students lose control of the ball, they get it back and keep dribbling to the endline. ★ Provide three or four balls per child and challenge students to get all the balls moving at the same time in the boundaried area.

Buschner: *Kicking Review*

Emphasize	Ideas for Lesson Development
Punting Kick hard.	★ Set up a zone or target for each pair of children. Students punt toward a target while a partner marks the zone; after five punts, they switch roles.

Emphasize	Ideas for Lesson Development
Collecting *Inside of foot* Inside of the foot faces the ball. Contact the middle of the ball. Give with the foot—trap an egg!	★ Students work with a partner: One student passes the ball to the other, who traps it. Challenge them to pass the ball using varied amounts of force.

Belka: *Aim and Go!*

GRADES 1-2

Sample Performance Task

Within a large boundaried area students travel, dribbling a ball with the feet at a comfortable speed that allows them to show control. If you wish, give pinnies to a small group of students that you will focus on for a time. At the signal, have the students give the pinnies to another group of students.

RUBRIC CLUES **To what extent do students**

- keep (or lose) control of the ball (i.e., keep it close)?
- bump into others or repeatedly go out of bounds?
- use the inside (or outside) of the foot to dribble with, not the toe?

Sample Portfolio Task

Students each trace one of their feet (with their shoes on) and color that part of it they should use to dribble a ball.

RUBRIC CLUES **To what extent do students**

- show, by coloring the inside (or outside) of the foot, they understand which part of the foot to use?

NASPE BENCHMARKS Continuously dribble a ball, using the hands or feet, without losing control. (1-2, #12)

Emphasize	Ideas for Lesson Development
Instep kick Stand a little behind, to one side (of the ball). (Kick with the) shoelaces (the top part of the instep). Kick hard.	★ Have students pair up: One student practices running up to and kicking a stationary ball to a large open area; the other partner retrieves the ball and places it back for the next kick. After five kicks, they switch roles. ★ Provide carpet squares or draw a box on the ground. Have students put their nonkicking foot on the bottom left of the box (if they kick with their right leg) before kicking; the ball goes on the upper right-hand corner of the box. ★ Put large targets (e.g., clowns, animals) on the walls and have the students kick to them. ★ Place two carpet squares about 8 to 10 feet away from each other. Pair up the students; one partner slowly rolls the ball to the other, the kicker. The roller partner retrieves the ball. After five kicks, they switch roles. If you desire, have the kickers see how many times they can run between the two squares before the rollers return to their square. ★ Place tug-of-war ropes or two chalk lines on the ground parallel to each other. They should be at least the length of a gym apart. Students pair up and decide who will kick first. At the signal, the first partner kicks a ball from behind the line, then continues to move to the ball and kick it to see how many kicks it takes to get the ball across the other line. After turning around and dribbling back to the original line, the other partner prepares to kick. Discuss what happens when a player uses great force to kick the ball: How does this make a difference in this activity?

Emphasize	Ideas for Lesson Development
Inside kick Stand a little behind, to one side (of the ball). Toes and knees out, like a duck.	★ Have students practice kicking a stationary ball along the ground toward a stationary partner or target. If possible, set up large plastic garbage cans, standing hoops, large stacked tin cans, or the like as targets for students to kick toward. ★ Have students practice kicking toward their partners using the inside of their foot; the carpet squares that they stand on should first be fairly close together. After each kick that a partner traps without going off the square, they move their squares backward. If a pass is missed, they bring the squares close together again and start over.

Ideas for Lesson Development

- ★ Set up six stations, two each of the following: (a) pass the ball back and forth to your partner, using the inside of your foot; (b) dribble around the cones, racing if you want to; (c) take turns defending and kicking toward a goal. Provide enough equipment at each station for all students to be active simultaneously.

Emphasize

Dribbling

Push, don't kick (the ball).

(Use) insides [or] outsides (of the feet).

Keep it close (to you).

Ideas for Lesson Development

- ★ Challenge students to dribble a ball inside a large boundaried area while moving at the fastest speed at which they can control it. At the signal, can they trap the ball before the count of 3? (If they cannot, they are dribbling too fast.)
- ★ Put a variety of tires, hoops, crates, and other items in the boundaried area. Challenge students to dribble around the items without touching them.

Emphasize

Punting

Hold (the ball shoulder-level).

Step (with the nonkicking leg).

Drop (the ball).

Kick (with the shoelaces—use the top portion of the foot).

Ideas for Lesson Development

- ★ Give students a variety of balls to punt with (e.g., nerf balls, playground balls, soft and regular footballs).
- ★ In self-space within a very large area, students practice punting balls into the air. Challenge them to catch their punts before they touch the ground.
- ★ Put up a "slanty" rope between standards; challenge children to punt over the rope at the height that most challenges them (a line can also be drawn or taped on a wall). Put up enough ropes so students have sufficient space to safely punt, or use this as one station among a set of kicking or manipulative skills stations.

KINDERGARTEN

Sample Performance Task

Students kick a stationary ball as hard as they can, either from a stationary or running start (they should be facing a large open area). Once they kick it, they should retrieve it, replace it on its poly spot or carpet square, and kick again. (Observe at least five trials.)

RUBRIC CLUES **To what extent do students**

- consistently make contact with the ball?
- kick, rather than push, the ball with the foot?

NASPE BENCHMARKS Kick a stationary ball, using a smooth, continuous running approach prior to the kick. (K, #12)

Emphasize	Ideas for Lesson Development
Instep [or] Inside kick Eyes (focus) on the ball.	★ Facing a large open area, each student stands and kicks a stationary playground ball using any part of the foot; provide a carpet square on which they set the ball after retrieving it. ★ Challenge students to run up to and kick a ball as it sits on the carpet square.

Emphasize	Ideas for Lesson Development
Dribbling Little pushes. (Use) insides (of the feet).	★ Encourage students to walk and "roll" the ball forward by using the inside of the foot.

Sample Overall Unit Outcomes

By the end of elementary school, students should be able to

- use the skills of throwing and catching in order to design and play a small-group game; and
- use the basic offensive and defensive strategies for keep-away games (i.e., creating and denying space) when playing in small groups.

THROWING AND CATCHING

Concepts and Skills	Learnable Pieces
Underhand throw	
	Face your target. (K, 1-2)
	Arm (swings) back—"tick." (K, 1-2)
	Arm (swings) forward—"tock." (K, 1-2)
	Step with the opposite foot. (1-2)
	Bend the knees as you step. (3-4)
	Point your fingers to the target. (3-4)
Overhand throw	
	Side (of your body to the target). (1-2)
	(Swing your arm) down, back, and up. (1-2)
	Step (with the opposite foot). (1-2)
	Hand (points straight) up. (K, 3-4)
	Twist your body (as the ball is thrown). (3-4)
	Point (your fingers) to the target. (3-4)
	Throw hard. (3-4)
Frisbees	
	Twist and untwist your body. (5-6)
	Snap your wrist on the release. (5-6)
Catching	
	Reach out to the ball. (K)
	Watch the ball. (K, 1-2)
	Thumbs together above your waist. (1-2)
	Pinkies together below your waist. (1-2)
	Move to meet the ball. (3-4)
	Give with your body. (3-4)
	Pull the ball in to your body. (5-6)

GRADES 5-6

Sample Performance Task

Groups of three students each make up three passing plays using throwing, catching, and traveling. Students draw their plays in the dust or on paper before practicing them. After a while, one partner becomes the defender (i.e., 2-on-1 situation); the partners take turns running and defending the plays.

RUBRIC CLUES To what extent do students

- throw and catch using correct form?
- on defense stay between the thrower and the catcher, positioned to intercept the ball?

Sample Portfolio Task

Ask students to demonstrate knowledge of throwing and catching by completing Figure 7.3.

RUBRIC CLUES To what extent do students

- show they understand the cues pertaining to throwing and catching?

NASPE BENCHMARKS Throw a variety of objects demonstrating both accuracy and distance (e.g., frisbees, deck tennis rings, footballs). (5-6, #1)

Consistently throw and catch a ball while guarded by opponents. (5-6, #7)

Design and play small-group games that involve cooperating with others to keep an object away from opponents (basic offensive and defensive strategy) (e.g., by throwing, kicking, or dribbling a ball. (5-6, #8)

Emphasize

Frisbees

Twist and untwist your body.

Snap your wrist on the release.

Ideas for Lesson Development

★ Have students practice throwing Frisbees back and forth with a partner.

★ Set up a Frisbee course using playground equipment, cones inside hoops, and so forth. Frisbees need to go over, between, or under something if possible. If you wish, give each student a map of the course and a score card.

Belka: *Mini Frisbee Golf*

Emphasize

Catching

Pull the ball in to your body.

Ideas for Lesson Development

★ Have students throw different objects, using varying degrees of force and speed, to a partner.

★ Have students work in pairs to throw and catch leading passes. Have one partner start by rolling a hula hoop, while the other tries to throw a ball overhand through it. Have them practice so the catcher doesn't have to stop in order to catch the ball.

★ Have pairs of students make up and practice different passing plays with one another. If you desire, have them work in groups of three: After "practice," one player becomes the defender. If they choose to, they may set up a goal area to move toward after catching.

Name ______________________ Class ______________

Catch This!

1. **What is one important thing to remember when you're trying to catch a ball?**

2. **What are two good hints to remember when throwing a ball?**

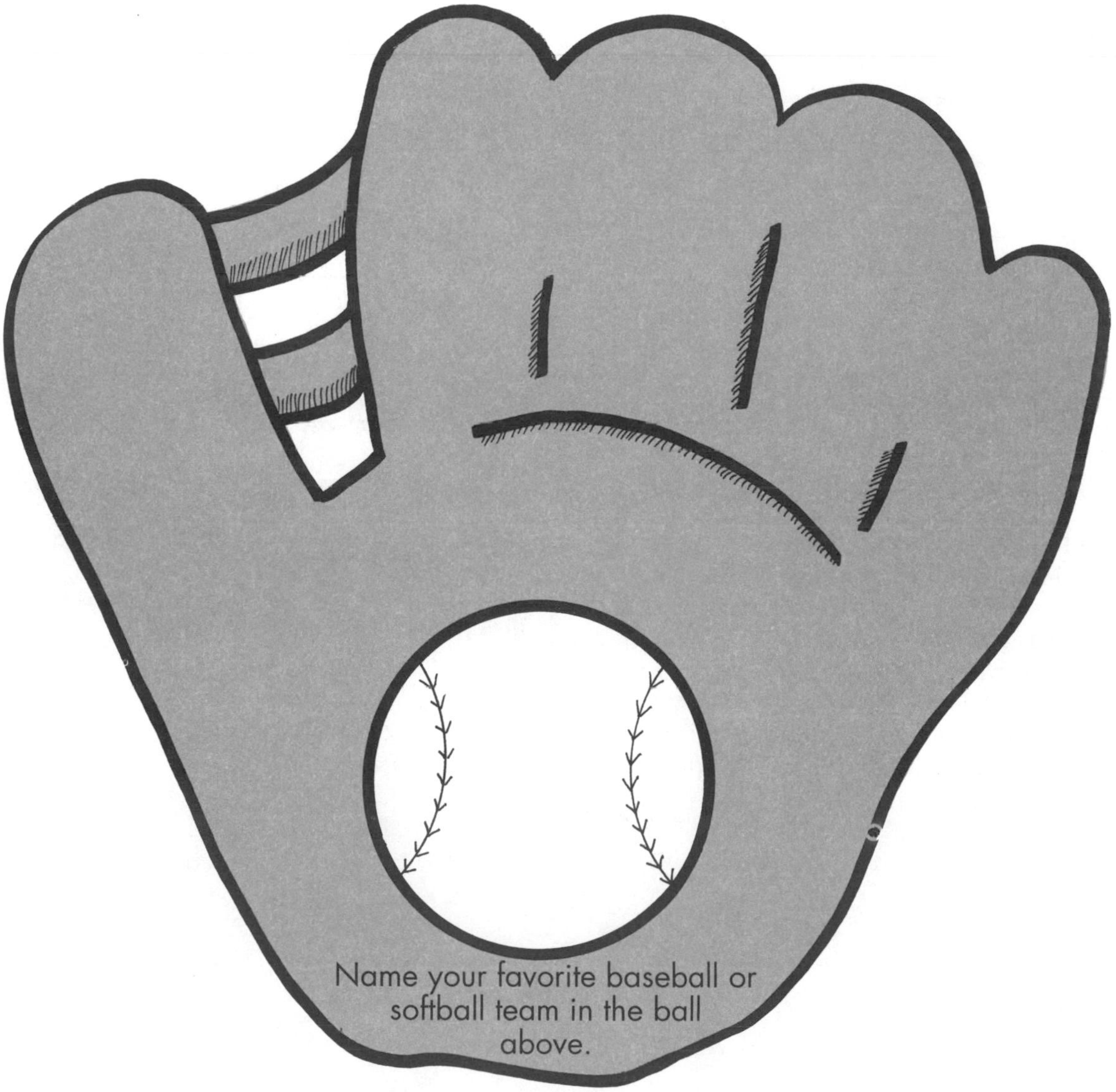
Name your favorite baseball or softball team in the ball above.

Figure 7.3 *Sample throwing and catching assessment sheet for Grades 5-6.*

Ideas for Lesson Development

- ★ Set up a large crash pad. Students jump off a box, crate, or other object and stretch to catch the ball, landing on the crash pad. The thrower should toss it so that the catcher really has to jump and stretch to catch it. You can use a regular mat instead of a crash pad; students have to roll after catching the ball.
- ★ Set up 2-on-2 or 3-on-3 modified Newcombe or deck tennis games, using Geo balls, yarn balls, and so forth. (Don't use volleyballs, or students will want to play volleyball!)

Belka: *Over and Under; The Route of It All; Predict-a-Bounce*

Emphasize

General space (see "Space Awareness," chapter 4)

Offense
Create space by moving to open areas to pass or receive the ball.

Defense
Deny space by keeping between the opponent and intended goal.

Ideas for Lesson Development

- ★ In an area about 20 × 20 feet students use throwing and catching to keep the ball away from opponents and to reach a designated goal area. Let students make up their own rules and boundaries; have them write these down.

GRADES 3-4

Sample Performance Task

Have students set up a 2-on-1 keep-away (Monkey-in-the-Middle) game; carpet squares can designate a minimum distance for the two outside partners. Using any types of throws and catching, the outside partners try to keep the ball away from the middle player. If the ball is caught or the "monkey" does not catch the ball after five throws, the middle player trades places with a student on the outside.

RUBRIC CLUES **To what extent do students**

- move to catch the ball?
- catch while guarded by an opponent?

Sample Portfolio Task

Students are to picture themselves in this situation: They are friends with the pitcher of their Little League baseball or softball team. Their friend is having trouble pitching to the batter, and the big game of the season is a week away. What are some hints they might give to help the friend pitch better? (Students should designate whether their friend pitches overhand or underhand.)

RUBRIC CLUES **To what extent do students**

- show an understanding of the cues for either the overhand or underhand throw?

NASPE BENCHMARKS Throw, catch, and kick using mature motor patterns. (3-4, #12)

Recognize fundamental components and strategies used in simple games and activities. (3-4, #20)

Describe essential elements of mature movement patterns. (3-4, #23)

Emphasize

Underhand throw

Bend the knees as you step.

Point your fingers to the target.

Ideas for Lesson Development

★ Set up stations for throwing, including a focus on using the underhand throw. Horseshoes (use stakes and deck tennis rings if you don't have horseshoes), bowling, and a large tic-tac-toe grid (use two different color bean bags) are just some of the stations you can use.

Emphasize

Overhand throw

Hand (points straight) up.

Twist your body (as the ball is thrown).

Point (your fingers) to the target.

Throw hard.

Ideas for Lesson Development

★ Discuss various pathways objects can move through in the air. Have students experiment throwing objects so they will move in straight or curved pathways. Discuss how these pathways relate to the object's speed in the air, its "hang" time, the object's weight, and its point of release. Relate these pathways to the way different objects are thrown in different sports (football, baseball, etc.)

★ Set up different-sized targets at varying distances from a line. Assign and label a point value for each target, depending upon its distance and size. (Make sure that there are targets of easy, medium, and hard difficulty so all students can gain points). Have students work with a partner to see if together they can reach a predetermined amount of points by the end of the class period; let students choose their target or targets and which objects they want to throw.

Belka: *Long Toss-n-Guard; Bounce and Field; Hoop Guard*
Buschner: *Spring Training*

Emphasize	Ideas for Lesson Development
Catching Move to meet the ball. Give with your body.	★ Have students throw and catch to themselves, challenging them to catch at different levels (high, middle, low), move in different directions to catch the object, and stretch or reach to catch. ★ Have a partner throw an object of choice to different places around the catcher's body, so that the catcher has to move (forward, backward, right, or left) to catch the ball. ★ Students can set up a 2-on-1, Monkey-in-the-Middle game; stress how the outside partners must move to get open. Discuss what the defensive player should do to catch the object.

Belka: *Trio Keep-Away*

GRADES 1-2

Sample Performance Task

Set up a variety of targets (boxes, large wall targets, hoops hung on a fence). Allow students to throw a beanbag to their choice of targets from a distance at least 5 feet away (use a jump rope on the ground to mark this). They may throw either underhand or overhand; observe them for at least five trials.

RUBRIC CLUES To what extent do students

- consistently step with the opposite foot when throwing, no matter whether they throw with an overhand or underhand throw?

Sample Portfolio Task

Students show their knowledge relative to correct throwing form by completing Figure 7.4.

RUBRIC CLUES To what extent do students

- show they understand how to step with the opposite foot when throwing a ball?

NASPE BENCHMARKS Throw a ball hard demonstrating an overhand technique, a side orientation, and opposition. (1-2, #10)

Emphasize	Ideas for Lesson Development
Underhand throw Face your target. Arm (swings) back—"tick." Arm (swings) forward—"tock." Step with the opposite foot.	★ Hang large targets (painted on canvas) 10 to 12 feet away from the wall in the gym (so balls won't bounce off the wall, going everywhere!). ★ Have students throw either underhand or overhand to a variety of targets. Here are some suggestions: Place hoops and tires on the ground in a line at progressively farther distances students can throw to. Post each letter of the alphabet on a 12 × 6 foot canvas target or area on the wall. Challenge students to spell their names by throwing to the correct letters. You also can arrange these letters in the form of a computer keyboard. Paint a calculator on a 5 × 6 foot target so students can dial (throw to) "9-1-1" or do easy math problems.

Name ______________________ Class ______________

How to Throw

Which picture shows the correct way for you to step when you throw a ball?

Circle it.

Figure 7.4 *Sample throwing and catching assessment sheet for Grades 1-2.*

Ideas for Lesson Development

Outline batters (boy and girl) on a 5 × 6 foot canvas, with the strike zone boxed in by a marker. Color in the box with crayon; iron it onto the material.

Set up large tin cans in pyramid fashion: Students throw and see how many cans they can knock over.

- ★ Make scoops out of milk cartons; students can throw underhand and catch yarn and tennis balls in them, either by themselves or with a partner.

Emphasize

Overhand throw

Side (of your body to the target).

(Swing your arm) down, back, and up.

Step (with the opposite foot).

Ideas for Lesson Development

- ★ Set up targets such as listed earlier (see Underhand throw) for students to throw to.
- ★ Pair up the students: One student holds up a hoop in various places around his or her body while the other, using a yarn or other soft ball, tries to throw the object through the hoop. Set a minimum distance for the throws, about 5 feet. Students accumulate points for each throw that goes through the hoop; after five tries, they switch roles.
- ★ Students work in pairs, one throwing to the targets and the other giving a point each time the thrower steps with the opposite foot. Partners (evaluators) award another point if the throwers also hit the target. Let students decide what distance to throw from.
- ★ Have students pair up and play the near/far game: Using an object appropriate to their ability to throw and catch, two students stand close, facing each other. Player A tosses the object to Player B; if B catches it, he or she takes a step backward. Player B then throws the object back to Player A; if caught, A takes a step backward. If the catcher misses, drops the object, or has to move more than one step away to catch the object, both partners return to their original positions close to one another and begin again. Observe for specific critical throwing and catching elements.

Buschner: *Carnival Throwing*

Emphasize

Catching

Watch the ball.

Thumbs together above your waist.

Pinkies together below your waist.

Ideas for Lesson Development

- ★ Students practice throwing and catching by themselves in self-space. Challenge them to clap one, two, three . . . times before they catch the ball; twist around and catch it; or add other movements before they catch it.
- ★ Challenge students to throw a ball up and catch it at a high level, medium level, or low level.
- ★ Challenge students to throw the ball up so they have to catch it at different places around their bodies (catch it on the left side, right side, etc.).
- ★ Put a clothespin on the shoelaces or a pants leg to remind students which of their feet is the "opposite" foot!

Buschner: *Egg Catching*

KINDERGARTEN

Emphasize	Ideas for Lesson Development
Catching Watch the ball. Reach out to the ball.	★ From a straddled sitting position, students roll a large ball to partners who catch it, using both hands. ★ Challenge students to roll and catch the ball both in front of and behind them when standing in a straddled position. ★ Have students throw and catch soft objects, such as nerf balls, yarn balls, and balloons, while they stand in self-space. Challenge them to clap one time before they catch the object.

Emphasize	Ideas for Lesson Development
Underhand throw Face your target. Arm (swings) back—"tick." Arm (swings) forward—"tock."	★ Put up large targets (clowns, animals) for students to throw at using an underhand throw. ★ Set up hoops or tires on the ground; allow students to throw soft objects such as beanbags or softballs toward them from their choice of distance.

Emphasize	Ideas for Lesson Development
Overhand throw Hand (points straight) up.	★ Challenge students to throw overhand to large targets.

Sample Overall Unit Outcome

By the end of elementary school, students should be able to

- use volleying skills, including the underhand, overhead, and the forearm (bump) pass, when playing or designing a small-group game.

VOLLEYING

Concepts and Skills	Learnable Pieces
Underhand	
	Bring your arm back. (K, 1-2)
	Step with the opposite foot. (1-2)
	Hit (the ball). (1-2)
	(Use the) heel of your hand. (1-2)
	Point your hand to the target. (3-4)
Overhead	
	Toss. (1-2)
	Hands above the head—high level. (1-2)
	Push your arms straight. (1-2)
	Step. (3-4)
	Bend the knees. (3-4)
	Hit using the fingerpads. (3-4)
	Move under the ball. (5-6)
	Stretch your body up. (5-6)
Forearm (bump) pass	
	Step (one foot in front). (3-4)
	Bend the knees. (3-4)
	Hands (point) down. (3-4)
	Arms like a paddle. (3-4)
	Move under the ball. (5-6)
	Point toward the target. (5-6)
	Stretch your body up. (5-6)

GRADES 5-6

Sample Performance Task

Students play a small-group game in an area about 20 × 20 feet, using underhand and overhead volleys and bump passes. Allow students to make up their own rules about the number of hits, height of the net, serving lines, catches, and points.

RUBRIC CLUES **To what extent do students**

- consistently volley, either to a teammate or across the net, using underhand and overhand volleys and bump passes?
- when they are on defense spread out equally to cover an area?
- when they are on offense hit the ball where others aren't?

Sample Portfolio Task

Ask students to describe strategies that are important both for the offense and defense to use in playing volleyball. Do they feel they can use these strategies in play?

RUBRIC CLUES **To what extent do students**

- show they understand the offensive and defensive strategies presented during instruction?

NASPE BENCHMARKS In a small group keep an object continuously in the air without catching it (e.g., ball, foot bag). (5-6, #6)

Emphasize

Forearm (bump) pass

Move under the ball.

Point toward the target.

Stretch your body up.

Ideas for Lesson Development

- ★ Challenge students to bump-pass a gently tossed object to a *different* area from where it came from. Thus, the passer must move in order to retrieve the ball.
- ★ Students partner up; the passer gently tosses an object to different places around the other partner, who must move to be in position to bump-pass or overhead-volley the ball back. After five tosses, they switch roles.
- ★ Using a medium-level rope or net, one student gently tosses the object to a partner, who bump-passes it back to the tosser. Challenge them eventually to bump-pass the object back to where the partner *is not*.

Belka: *Over Long and Short*

Emphasize

Overhead

Move under the ball.

Stretch your body up.

Ideas for Lesson Development

- ★ Using a medium-level rope or net, students overhead-volley a ball back to the partner who tossed it. As their skills increase, challenge players to volley the ball back and forth.

Emphasize	Ideas for Lesson Development
General space (see "Space Awareness," chapter 4) *Offense* Hit the ball to where opponents aren't standing. *Defense* Be ready to move. Partners equally cover the area.	★ Students set up and play small-group games that involve using overhead and underhand volleying and bump passing to keep the ball in play as long as possible. ★ Challenge students to eventually start passing to where the defense is *not*. Allow students to determine the game rules, hits, serve lines, and so forth.

GRADES 3-4

Sample Performance Task

Mark off two large (about 4 feet) squares adjacent to each other. Students take turns underhand volleying (striking) an appropriate ball that can be bounced back and forth, always trying to return the ball to the opposite square after one or no bounces. If a ball cannot be returned after one bounce or if it goes out of the square, the other partner starts a new series by an underhand serve.

RUBRIC CLUES **To what extent do students**

- consistently volley or strike the ball using an underhand striking pattern?

Sample Portfolio Task

Students describe a sport or activity that uses volleying. What is a hint to remember when volleying?

RUBRIC CLUES **To what extent do students**

- give examples that show they understand the skills specific to volleying?
- show they clearly understand the cues for volleying?

NASPE BENCHMARKS Strike a softly thrown, lightweight ball back to a partner using a variety of body parts and combinations of body parts (e.g., the bump volley as in volleyball, the thigh as in soccer). (3-4, #6)

Describe essential elements of mature movement patterns. (3-4, #23)

Emphasize	Ideas for Lesson Development
Underhand Point your hand to the target.	★ Put a net up against a wall; students can serve or volley to the wall above the net, almost like the real thing! ★ Challenge students to volley or strike an object using at least two different body parts in succession. ★ See if students can volley or strike a lightly tossed object to a partner using different body parts.

Ideas for Lesson Development

- ★ Put large targets or hoops on the floor on the other side of a low net. Students practice serving the ball underhand, trying to get it to a certain target. If you wish, assign point values to the targets and encourage students to work together with a partner to reach a certain amount of points.
- ★ Set up a two-square court, or make a low jump-rope net. Students take turns underhand striking an appropriate object back and forth across the line or net to their partners, allowing one bounce before returning it.
- ★ In groups of four, students set up and volley in a four-square situation.

Belka: *Across the Line*

Emphasize

Overhead

Step.

Bend the knees.

Hit using the fingerpads.

Ideas for Lesson Development

- ★ Set up large targets at varying heights on a wall. Students can practice self-tossing, then overhand volleying an appropriate object to the targets or a partner.
- ★ Without them using any type of net, have students practice softly tossing an appropriate object to a partner, who overhead-volleys it back. After five volleys, they switch roles.

Emphasize

Forearm (bump) pass

Step (one foot in front).

Bend the knees.

Hands (point) down.

Arms like a paddle.

Ideas for Lesson Development

- ★ Have students explore why the various cues are important. For example, ask them what happens if you volley the ball without bending the knees. "Now try it bending your knees, to see the difference." Encourage them to figure out why the ball sometimes flies backward when you hit it: What do the hands have to do when hitting high balls?
- ★ Students softly toss an appropriate object to a partner, who practices bump (forearm) passing it back.

GRADES 1-2

Sample Performance Task

Have students set up jump ropes and crates or cones as a low net. Students underhand-volley or strike a soft, lightweight ball back and forth over the jump ropes; partners catch the ball and underhand-strike it back over. Students can stand any distance they choose from the ropes.

RUBRIC CLUES **To what extent do students**

- demonstrate they can use one or more of the specific cues related to the underhand throw or strike?

Sample Portfolio Task

Ask students to draw a picture of themselves on a piece of paper, then make an "x" on the different body parts they can use to strike or volley a balloon or other soft ball.

RUBRIC CLUES **To what extent do students**

- give examples of body parts that are feasibly used for volleying and striking?

NASPE BENCHMARKS Use at least three different body parts to strike a ball toward a target. (1-2, #13)

Emphasize

Underhand

Bring your arm back.

Step with the opposite foot.

Hit (the ball).

(Use the) heel of your hand.

Ideas for Lesson Development

- ★ Give students a choice of balls to use for volleying. Punch balls, helium-quality balloons, and the new lightweight, oversize volleyball trainers make volleying less threatening and more motivating. Allow the students to trade balls to keep up their interest.
- ★ Discuss how a volley is not a push or slap, but a solid "pop" using the hand or other body part (force is not absorbed by the body part). Challenge students to see how many different body parts they can use to volley a soft, lightweight ball while keeping it in self-space. Challenge them to use their head, elbows, knees, and foot.
- ★ Have students experiment with how they must strike the object to make it go up, forward, back over their head, or in any other direction.
- ★ Have students practice the underhand, striking a soft object upward with the hand while keeping it in self-space.
- ★ Challenge students to travel slowly through general space, striking an object underhand (upward) using their hands. See if they can keep control of the objects by taking only one or two steps to get to the ball.
- ★ Using a ball that bounces, have students bounce and then "pop" it upward using the heels of their hands. Challenge them to catch a ball after one bounce or before it bounces at all, then pop it again (the sequence becomes bounce, pop, [bounce], catch). They can also try to continuously pop the ball without catching it at all (bounce, pop, bounce, pop). Challenge them to pop the ball upward using different body parts.
- ★ On a fence or wall set up large targets of varying sizes and heights. Challenge students to strike an object underhand to the targets, from whatever distance they wish.
- ★ String up a "slanty" rope between standards. Pair up the students and have them take turns underhand striking and catching an object.

Emphasize

Overhead

Toss.

Hands above the head—high level.

Push your arms straight.

Ideas for Lesson Development

- ★ Have students practice overhead volleying and catching with self-tossed lightweight balls or balloons, keeping them in self-space.
- ★ Set up a low net; students take turns overhead volleying a self-tossed ball over the net to their partner, who catches and returns it doing the same.

KINDERGARTEN

Emphasize	Ideas for Lesson Development
Underhand Bring your arm back.	★ Students each underhand strike a balloon upward while keeping it in self-space. See if the children can do this with both the right and left hands. ★ Challenge students to strike balloons with their heads, elbows, knees, and other body parts. ★ Challenge students to move slowly through general space while they use their hands to keep balloons off the ground.

Sample Overall Unit Outcomes

By the end of elementary school, students should be able to

- use the individual skills of the underhand, forehand, and backhand strikes in appropriate situations, and
- use combinations of underhand, forehand, and backhand strikes in appropriate game situations.

STRIKING WITH SHORT-HANDLED IMPLEMENTS

Concepts and Skills	Learnable Pieces
Underhand	
	Watch the ball. (K)
	Paddle back. (K)
	Shake hands with the paddle. (K, 1-2)
	Firm wrist and elbow. (1-2)
	Hit the ball on its way down. (1-2)
Forehand	
	(Turn your) side to the target. (1-2)
	(Start with or bring the) paddle or racket back. (1-2)
	Firm wrist and elbow. (1-2)
	Extend the arm (as you swing). (3-4)
	Level swing. (3-4)
	Step into the swing. (5-6)
	Paddle to the target. (5-6)
Backhand	
	Arm across the body. (3-4)
	(Turn to) other side to the target. (3-4, 5-6)
	Step into the swing. (5-6)
	Extend the arm (as you swing). (5-6)
	Level swing. (5-6)
	Paddle to the target. (5-6)

GRADES 5-6

Sample Performance Task

Mark a "net" line on a wall toward which students use forehand and backhand strikes to hit a rebounding ball. Allow students to choose the distance at which they stand, as well as the size of racket.

RUBRIC CLUES To what extent do students

- demonstrate the cues presented in class for the forehand and backhand strikes?

Sample Portfolio Task

After they have participated in experiences related to striking, students are asked to reflect in writing on what they feel they have learned or understood more as a result of their experiences. What has helped them to learn or improve?

RUBRIC CLUES To what extent do students

- show they understand the concepts and skills presented in class?

NASPE BENCHMARKS Continuously strike a ball to a wall or a partner, with a paddle, using forehand and backhand strokes. (5-6, #2)

Recognize that time and effort are prerequisites for skill improvement and fitness benefits. (5-6, #18)

Emphasize

Forehand

Step into the swing.

Paddle to the target.

Ideas for Lesson Development

- ★ Challenge students to strike a ball rebounding from a wall with their rackets or paddles, using forehand strikes.
- ★ Set up a low net; ask students to bounce, then strike a ball toward different targeted areas on the other side of the net. Make sure the targeted areas are large and that they vary in distance and angle from the net.
- ★ Encourage students to move into a ready position after each strike, prepared to move to where the ball will be going.

Belka: *Three-Court Tennis*

Emphasize

Backhand

(Turn to) other side to the target.

Step into the swing.

Extend the arm (as you swing).

Level swing. [Use this only if it is appropriate for students' skill level.]

Ideas for Lesson Development

- ★ Have a partner gently toss a ball; the "striker" uses a backhand motion to strike the ball.

Emphasize

Paddle to the target. [Use this only if it is appropriate for students' skill level.]

GRADES 3-4

Sample Performance Task

Students are to bounce and then use a forehand strike to move a small, lightweight ball toward a large target on the wall or ground. Allow students to choose how far they stand from the wall and what type of paddle or racket they will use.

RUBRIC CLUES **To what extent do students**

- consistently demonstrate the ability to use (one or all of) the cues presented in class?

Sample Portfolio Task

Ask students each to write a letter to a favorite tennis player. Their letters should include an important hint to remember for hitting a forehand strike and a backhand strike.

RUBRIC CLUES **To what extent do students**

- show they understand the important cues presented in class?

NASPE BENCHMARKS Consistently strike a softly thrown ball with a bat or paddle, demonstrating an appropriate grip, side to the target, and swing plane. (3-4, #7)

Describe essential elements of mature movement patterns. (3-4, #23)

Emphasize

Forehand

Extend the arm (as you swing).

Level swing.

Ideas for Lesson Development

★ One way to teach the correct forehand grip is to have students each place the racket flat on the ground, put the hand flat on the paddle face, and slide it down the handle. For the backhand have students each place the racket under the nonpreferred arm, then reach over and grab it using the striking hand.

★ Set up low jump-rope "nets" with cones or crates, or mark or tape a "net" on a wall. Students can each practice forehand striking a lightweight ball using a paddle or racket to a partner or the wall.

★ Set up low jump-rope "nets" with cones or crates, or mark or tape a "net" on a wall. Students can each practice forehand striking a lightweight ball using a paddle or racket to a partner or the wall.

★ Place large targets on the wall for students to strike to. Allow them to choose where they will stand.

★ Pair up students. Have a partner gently toss a soft, lightweight ball to the "striker." Put a hoop or jump-rope circle down in an appropriate place for students to aim at when tossing.

Emphasize	Ideas for Lesson Development
Backhand (Turn to) other side to the target. Arm across the body.	★ Have students each practice bouncing then striking a soft, lightweight ball using a backhand motion toward a large open area, partner, or wall. ★ Have a partner drop a ball in the appropriate place for students to backhand-strike it.

GRADES 1-2

Sample Performance Task

Students bounce and then strike a soft, lightweight ball from behind a jump-rope line to the general area of their partners, who stand in an open area and try to catch it. Students can strike with either a hand or other lightweight paddle. Each person can get five strikes, then must switch roles.

RUBRIC CLUES **To what extent do students**

- consistently demonstrate (one or all of) the cues specific to the forehand strike?

Sample Portfolio Task

Ask students to list four body parts that figure importantly in striking, such as hand, eyes, side of body, and arm.

RUBRIC CLUES **To what extent do students**

- show they understand the cues for striking?

NASPE BENCHMARKS Strike a ball repeatedly with a paddle. (1-2, #14)

Emphasize	Ideas for Lesson Development
Underhand Shake hands with the paddle. Firm wrist and elbow. Hit the ball on its way down.	★ In self-space students each try to flip a beanbag "pancake" over and to catch it on the paddle. Can they travel slowly and do this? ★ Ask students each to stay in self-space while continuously bouncing then striking a small, lightweight ball upward with a hand or other lightweight paddle (i.e., bounce, strike, bounce, strike, etc.). ★ Challenge students each to stay in self-space while continuously striking a small, lightweight ball upward. How many times can each hit the ball in a row, without losing control of it?

Emphasize	Ideas for Lesson Development
Forehand (Turn your) side to the target. (Start with or bring the) paddle or racket back. Firm wrist and elbow.	★ Prepare and suspend balls in this manner: Cut a small slit in the sides of two tennis balls. Use a darning needle to string the balls onto a long piece of Weed-Eater string, which can be suspended between two standards. Add a small (half-inch) brass ring between the two balls (the two balls will keep the suspended ball you use from moving along the rope). Then, tie a string to the brass ring using a hangman's knot. Draw this string through two small slits on another (suspended) tennis ball, or suspend a Wiffle ball. You can suspend many such sets and move them along the line to fit your space and needs.

Ideas for Lesson Development

- Challenge students to continuously strike a suspended ball, either by hand or with a lightweight paddle, using a forehand motion. How many times in a row can each strike the ball?
- Have students bounce and then strike a ball either by hand or with a lightweight paddle toward a partner, wall, or hoop (or tire) set on the ground as a target.

KINDERGARTEN

Emphasize	Ideas for Lesson Development
Underhand Shake hands with the paddle. Watch the ball. Paddle back.	★ Challenge students each to balance a beanbag on a paddle and move through general space without dropping it. ★ Using either a hand or lightweight paddle (nylon or "lollipop"), have students each practice repeatedly striking a balloon with an underhand motion. ★ Challenge students to strike underhand a Wiffle ball suspended from a bar or rope by hand, with a hand paddle, or with some other lightweight paddle.

Sample Overall Unit Outcomes

By the end of elementary school, students should be able to

- strike in appropriate practice situations, using a variety of long-handled implements, and
- use the skills of striking with long-handled implements to play or design small-group games.

STRIKING WITH LONG-HANDLED IMPLEMENTS

Concepts and Skills	Learnable Pieces
Batting	
	Tee in front, side to the target. (K, 1-2)
	Shake hands with the bat, your favorite hand on top. (1-2)
	Twist, untwist (your hips lead). (1-2)
	Stand bat's length away (from the tee or plate). (1-2)
	Step in the direction of the ball. (3-4)
	Level, stretched stroke. (3-4)
	Extend to the target. (5-6)
Hockey and golf strike	
	Shake hands with the stick, your favorite hand on top. (1-2)
	Small swings, side to side. (hockey only) (1-2)
	Side to the target—ball in front of you. (1-2, 3-4)
	Large swing, side to side. (golf only) (3-4)
	Twist, untwist (your hips and shoulders turn). (3-4)
	Hit underneath the ball. (golf only) (5-6)
	Extend to the target. (5-6)
Hockey dribble	
	Use both sides of the stick. (1-2)
	Ball in front of you. (1-2)
	Small taps. (1-2, 3-4)
	Keep it close. (3-4)
	Look up. (5-6)

GRADES 5-6

Sample Performance Task

Have small groups (three to four students each) design and play a small-group game using dribbling and passing with a hockey stick to move a Wiffle ball (you can adjust the type stick and ball) toward a goal area. Allow students to choose boundaries, size of the goal area, and rules.

RUBRIC CLUES To what extent do students

- successfully use the skills of dribbling and passing?
- choose boundaries and rules appropriate to their skill levels?
- successfully use offensive and defensive strategies to create and deny space?

Sample Portfolio Task

Ask students to list all the sports and activities they know that involve the use of striking. Which of these do or would they enjoy playing or learning? How might their experiences in physical education help them be successful in these activities?

RUBRIC CLUES To what extent do students

- show they understand the skills of striking?

NASPE BENCHMARKS Consistently strike a ball, using a golf club or a hockey stick, so that it travels in an intended direction and height. (5-6, #3)

Emphasize

Batting

Extend to the target.

Ideas for Lesson Development

★ Make large target areas (using chalk lines, etc.) and assign each a number of points. Challenge students to strike a ball with the bat toward certain areas and see how many points they and a partner can earn.

★ Modified striking game—half of the class is up to bat; the other half is in the field (no out-of-bounds). Give paddles or rackets to half of the fielders. At one time, half of the batters strike and try to run around two cones set up in the field. Each time the group of batters runs around the cones, they get one point. Meanwhile, the fielders without rackets must get the balls to the fielders who have the implements. These fielders try to strike the balls into a large target (9 × 12 feet on the wall, or a large area set up behind the batters). Fielders can strike from anywhere to get the balls to the target. After all the balls are in (or have been hit to) the target, the fielders give their paddles to the other half of the fielders to use, and the other half of the batters go to bat. Each person gets to bat twice before fielders and batters switch roles.

Belka: *300; Strategy Fielding*

Emphasize	Ideas for Lesson Development
Hockey and golf strike Hit underneath the ball (golf only). Extend to the target.	★ Set up zones of varied distances away from a starting line (the "driving range"). Challenge each student to strike a small Wiffle-type ball for distance toward the zones; a partner can retrieve balls and then switch roles after five strikes.

Emphasize	Ideas for Lesson Development
Hockey dribble Look up. **General space** (see "Space Awareness," chapter 4) *Offense* Keep your body between the ball and the defender.	★ In a large boundaried area, challenge each student to dribble a Wiffle-type ball with hockey sticks and change speeds according to the drum or tambourine beat or a signal. ★ Put obstacles, such as crates, boxes, and cones, in general space; challenge students to dribble as quickly as possible through general space without colliding with others or with obstacles. ★ Modified Trees in the Forest—have defenders stand in hoops spread throughout general space; the other students move through the area, trying not to lose control of the ball. ★ Set up an obstacle course with cones, crates, and boxes that students must dribble through; have a large goal set up at the end toward which they can then strike.

Emphasize	Ideas for Lesson Development
General space (see "Space Awareness," chapter 4) *Offense* Keep your body between the ball and the defender. Create space by moving to open areas to pass or receive the ball. *Defense* Deny space by keeping between the opponent and intended goal.	★ Have students design and play small-group games (2-on-2, 2-on-3, 3-on-3) that involve dribbling and shooting with a hockey stick toward a goal area. A goal defender can be part of each team. Allow students to determine their own rules, boundaries, and goal size.

GRADES 3-4

Sample Performance Task

Students use hockey sticks to strike a Wiffle-type ball toward targets of varied sizes and distances. They choose the targets they wish to strike.

RUBRIC CLUES To what extent do students

- demonstrate the cues related to striking to targets with a long-handled implement?

Sample Portfolio Task

Ask students to reflect about the cues they use in batting by completing Figure 7.5.

RUBRIC CLUES To what extent do students

- show they understand the cues for batting?

Name ______________________________ Class ____________________

What's Your Batting Average?

What's a game that uses striking?

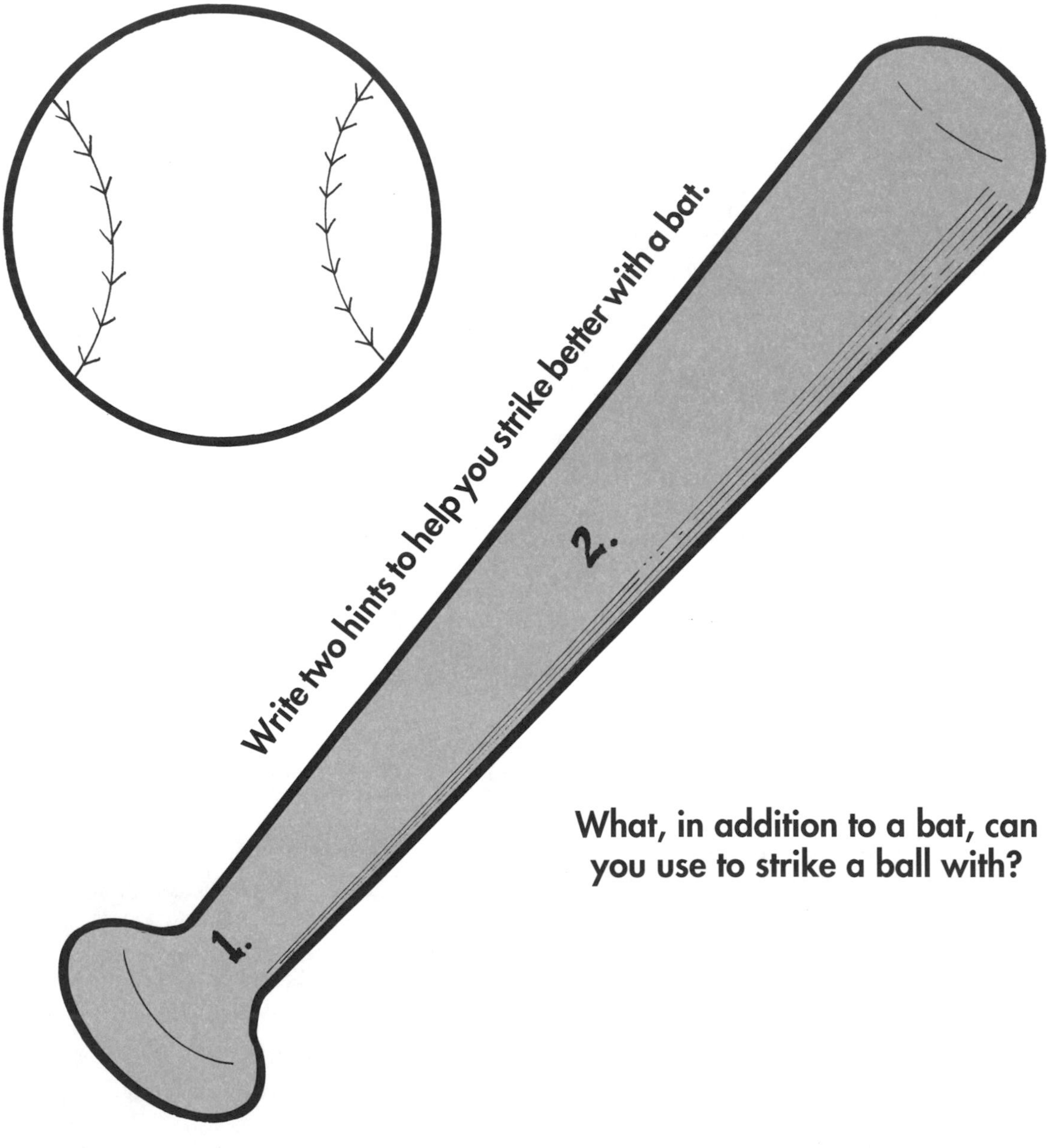
Write two hints to help you strike better with a bat.
1.
2.

What, in addition to a bat, can you use to strike a ball with?

Figure 7.5 *Sample striking with long-handled instrument assessment sheet for Grades 3-4.*

Emphasize	Ideas for Lesson Development
Batting Step in the direction of the ball. Level, stretched stroke.	★ Students can take turns hitting off a tee to two partners in the field; after five strikes, they switch roles. Put out a variety of equipment, such as bases, poly spots, and carpet squares, so that the students can make up their own games, if they so wish. ★ Discuss what makes a good underhand pitch; allow students to practice pitching toward a home plate. Then, in groups of three or four, have the students each practice the roles of batter, fielder, and pitcher.

Buschner: *Step and Swing*

Emphasize	Ideas for Lesson Development
Hockey strike Side to the target—ball in front of you. Twist, untwist (your hips and shoulders turn).	★ Standing a distance of choice away from each other, have pairs of students practice striking a Wiffle-type ball along the ground to a partner. Once they can strike the ball so their partners don't have to move more than a step away from position to trap it, challenge them to work from greater distances. ★ Set up a variety of targets (large tin cans on their sides, hoops, goals) that students can strike toward from a distance they choose. Assign point values to the targets if you wish. ★ Set up several goals in a large boundaried area. Have pairs of students practice dribbling, then shooting, toward any goal area they wish. Several pairs of students can be working in the area simultaneously, as long as there is at least one goal for each pair and a large enough space for them all to move around safely. If you wish, have students work in groups of three, with one as goal defender. You can specify time limits for them to rotate to the field, as a fielder becomes a goal defender.

Emphasize	Ideas for Lesson Development
Golf strike Side to the target—ball in front of you. Large swings, side to side. Twist, untwist (your hips and shoulders turn).	★ Have students strike a small Wiffle-type ball toward a large open area; partners use cones to mark the farthest distance hit. After five strikes, partners switch roles.

Emphasize	Ideas for Lesson Development
Hockey dribble Small taps. Keep it close.	★ Many long-handled, hockey-type sticks are on the market today: Plastic hockey sticks, Pillo-Pollo sticks, and golf sticks or clubs are a few examples. Encourage students to practice their skills with as many different implements as possible. ★ In a large boundaried area, have students each dribble a Wiffle-type ball with a hockey-type stick and at the signal change the direction, or pathway, they are traveling on.

GRADES 1-2

Sample Performance Task

From a tee or large cone students each strike a large Wiffle-type ball with a plastic bat to a fielder standing in a large open area.

RUBRIC CLUES To what extent do students

- demonstrate the cues presented in class that relate to striking with a bat?

Sample Portfolio Task

Give students a portfolio worksheet showing the front view of a person preparing to swing a bat. Ask the students to designate the part of the body that would face the batting tee (see Figure 7.6).

RUBRIC CLUES To what extent do students

- designate the side as the correct body part to face the tee?

NASPE BENCHMARKS Consistently strike a ball with a bat from a tee or cone, using a correct grip and side orientation. (1-2, #15)

Emphasize

Batting

Shake hands with the bat, your favorite hand on top.

Tee in front, side to the target.

Stand bat's length away (from the tee or plate).

Twist, untwist (your hips lead).

Ideas for Lesson Development

★ Stress the protocol of using long-handled implements to students: Always look around to make sure you have plenty of space to swing and always keep your hockey-type stick at a low level.

★ Students can each practice hitting a Wiffle-type ball off a tee with a plastic or lightweight bat to a partner who fields.

★ Allow students, in groups of two or three, to make up their own game when batting. Poly spots and carpet squares can be used as bases.

Emphasize

Hockey strike

Shake hands with the stick, your favorite hand on top.

Side to the target—ball in front of you.

Small swings, side to side.

Ideas for Lesson Development

★ Have students each practice hitting a Wiffle-type ball with a hockey-type club to a hoop on the ground or to some other target, such as foam pins or 2-liter bottles with the bottoms filled with sand.

★ Divide the class in half: Each half stands behind a line. On a third line (centered about 12 feet away from each line) set up three to four targets (e.g., 2-liter plastic bottles) in front of each student. On the signal, students strike toward their targets. When one side has all their targets down, they set them up and begin again. This activity can also be done in a small-group situation.

Name ______________________ Class ______________

How Should You Bat?

Circle the part of your body that should face the *tee* or *pitcher* when you bat.

front **back** **top** **side** **bottom**

Figure 7.6 *Sample striking with long-handled instrument assessment sheet for Grades 1-2.*

Emphasize	Ideas for Lesson Development
Hockey dribble Use both sides of the stick. Ball in front of you. Small taps.	★ In a large open area, have students practice dribbling a Wiffle-type ball with a hockey stick. Set up a large goal area they can practice striking toward. ★ Paint or chalk large designs of different pathways. Challenge students to dribble their balls on the pathways, moving as quickly as they can while keeping control of the balls.

KINDERGARTEN

Emphasize	Ideas for Lesson Development
Batting Tee in front, side to the target.	★ Set up 6-inch playground balls on large cones for students to strike, using their hands like bats. Students practice in pairs. Have a partner catch the ball; each batter gets three strikes before they become a catcher.

CHAPTER 8 *Fitness*

Sample Overall Unit Outcome

By the end of elementary school, students should be able to

- apply to situations in their daily lives, as much as possible, the basic concepts relating to physical fitness in general.

INTRODUCTION TO FITNESS

Concepts and Skills	Learnable Pieces
Being active is important for your body.	
	Being active is good for your body. (K)
	Being active is a healthy habit. (1-2)
	Being active helps you look and feel good, and it helps your heart, bones, and muscles become strong and healthy. (3-4)
	Being active is the only way to become physically fit. (3-4, 5-6)
You can be active in many different ways.	
	Playing is a fun way to be active. (K)
	Moving, playing, working, and exercising are ways you can be active. (1-2, 3-4)
	There are many fun ways to become active and fit. (3-4, 5-6)
	Sometimes it's not easy to be active. (5-6)
It is important to be physically fit.	
	Being physically fit means your heart, bones, and muscles are strong and healthy. (1-2)
	Being physically fit means you look good, feel good, and have lots of energy to play and work at home and in school. (3-4)
	The only way to become physically fit is to be active. (5-6)
	Being physically fit means you have good aerobic endurance, muscle strength, flexibility, and body fat levels. (5-6)
Physical fitness tests assess your body's fitness levels.	
	Fitness tests help you find out how fit your body is and whether you need to improve your activity level. (3-4, 5-6)

GRADES 5-6

Sample Portfolio Task

Ask students to describe whom they consider more physically active—people in the present or people who lived 100 years ago. Why do they think so?

RUBRIC CLUES **To what extent do students**

- show their understanding by appropriately using terms and examples?
- use examples to back up their viewpoints?

Emphasize

Being active is important for your body.

Being active is the only way to become physically fit.

Ideas for Lesson Development

- ★ Discuss with the class that when you are active by moving, playing, working, and exercising, you help yourself become physically fit. Being active is the only way you can get to become or remain physically fit.
- ★ Relate to students how being active helps the body become better, just like doing homework and studying helps the mind become smarter. Being active is a smart way to take care of the body!
- ★ Ask questions to facilitate discussion and review, such as these: (a) What is the only way you can become physically fit? (b) What are some ways people, especially on TV, try to make you think you can become physically fit, ways that really don't work?

Emphasize

You can be active in many different ways.

There are many fun ways to become active and fit.

Ideas for Lesson Development

- ★ Discuss with students the many fun ways they can move, exercise, and be active at home and in school. Ask them for examples: Jumping rope, jogging, dancing, swimming, doing push-ups, throwing and catching, and playing tag are just a few possibilities.
- ★ Discuss how gardening, walking, and working around the house or farm help people stay active and become physically fit, too.
- ★ Discuss some ways that make being active and exercising more fun, such as exercising with a friend, your pet, parents, and siblings, or exercising to music.
- ★ Ask students to describe in writing their favorite way of being active and becoming physically fit. Post these on a bulletin board where everyone can see them.
- ★ Ask questions to facilitate discussion and review, such as the following: (a) Name some things you like to do that are plain fun. Do you think you get more fit by doing them? (b) What can you do to make exercising more fun? (c) What kinds of things do you like to do to play and be active at home or in school? (d) Does being active only mean participating in sports? What can you do to be active if you don't like playing sports?

Sometimes it's not easy to be active.

- ★ Discuss with students when exercising or being active might be hard: when they have too much homework, when they don't feel good, when the level of exercise is difficult for them, and when they become tired.

Ideas for Lesson Development

- ★ Let students know that it's OK not to always feel good during or after exercising: Sometimes it does hurt some or make them tired. Discuss the difference between something being hard and hurting a little, versus activity that makes you feel very bad and seriously hurt.
- ★ Discuss how the body has to get used to playing and exercising hard. If people do too much at once, they may not feel well. It's better to start out a little less strenuously!
- ★ Have students write a paragraph for their exercise or class journal that describes feeling good when they were exercising or being active. What made them feel good? Then have them describe a time they didn't feel well when exercising or being active.
- ★ Ask questions to facilitate discussion and review, such as the following: (a) What are some ways you might feel when you're participating in physical activity? Do you think they all are OK? (b) Is exercising always easy? Does it always feel good to exercise? (c) How do you know when you've done too much? (d) What are some ways that you can help yourself not think that exercising is overly hard?

Emphasize

It is important to be physically fit.

Being physically fit means you have good aerobic endurance, muscle strength, flexibility, and body fat levels.

The only way to become physically fit is to be active.

Ideas for Lesson Development

- ★ Ask students who they think is physically fit. Why do they think that? How did this person become physically fit?
- ★ Discuss with students how being fit helps you be the best person you can be; being fit is the way you take care of your body.
- ★ Ask students to write a private letter about themselves to their portfolio discussing how physically fit they feel. What are some ways they think they are or aren't fit? Can they improve their physical fitness? Would they like you to help them in any special ways? How might they improve their fitness levels, if need be? (Be sure to discuss that there is not a right and a wrong answer to this task: What's important is being honest in the writing.)

Ratliffe: *Shape Up; Health-Related Circuit*

Emphasize

Physical fitness tests assess your body's fitness levels.

Fitness tests help you find out how fit your body is and whether you need to improve your activity level.

Ideas for Lesson Development

- ★ Discuss how the fitness tests students take are ways to discover how fit their body is. They tell them if they need to be more active to become stronger and healthier.
- ★ Ask questions to facilitate discussion and review: (a) Are there other ways besides taking tests to find out how strong and fit you are? (b) What are some ways you can test yourself at home to find out how fit your body is?

GRADES 3-4

Sample Portfolio Task

Students are asked to write about someone whom they consider physically fit. What makes that person seem physically fit? What does that person do to become physically fit? Would they like to be like that person?

RUBRIC CLUES **To what extent do students**

- use correct terms and explanations to describe physical fitness?
- give examples of behaviors that can lead to physical fitness?

NASPE BENCHMARKS Describe healthful benefits that result from regular and appropriate participation in physical activity. (3-4, #24)

Emphasize

Being active is important for your body.

Being active helps you look and feel good, and it helps your heart, bones, and muscles become strong and healthy.

Being active is the only way to become physically fit.

Ideas for Lesson Development

★ Discuss with students why it is important to be active in life. Why is it not good to be a "couch potato"? Relate being active to the body's becoming strong and healthy. Talk about how just as you need to study to help be smart, you need to be active to help be fit.

★ Ask questions to facilitate discussion and review: (a) Why do you think it is good for you to play and be active? (b) What happens if you aren't very active or if you don't move or play very much?

Emphasize

You can be active in many different ways.

Moving, playing, working, and exercising are ways you can be active.

There are many fun ways to become active and fit.

Ideas for Lesson Development

★ Discuss how moving, playing, and exercising are ways to be active. Ask students to describe specific ways they are active in everyday life.

★ Ask students to name the different things they do to be active and fit, such as jumping rope, jogging, dancing, swimming, doing push-ups, playing tag, and throwing footballs. Categorize these according to where they can be done: at home, in the community, or at school.

★ Ask students what makes exercising or being active fun for them (some examples might include exercising with a friend, parents, or brothers and sisters; putting on music; and exercising with a pet dog).

★ Ask students for fun suggestions of what they can do to be active with their family.

★ Give students an assignment in which they each must exercise or do something active with a parent or big brother or sister one time during the week. What they do and for how long is up to them. Have them write a note to their portfolio describing what they did.

Ratliffe: *Shape Up*

Emphasize

It is important to be physically fit.

Being physically fit means you look good, feel good, and have lots of energy to play and work at home and in school.

Ideas for Lesson Development

★ Discuss what it means to be physically fit. Ask questions to facilitate discussion: (a) Who do you know who is physically fit? Why? (b) What do you think it means to be physically fit? Why? (c) Are you fit only if you are skinny? Why or why not?

★ Have students glue pictures of people they think look physically fit (from home, magazines, etc.) onto a piece of paper and label who it is. Put these up on a bulletin board. Use a title, such as "Look Whoooo's Physically Fit." (Show an owl pointing to the slogan.)

Ratliffe: *Health-Related Circuit*

Emphasize

Physical fitness tests assess your body's fitness levels.

Fitness tests help you find out how fit your body is and whether you need to improve your activity level.

Ideas for Lesson Development

★ Point out to the students that just as they take math or spelling tests, they can take physical fitness tests to see how fit their bodies are. Talk about how the results will let them see if they need to be more active.

GRADES 1-2

Sample Portfolio Task

Ask students to draw pictures of themselves on large blank paper participating in a favorite activity that helps each become physically fit. On a separate piece of ruled paper, the child should explain what he or she is doing in the drawing and why it is fun, if possible.

RUBRIC CLUES **To what extent do students**

- draw an activity that involves being active?

Emphasize

Being active is important for your body.

Being active is a healthy habit.

Ideas for Lesson Development

★ Discuss how being active is a healthy habit, like brushing your teeth, combing your hair, resting, and eating. Being active is something that should happen every day.

Ratliffe: *Activity Benefits*

Emphasize	Ideas for Lesson Development
You can be active in many different ways. Moving, playing, working, and exercising are ways you can be active.	★ Ask students to tell you things they do at home and school to be active. What do they think helps the heart, muscles, and bones grow strong? Talk about how fun these activities are to do. ★ Have students draw pictures of themselves doing something that helps them to be active and fit.

Ratliffe: *Be Active!*

Emphasize	Ideas for Lesson Development
It is important to be physically fit. Being physically fit means your heart, bones, and muscles are strong and healthy.	★ Ask students to tell you about someone they think is physically fit. Discuss how these people got to be fit: they are active and they exercise. Do they think a person becomes fit by being active only once in a while or often? how often? (Almost every day.) Ask students if they think the people they named were active and exercised when they were in first or second grade. What kinds of things do they think these fit people did? ★ Discuss with students how their hearts, muscles, and bones grow bigger and stronger every time they play and exercise.

KINDERGARTEN

Sample Portfolio Task

Ask students to draw pictures of themselves participating in their favorite play or exercise activities. (These drawings are not to be assessed.)

Emphasize	Ideas for Lesson Development
Being active is important for your body. Being active is good for your body.	★ After participating in a fun activity with students (such as parachute play or jumping rope), discuss that some fun activities also help their bones and muscles become stronger. ★ Ask students to tell you someone who has big muscles or is very fit; discuss how this person got to be so strong by being active.

Emphasize	Ideas for Lesson Development
You can be active in many different ways. Playing is a fun way to be active.	★ Ask students to tell you activities that are fun to do and help their muscles get stronger. Mention an activity and have them raise their hands if they think it helps them become strong (e.g., jumping rope, playing tag, swimming, dancing, playing on the playground). ★ Walt Disney's *Mousercize* record album has a collection of fun, active aerobic routines introduced by various Disney characters. The "Medley" song is a wonderful activity to do with preschoolers and kindergartners.

Sample Overall Unit Outcome

By the end of elementary school, students should be able to

- apply to situations in their daily lives, as much as possible, the basic concepts of cardiorespiratory fitness.

CARDIORESPIRATORY FITNESS

Concepts and Skills	Learnable Pieces
Your heart is an important muscle.	
	Your heart is special because it is always beating. (K)
	Your heart is in your chest. (K, 1-2)
	It is the size of your fist covered by your other hand. (K, 1-2)
	Your heart is a strong, special muscle that is a pump. (1-2)
	Your heart pumps blood to your muscles and your body. (1-2)
	Your heart grows bigger as you grow bigger. (1-2)
Your heart acts differently when you exercise.	
	When you exercise, your muscles need more oxygen and energy to keep moving. (3-4)
	Your heart beats faster when you exercise so it can take oxygen from your lungs and food energy from your blood to your muscles. (5-6)
You can listen to your heart beat.	
	You can feel your heart beat by putting your hand on your chest. (K)
	You can feel your heart beat at your wrist, your neck, or your chest. (1-2)
	Your heart beats slowly when you sit, sleep, and rest. (K, 1-2)
	Your heart beats fast when you move, play, and exercise. (K, 1-2)
	Your heart rate tells you how hard your heart is working. (3-4)
	Your heart rate, or pulse, is how many times your heart beats in 1 minute. (3-4, 5-6)
	You can find out your heart rate by counting how many times your heart beats in 6 seconds and then multiplying this by 10. (3-4, 5-6)
	Take your heart rate about 5 minutes after you've been exercising hard. By then it should almost be back to your normal heart rate. (5-6)

(continued)

Concepts and Skills	Learnable Pieces
It is important to have good aerobic endurance.	
	Your heart gets stronger when you play and exercise. (1-2) Endurance means your heart and muscles can move and exercise for a long period of time—like your PE time. (3-4) Just like your other muscles, your heart gets stronger and has more endurance when you exercise and gets weaker when you don't exercise. (3-4, 5-6) Aerobic endurance helps keep your body strong and fit and it keeps up your energy. (3-4, 5-6) Aerobic endurance refers to how good a shape your heart, lungs, and muscles are in. (5-6) If your heart, lungs, and muscles can be active for a long period of time—about 20 minutes—without your getting very tired, you probably have good aerobic endurance. (5-6) Without good endurance, you cannot be physically fit. (3-4, 5-6)
There are many ways to exercise aerobically.	
	Running, playing tag, and jumping rope are things your heart likes for you to do. (K, 1-2) Watching too much TV and playing too many indoor games can keep you from having a strong heart (1-2) and good endurance. (3-4) You improve your endurance by doing things that keep you moving for at least 20 minutes. (3-4) You get aerobic endurance by playing and exercising in activities that make your heart, lungs, and muscles work harder and faster for about 20 minutes. (5-6) Biking, swimming, jumping rope, and playing tag are examples of aerobic activities. (5-6) It is best to do aerobic activities at least three times a week for at least 20 minutes each time. (5-6) If you don't stay active, your aerobic endurance will decrease. (3-4, 5-6)

Concepts and Skills	Learnable Pieces
You should be smart and safe when you exercise aerobically.	
	You should warm up before you exercise aerobically and cool down afterward. (5-6)
	If you haven't been exercising much, you will need to gradually work up to being active for 20 minutes. (5-6)
There are different ways you can test your aerobic endurance.	
	You take the mile-run test to see how strong your heart is. (1-2)
	The mile-run test can tell you if you need to be more active. (3-4)
	The mile run is a way to test the aerobic endurance of your heart, lungs, and muscles. (3-4, 5-6)
	Seeing how far you can run, walk fast, ride your bike, and how many times you can jump rope are ways to test your (aerobic) endurance at home. (3-4, 5-6)

GRADES 5-6

Sample Portfolio Task

Students are to explain in their own words what the term *aerobic* exercise means and to describe why it is important. They should then relate it to their lives by giving examples or keeping a log of aerobic activities they participate in.

RUBRIC CLUES **To what extent do students**

- show a correct understanding of the word *aerobic*?
- use appropriate, accurate examples to enhance their explanations?

NASPE BENCHMARKS Correctly demonstrate activities designed to improve and maintain muscular strength and endurance, flexibility, and cardiorespiratory functioning. (5-6, #15)

Emphasize

Your heart acts differently when you exercise.

Your heart beats faster when you exercise so it can take oxygen from your lungs and food energy from your blood to your muscles.

Ideas for Lesson Development

- ★ Discuss the heart pathway with students—how oxygen is taken in by the lungs from the air and passed into the blood, which is pumped through the body, passing along oxygen and energy from food they eat. Explain how once the muscles use the oxygen, only carbon dioxide is left over, which enters the blood and then is exhaled through the lungs.
- ★ Talk with the classroom teachers to see when they teach the "body" units in health or science. You may be able to coordinate teaching much about the heart and lungs between physical education and other classes.
- ★ Read the American Heart Association's *Heart Treasure Chest* for a variety of ideas for teaching about the heart.
- ★ Borrow a model of the heart and lungs from a local community college or high school biology department to show your students how they look inside.

Ratliffe: *Heart Pump Circuit*

Emphasize

It is important to have good aerobic endurance.

Aerobic endurance refers to how good a shape your heart, lungs, and muscles are in.

Aerobic endurance helps keep your body strong and fit and it keeps up your energy.

Ideas for Lesson Development

- ★ After explaining how aerobic endurance involves the heart, lungs, and muscles working together, ask students if they think a marathoner has good aerobic endurance. How do they know that? What about someone who plays a whole soccer game every Saturday morning? Ask them to give other examples of people with endurance (not necessarily athletes).
- ★ Discuss the benefits of good aerobic endurance and whether it is likely to come with being a couch potato. With aerobic endurance do you have lots of energy, or a little? Do you get sick frequently?
- ★ Encourage students to "keep on moving" for as long a period as they can. They should see if they can increase the time they can stay active and moving, without sitting down or resting. Relate the increased amounts of time with increased aerobic endurance.

Emphasize

If your heart, lungs, and muscles can be active for a long period of time—about 20 minutes—without your getting very tired, you probably have good aerobic endurance.

Ratliffe: *Keeping the Pipes Clean*

Just like your other muscles, your heart gets stronger and has more endurance when you exercise and gets weaker when you don't exercise.

Without good endurance, you cannot be physically fit.

- ★ Discuss how aerobic endurance is only one aspect of being physically fit, but perhaps the most important aspect. Ask for reasons why this might be so.
- ★ Relate how the heart must be exercised to stay in shape, just like other muscles.

Emphasize

There are many ways to exercise aerobically.

You get aerobic endurance by playing and exercising in activities that make your heart, lungs, and muscles work harder and faster for about 20 minutes.

It is best to do aerobic activities at least three times a week for at least 20 minutes each time.

Biking, swimming, jumping rope, and playing tag are examples of aerobic activities.

If you don't stay active, your aerobic endurance will decrease.

Ideas for Lesson Development

- ★ Discuss the word *aerobics*. What does it mean? Why is aerobic exercise (in fitness centers) so named? Relate the word *aerobics* to the increased work of the heart and lungs.
- ★ Ask for examples of exercises or activities that can help increase aerobic endurance. Can each of the examples be done for at least 20 minutes?
- ★ Write a list of activities on the board. Ask the class to group or classify them according to whether each helps increase aerobic endurance.
- ★ Start a Heart Smart Club. If a student exercises aerobically three times a week, he or she writes down the activity and time; every Monday, post these heart-smart descriptions on a bulletin board. You can post each student's photo with his or her activity sheet (take a picture or have the student bring one from home).
- ★ Ask questions to facilitate discussion and review: (a) What does it mean if an activity is aerobic? What body parts does this involve? (b) How long should you work, play, and be active to get aerobic or cardiorespiratory fitness benefits? (c) Can you "save up" aerobic endurance if you do a lot of activity, then stop, and still derive benefits? (d) What are some aerobic activities that you like to do?

Ratliffe: *Run to the Front*

Emphasize	Ideas for Lesson Development
You should be smart and safe when you exercise aerobically. If you haven't been exercising much, you will need to gradually work up to being active for 20 minutes. You should warm up before you exercise aerobically and cool down afterward.	★ Discuss how, before doing heavy aerobic exercising, you should warm up the heart and other muscles by walking, circling the arms and legs, and then stretching the arms and legs. Then, after finishing, you should cool down by walking, circling the arms, and again stretching.

Emphasize	Ideas for Lesson Development
You can listen to your heart beat. Your heart rate, or pulse, is how many times your heart beats in 1 minute. You can find out your heart rate by counting how many times your heart beats in 6 seconds, and then multiplying this by 10. Take your heart rate about 5 minutes after you've been exercising hard. By then it should almost be back to your normal heart rate.	★ Have students take their heart rates before and during a vigorous activity. Use a large conversion chart that shows the number of times they might count in 6 seconds, and what these numbers mean in terms of a minute. After a few minutes' rest, have students again take their pulses to see how much they have slowed. ★ Have students guess their heart rates when they are resting and when they have been exercising hard. Then have them take their pulses to see how close they guessed.

Emphasize	Ideas for Lesson Development
There are different ways you can test your aerobic endurance. The mile run is a way to test the aerobic endurance of your heart, lungs, and muscles. Seeing how far you can run, walk fast, ride your bike, and how many times you can jump rope are ways to test your (aerobic) endurance at home.	★ Discuss how the mile-run test lets them see how much aerobic endurance they have—it is given not just for the teachers to be mean! ★ Set up *heart-smart* stations: jumping rope, walking or jogging on a fitness trail, dancing to music, hula hooping, playing tag, Frisbee, or football, and so forth. On a Heart Day, challenge students to choose the stations they wish and to keep moving and being active for as long as they can. They should try to work up to the entire class period. This is a good change of pace and a day when you can talk to individual students about their portfolios and fitness scores.

GRADES 3-4

Sample Portfolio Task

Students list four activities that can help them improve their endurance and four activities that cannot. They should circle the items on either of their lists that they participated in within the past week, either in or out of school.

RUBRIC CLUES **To what extent do students**

- list appropriate examples of activities that are, or are not, good for improving endurance?
- name four examples for each category?

Emphasize

Your heart acts differently when you exercise.

When you exercise, your muscles need more oxygen and energy to keep moving.

Ideas for Lesson Development

★ Discuss how the muscles need oxygen and energy to move, and how during exercise they need even more—which is why the heart beats faster during exercise.

★ Explain how oxygen from the air goes into the lungs and then into the blood. So, when we move a lot, our lungs breathe faster because the muscles need more oxygen.

Ratliffe: *Heart Pump Circuit*

Emphasize

It is important to have good aerobic endurance.

Endurance means your heart and muscles can move and exercise for a long period of time—like your PE time.

Just like your other muscles, your heart gets stronger and has more endurance when you exercise and gets weaker when you don't exercise.

Aerobic endurance helps keep your body strong and fit and it keeps up your energy.

Without good endurance, you cannot be physically fit.

Ideas for Lesson Development

★ Compare endurance to the Energizer Bunny—it lets you keep going and going!

★ Ask students who they sense has good endurance. Why? Give examples for them to reflect on, such as Michael Jordan and Joe Montana.

★ Set up heart-smart stations as described earlier. Relate the students' participation in the activities to their endurance.

★ Discuss how endurance might be the most important part of fitness.

★ Ask questions to facilitate discussion and review: (a) If someone's heart works harder when she plays for a few minutes, and then she gets so tired she can't play anymore, do you think she has good endurance? (b) If you can keep moving for 20 minutes or more, about your PE class time, do you think that means your heart has good endurance?

Ratliffe: *Keeping the Pipes Clean*

Emphasize

There are many ways to exercise aerobically.

You improve your endurance by doing things that keep you moving for at least 20 minutes.

Watching too much TV and playing too many indoor games can keep you from having good endurance.

If you don't stay active, your aerobic endurance will decrease.

Ideas for Lesson Development

★ Ask students to tell you some activities that they can do for 20 minutes or more (e.g., walking, running, riding bikes, swimming, playing tag). Discuss how these develop endurance because they keep you moving for at least 20 minutes.

★ Discuss the kinds of activities that aren't very active and that might keep students from having good endurance (such as watching TV and playing indoor games). Acknowledge that doing this is OK some of the time but, just like many other things, too much is not good.

★ Challenge students to keep logs for 1 week of the activities they do to help their endurance. At the end of the week they should think about their habits: Do they need to be more active? Discuss ways they can start to be more active.

★ Ask students to bring in pictures from magazines or photos from home showing people participating in helpful or unhelpful activities for the heart. Post the pictures on a bulletin board.

Ratliffe: *Fitness Club; Run to the Front*

Emphasize

You can listen to your heart beat.

Your heart rate tells you how hard your heart is working.

Your heart rate, or pulse, is how many times your heart beats in 1 minute.

You can find out your heart rate by counting how many times your heart beats in 6 seconds and then multiplying this by 10.

Ideas for Lesson Development

★ Discuss how the heart rate tells how fast or slow the heart is beating, or working. A fun fact is that at rest the heart should beat less than 100 times in a minute. During exercise, the heart beats very fast—much more than 100 times a minute.

★ Have students practice taking their heart rates right before, during, and after exercising. Discuss why it was higher during exercise, and why it slowed down afterward.

Emphasize

There are different ways you can test your aerobic endurance.

The mile run is a way to test the aerobic endurance of your heart, lungs, and muscles.

The mile-run test can tell you if you need to be more active.

Ideas for Lesson Development

★ Discuss how the mile-run test is used to see if the heart has good endurance. What if it doesn't? What can the results tell?

★ Encourage students to "keep on moving" at home and test themselves periodically. Challenge them to do this not because they will be tested in class, but because they are helping themselves by getting in shape.

Emphasize

Seeing how far you can run, walk fast, ride your bike, and how many times you can jump rope are ways to test your (aerobic) endurance at home.

GRADES 1-2

Sample Portfolio Task

Ask students to draw themselves doing their favorite heart-smart activities (which help get their hearts in shape). If you wish, have them also explain briefly what they are doing in the drawings.

RUBRIC CLUES **To what extent do students**

- give examples of an activity that can make the heart stronger?

Emphasize

Your heart is an important muscle.

Your heart is in your chest.

It is the size of your fist covered by your other hand.

Your heart grows bigger as you grow bigger.

Ideas for Lesson Development

★ If possible, bring in a model of the heart (or show a picture of it) to help students understand that the heart is what makes the noise they hear in their chests!

Ratliffe: *Listening to Your Heart*

Your heart is a strong, special muscle that is a pump.

Your heart pumps blood to your muscles and your body.

★ Discuss how the heart pumps blood all over the body—to the muscles, stomach, eyes, and everything.

★ Relate to students that the heart is special because it always pumps blood—even while we sleep.

Emphasize

You can listen to your heart beat.

You can feel your heart beat at your wrist, your neck, or your chest.

Ideas for Lesson Development

★ After a vigorous activity, have students each feel their own, and a partner's, heart. Discuss why the heart was beating faster.

★ Have students each make a fist and squeeze it however fast they think the heart pumps at rest, and then during exercise.

Emphasize	Ideas for Lesson Development
Your heart beats slowly when you sit, sleep, and rest. Your heart beats fast when you move, play, and exercise.	★ Borrow stethoscopes from a local doctor's office, health office, or nursing program at the community college. Allow students to listen to each other's heart through the stethoscope. **Ratliffe:** *Listening to Your Heart*

Emphasize	Ideas for Lesson Development
It is important to have good aerobic endurance. Your heart gets stronger when you play and exercise.	★ Discuss how the heart, like other muscles, gets stronger when we do things to help it out, like playing and exercising.

Emphasize	Ideas for Lesson Development
There are many ways to exercise aerobically. Running, playing tag, and jumping rope are things your heart likes for you to do. Watching too much TV and playing too many indoor games can keep you from having a strong heart.	★ Ask students for ideas of activities they can do to help get a strong heart. Give examples that are inactive or active, to see if they can tell the difference (e.g., playing video games, watching TV, playing tag, jumping rope). ★ Make a bulletin board titled "Look Whoooo's . . . Heart Smart" (get an owl from a classroom teacher if you can). Use pictures that students have drawn of themselves participating in heart-smart activities. **Ratliffe:** *Fitness Club*

Emphasize	Ideas for Lesson Development
There are different ways you can test your aerobic endurance. You take the mile-run test to see how strong your heart is.	★ Set up a "superstars" jogging/walking club to help students prepare for the mile-run test. Students can earn their way into the Batman, Spiderman, Superman, or Wonder Woman Club, depending on the number of laps they walk or jog. Stickers and certificates are good awards. You may also decide to give decorated pencils as awards for joining the "higher" clubs. (And yes, even boys belong to the Wonder Woman Club!) **Ratliffe:** *Endurance Challenge*

KINDERGARTEN

Emphasize

Your heart is an important muscle.

Your heart is special because it is always beating.

Your heart is in your chest.

It is the size of your fist covered by your other hand.

Ideas for Lesson Development

- ★ Have students feel their hearts while they are sitting and then after they exercise. Talk about how the heart is a special muscle.

Emphasize

You can listen to your heart beat.

You can feel your heart beat by putting your hand on your chest.

Your heart beats slowly when you sit, sleep, and rest.

Your heart beats fast when you move, play, and exercise.

Ideas for Lesson Development

- ★ Have students make fists and show you how fast their hearts pump when they are sleeping . . . running fast . . . writing at their desks in the classroom . . . watching TV . . . playing on the playground . . . dancing to music, and so forth.
- ★ Have students each put a hand on a partner's chest and try to feel the heart beat. Do this before and after a vigorous activity.

Ratliffe: *Listening to Your Heart*

Emphasize

There are many ways to exercise aerobically.

Running, playing tag, and jumping rope are things your heart likes for you to do.

Ideas for Lesson Development

- ★ Use Disney's *Mousercise* as a fun activity that can help the heart.

Sample Overall Unit Outcome

By the end of elementary school, students should be able to

- apply to situations in their daily lives, as much as possible, the basic concepts relating to the components of muscular strength and endurance.

MUSCULAR STRENGTH AND ENDURANCE

Concepts and Skills	Learnable Pieces
Muscles are an important part of the body.	
	You have hundreds of muscles in your body. (K, 1-2)
	Muscles help you move, stand up straight, and have good posture. (1-2)
	Muscles help you lift things. When you lift objects, you should bend your knees. (3-4)
	Muscles help you move, hold you up, and protect the bones and organs inside your body. (3-4, 5-6)
It is important to have good muscle strength.	
	Firm muscles are strong, healthy muscles. (3-4)
	Muscle strength relates to how strong your muscles are. (5-6)
	Good muscle strength helps your body look good and feel good. (5-6)
	You need strong muscles to become physically fit. (5-6)
It is important to have good muscle endurance.	
	Muscle endurance relates to how long your muscles can work and play without getting too tired. (3-4, 5-6)
	Having good muscle endurance is a part of being physically fit. (5-6)
You can achieve muscle strength and endurance in many different ways.	
	Playing, exercising, and using your muscles can help make them big and strong! (K)
	You help your muscles become strong and healthy by playing, moving, exercising, and being active. (1-2, 3-4)
	Certain activities will help certain muscles become stronger and have more endurance. (5-6)
	Swimming, bike-riding, walking, and soccer can help increase the strength and endurance of your leg muscles. (5-6)

Concepts and Skills	Learnable Pieces
	Swimming, climbing, push-ups, pull-ups, and jumping rope can help increase the strength and endurance of your arm and shoulder muscles. (5-6)
Exercise is good for your muscles.	
	When you exercise, you don't get more muscles, but the muscles you have become stronger and bigger. (5-6) The more you exercise and are active, the stronger your muscles become and the more endurance you have. (5-6)
There are different ways you can test your muscle strength and endurance.	
	You take the pull-ups test to see how strong your arms and shoulders are. (1-2, 3-4, 5-6) You take the curl-ups test to see how strong your abdominal muscles are. (1-2, 3-4, 5-6) You can test arm muscle strength at home by seeing how many push-ups and pull-ups you can do. (3-4, 5-6)

GRADES 5-6

Sample Portfolio Task

Give students a list of about 10 different activities. Ask them to rate each activity good or poor for helping to increase muscle strength or endurance. They should briefly explain why they rate the activity good or poor.

RUBRIC CLUES **To what extent do students**

- correctly rate each activity?
- give a logical explanation for their ratings, even if they were rated incorrectly?

Emphasize

Muscles are an important part of the body.

Muscles help you move, hold you up, and protect the bones and organs inside your body.

Ideas for Lesson Development

- ★ Get a life-size chart of the human body showing the muscles.
- ★ Discuss how muscles cover the bones; without them, we would get injured much more easily.

Ratliffe: *The Muscle Circuit*

Emphasize

It is important to have good muscle strength.

Muscle strength relates to how strong your muscles are.

Good muscle strength helps your body look good and feel good.

You need strong muscles to become physically fit.

Ideas for Lesson Development

- ★ Ask students for examples of people with good muscle strength. Most likely, they will name athletes; lead them to think about others in their community who have muscle strength (e.g., construction workers, firemen).
- ★ Discuss how everyone needs to have good muscle strength, even nonathletes and people whose work is nonphysical. Ask students to think of why muscle strength is important for office workers who sit all day (for posture), for homemakers (to clean, lift), and so forth.
- ★ Ask students why they think muscle strength is important in their own everyday lives. What does it help them do? What couldn't they do as well if they had poor muscle strength? Try to get them to think beyond activities in physical education.

Emphasize

It is important to have good muscle endurance.

Muscle endurance relates to how long your muscles can work and play without getting too tired.

Having good muscle endurance is a part of being physically fit.

Ideas for Lesson Development

- ★ Discuss how muscle endurance is similar to aerobic endurance in relating to the muscles' working for long periods of time.
- ★ Discuss why muscle endurance is important: so we can remain active without tiring.
- ★ Ask students to list at least two things they do in their everyday lives that require muscle endurance. Challenge them to add another activity to their lists over the next month.

Emphasize

You can achieve muscle strength and endurance in many different ways.

Certain activities will help certain muscles become stronger and have more endurance.

Swimming, bike-riding, walking, and soccer can help increase the strength and endurance of your leg muscles.

Swimming, climbing, push-ups, pull-ups, and jumping rope can help increase the strength and endurance of your arm and shoulder muscles.

Ideas for Lesson Development

★ Discuss how certain activities make specific muscles stronger—not all muscles. Name an activity, and see if students can figure out which muscle group(s) it helps most.

★ Ask students to list other activities that help develop muscle strength and endurance, such as walking fast, playing basketball, in-line skating, and weight-lifting.

Ratliffe: *Muscle of the Month*

Emphasize

Exercise is good for your muscles.

When you exercise, you don't get more muscles, but the muscles you have become stronger and bigger.

The more you exercise and are active, the stronger your muscles become and the more endurance you have.

Ideas for Lesson Development

★ Many students, especially girls, become very conscious of their bodies at this age. Relate that exercising won't make you get more and more muscles, just firmer ones.

Emphasize

There are different ways you can test your muscle strength and endurance.

You take the pull-ups test to see how strong your arms and shoulders are.

You take the curl-ups test to see how strong your abdominal muscles are.

Ideas for Lesson Development

★ Partner pull-ups are fun: One partner lies prone on his back on the floor, and the other partner (of similar size and weight) stands over him, extends his arms, grasps the partner's hands, and pulls him up.

★ Secure a bat between two solid chairs. Students can lie under this to practice pull-ups without a pull-up bar. If possible, have family members or friends sit on the chairs to keep them securely anchored to the floor.

Emphasize

You can test arm muscle strength at home by seeing how many push-ups and pull-ups you can do.

GRADES 3-4

Sample Portfolio Task

Ask students to describe two things they do at home, either around the house or yard or in sports, that use their muscles and help them develop or maintain strong muscle strength. Ask them to also describe two things that their moms or dads do at home or work to use and develop the muscles.

RUBRIC CLUES **To what extent do students**

- accurately give examples of developing muscle strength?

Emphasize

Muscles are an important part of the body.

Muscles help you move, hold you up, and protect the bones and organs inside your body.

Muscles help you lift things. When you lift objects, you should bend your knees.

Ideas for Lesson Development

- ★ Discuss the role of muscles in posture. Have students put their hands on their abdomens, then "slouch" while sitting to feel how the abdominal muscles help hold them up.
- ★ Discuss how bending the knees when lifting items helps keep the back muscles from being hurt.
- ★ Set up some heavy items that students can practice lifting, at the same time challenging them to see how strong their muscles are! Examples can include jumping boxes made from tin cans (see "Jumping and Landing" in chapter 5) or crates filled with objects.

Emphasize

It is important to have good muscle strength.

Firm muscles are strong, healthy muscles.

Ideas for Lesson Development

- ★ Ask students for suggestions of people they know who have strong, firm muscles.
- ★ Discuss how the healthiest muscles are firm, not weak and flabby.
- ★ Relate good muscle strength to high levels of fitness.
- ★ Have students cut out pictures of people who show good muscle strength; tack these up on a bulletin board.

Ratliffe: *The Muscle Circuit*

Emphasize	Ideas for Lesson Development
It is important to have good muscle endurance. Muscle endurance relates to how long your muscles can work and play without getting too tired.	★ Discuss how strong, healthy muscles can continuously move for a long time—at least 20 minutes (about the length of PE time). ★ Ask students to suggest activities that keep them moving and can contribute to muscle endurance (e.g., biking, walking fast, running).

Emphasize	Ideas for Lesson Development
You can achieve muscle strength and endurance in many different ways. You help your muscles become strong and healthy by playing, moving, exercising, and being active.	★ Discuss the types of things that students can do to develop muscle strength and endurance. ★ List activities on the board; ask students which ones are beneficial for achieving muscle strength and endurance.

Emphasize	Ideas for Lesson Development
There are different ways you can test your muscle strength and endurance. You take the pull-ups test to see how strong your arms and shoulders are. You take the curl-ups test to see how strong your abdominal muscles are. You can test arm muscle strength at home by seeing how many push-ups and pull-ups you can do.	★ As a fitness warm-up one time a week have students practice sit-ups or push-ups and count how many they do. Have them write the number down, then graph how many they have done over a period of time.

GRADES 1-2

Sample Portfolio Task

Ask students to cut out and glue on paper photos or pictures from the paper and magazines (from home or school) showing examples of people using their muscles. On each picture the students should label the general muscles of the body that are working (e.g., arm muscles, leg muscles). If pictures are unavailable, students can draw examples.

RUBRIC CLUES **To what extent do students**

- give examples that show the muscles in use?
- accurately label each picture?

Emphasize	Ideas for Lesson Development
Muscles are an important part of the body. Muscles help you move, stand up straight, and have good posture. You have hundreds of muscles in your body.	★ Have students put their hands on their backs and abdomens as they slouch and then straighten up—to get a feel of how their muscles help them pull up and sit up straight.

Emphasize	Ideas for Lesson Development
You can achieve muscle strength and endurance in many different ways. You help your muscles become strong and healthy by playing, moving, exercising, and being active.	★ Discuss how, like the heart, other muscles get strong when we move, play, and exercise them. ★ Ask students for ideas of activities they can do to promote their muscle strength. Ratliffe: *Muscle Time*

Emphasize	Ideas for Lesson Development
There are different ways you can test your muscle strength and endurance. You take the pull-ups test to see how strong your arms and shoulders are. You take the curl-ups test to see how strong your abdominal muscles are.	★ Ask students questions about assessment, such as the following: (a) Do you know which test tells us how strong our arms and shoulders are? (b) What other things can you do to tell you how strong these muscles are? (c) Do you know which test tells us how strong our abdominal muscles are? (d) Do you know any other ways for us to know how strong the abdominal muscles are?

KINDERGARTEN

Emphasize	Ideas for Lesson Development
Muscles are an important part of the body. You have hundreds of muscles in your body.	★ Name a muscle area (e.g., arm, leg) and have students quickly point to it. ★ Play Simon-says with muscles: Show me where your leg muscle is . . . arm muscle . . . abdominal muscles. . . .

Emphasize	Ideas for Lesson Development
You can achieve muscle strength and endurance in many different ways. Playing, exercising, and using your muscles can help make them big and strong!	★ Discuss activities students can do to make their muscles strong, such as playing outdoors, jumping rope, and skipping.

Sample Overall Unit Outcome

By the end of elementary school, students should be able to

- apply to situations in their daily lives, as much as possible, the basic concepts related to the component of flexibility.

FLEXIBILITY

Concepts and Skills	Learnable Pieces
It is important to have good flexibility.	
	Your muscles like to be stretched every day. This keeps them from getting hurt and makes them feel good. (K, 1-2)
	Flexibility means you can easily move your muscles and joints. (3-4, 5-6)
	Flexibility allows you to move your body easily and protects your muscles from getting stretched too far and hurt. (5-6)
	Being flexible is part of being physically fit. (5-6)
It is important to stretch correctly.	
	Stretch until you feel a pull; then let off a little, so it doesn't hurt. (1-2, 3-4)
	When you stretch, remember to hold the stretch—don't bounce! (1-2, 3-4)
	You should hold a stretch at least for a count of 10. (1-2, 3-4)
	If you stretch with your legs together, keep your knees bent a little, so you don't hurt your back. (1-2, 3-4)
	You should stretch your muscles before you do much exercise, to get them warmed up and ready to move. (3-4, 5-6)
	You should especially stretch the muscles you will be using most. (5-6)
	After you exercise, you should again gently stretch your muscles. (5-6)
You can improve your flexibility in many different ways.	
	You should stretch a little every day to help your flexibility the most. (3-4, 5-6)
	Certain stretches will help certain muscles become more flexible. (5-6)
There are different ways to test your flexibility.	
	You take the sit-and-reach test to determine the flexibility of your lower back and leg muscles. (1-2, 3-4, 5-6)

GRADES 5-6

Sample Portfolio Task

Ask students to give two examples of how flexibility is needed in sports and to explain why it is important in these situations. Then ask them to give two examples of how flexibility is needed in everyday life and why it is important.

RUBRIC CLUES **To what extent do students**

- show they understand what flexibility is and how it is important?

Emphasize

It is important to have good flexibility.

Flexibility means you can easily move your muscles and joints.

Flexibility allows you to move your body easily and protects your muscles from getting stretched too far and hurt.

Being flexible is part of being physically fit.

Ideas for Lesson Development

★ Discuss how flexibility allows us to move our joints and muscles easily. "Just think what would happen if we couldn't stretch!" Give the example of falling off a bike—if the arm that was landed on got stretched in a strange way, flexibility would allow it to stretch without injury.

★ Ask students for examples in sports and everyday life where flexibility is important.

★ Discuss how flexibility is part of being fit; everyone should have *at least* minimal flexibility. This doesn't mean that everyone needs the flexibility of a gymnast, but some flexibility will help to keep the body feeling good.

Ratliffe: *Stay Flexed!*

Emphasize

It is important to stretch correctly.

You should stretch your muscles before you do much exercise, to get them warmed up and ready to move.

You should especially stretch the muscles you will be using most.

After you exercise, you should again gently stretch your muscles.

Ideas for Lesson Development

★ Discuss why it is important to stretch, even a little, before undertaking a lot of exercise. Use a piece of clay to demonstrate how it will just break apart when cold—and how it will stretch when it is worked and warmed up.

★ Discuss how stretching is specific to certain muscles; we should stretch the ones we will be using the most. Cite a few examples of activities, and ask students which muscles are used most in each activity.

★ Discuss how the best way to increase flexibility is to stretch after exercise, because the muscles are warmed up and ready to stretch. Stretching after exercise can also help cool down the muscles.

Emphasize	Ideas for Lesson Development
You can improve your flexibility in many different ways. Certain stretches will help certain muscles become more flexible. You should stretch a little every day to help your flexibility the most.	★ Practice specific stretches that help particular muscle groups. ★ Discuss how flexibility decreases if it isn't worked on, and it is best to practice stretching as often as possible—even every day.

Ratliffe: *Stretch It!*

Emphasize	Ideas for Lesson Development
There are different ways to test your flexibility. You take the sit-and-reach test to determine the flexibility of your lower back and leg muscles.	★ Discuss how everyone needs a minimal level of flexibility in the lower back to stay healthy; the sit-and-reach test helps to tell if the lower back has that minimum flexibility. ★ On a "choice" or free day, put out the sit-and-reach boxes so students can test each other, if they wish. They'll enjoy being "the teacher" and helping one another. ★ Discuss stretches students can do at home if they wish to improve flexibility.

GRADES 3-4

Sample Portfolio Task

Ask students to show their knowledge of what flexibility means by completing Figure 8.1.

RUBRIC CLUES **To what extent do students**

- show an accurate understanding of what flexibility means and how to stretch correctly?

Emphasize	Ideas for Lesson Development
It is important to have good flexibility. Flexibility means you can easily move your muscles and joints.	★ Discuss what flexibility means and how it allows people to easily move their muscles and joints. ★ Ask students for examples of people who have good flexibility. ★ Have students find pictures of athletes in the paper, magazines, and elsewhere that show good flexibility. Post them on a Flexibility bulletin board. ★ Questions to facilitate discussion and review include the following: (a) What does it mean if you are very flexible? (b) What kinds of athletes have especially good flexibility? Why do you think so? (c) Can you think of other occupations where people have good flexibility? Why?

Name ______________________ Class ______________

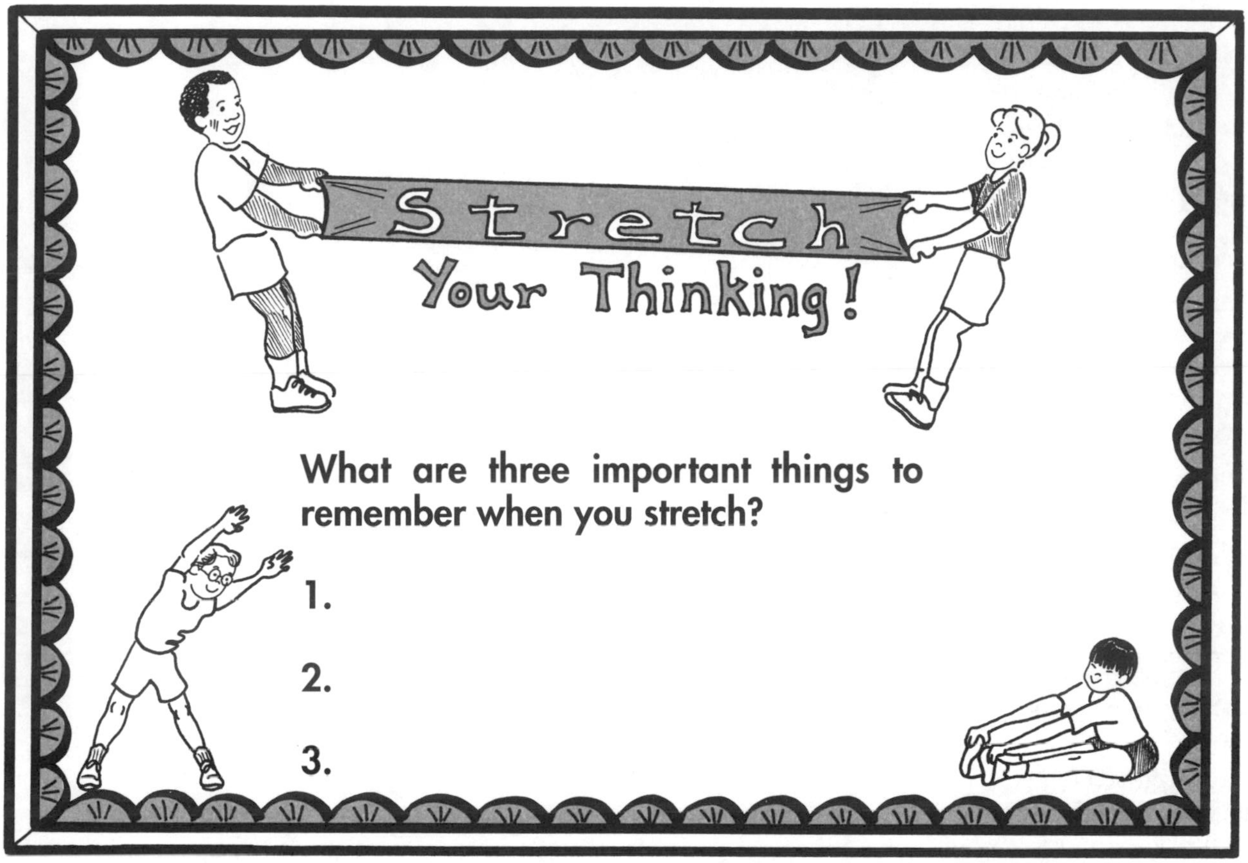

What are three important things to remember when you stretch?

1.

2.

3.

Describe something that flexibility helps you do better.

Figure 8.1 *Sample flexibility assessment sheet for Grades 3-4.*

Emphasize	Ideas for Lesson Development
It is important to stretch correctly. Stretch until you feel a pull; then let off a little, so it doesn't hurt. When you stretch, remember to hold the stretch—don't bounce! You should hold a stretch at least for a count of 10. If you stretch with your legs together, keep your knees bent a little, so you don't hurt your back. You should stretch your muscles before you do much exercise, to get them warmed up and ready to move.	★ Show students how to practice stretching different muscles correctly; discuss why this is important and have them practice the stretches.

Ratliffe: *Stay Flexed!; Stretch It!*

Emphasize	Ideas for Lesson Development
You can improve your flexibility in many different ways. You should stretch a little every day to help your flexibility the most.	★ Discuss how students can make stretching a habit—stretching when they wake up, before they go to bed, or at other regular times.

Emphasize	Ideas for Lesson Development
There are different ways to test your flexibility. You take the sit-and-reach test to determine the flexibility of your lower back and leg muscles.	★ Discuss why students take the sit-and-reach test. After the first test, allow them to practice and test themselves. Give them an "official" test at any time during the year when they are trying to improve their scores. Set aside one day a week or month to test students "officially"; let them know that they will be tested by you at least once before a date you set toward the end of the year.

GRADES 1-2

Emphasize

It is important to have good flexibility.

Your muscles like to be stretched every day. This keeps them from getting hurt and makes them feel good.

Ideas for Lesson Development

★ Try a ball gymnastics routine with students to work on flexibility. Use a large or small playground ball and slow music. Students match your movements as you move the ball slowly around your neck, down and back up your arms, around your waist, stretching to move the ball out to both sides, rolling the ball down and up your legs (don't lock the knees), down and up one leg (straddle your legs), down the other, touch the ball to the ground and raise it above the head, sit on the ground and touch the ball to your toes (feet straddled, then together), and roll the ball to the toes and back to the waist. Students also can sit with partners, their straddled feet touching; partners pass the ball to each other, leaning forward to get it. They can roll the ball to their feet while the partners reach to roll it down one leg and then over to the other.

Emphasize

It is important to stretch correctly.

Stretch until you feel a pull; then let off a little, so it doesn't hurt.

When you stretch, remember to hold the stretch—don't bounce!

You should hold a stretch at least for a count of 10.

If you stretch with your legs together, keep your knees bent a little, so you don't hurt your back.

Ratliffe: *Stretching Yourself*

Emphasize

There are different ways to test your flexibility.

You take the sit-and-reach test to determine the flexibility of your lower back and leg muscles.

Ideas for Lesson Development

★ While some students are practicing or taking the sit-and-reach test, divide students into other stations where they practice different activities (e.g., bear walk/caterpillar station, a station with stretching cards, and so forth).

KINDERGARTEN

Emphasize	Ideas for Lesson Development
It is important to have good flexibility. Your muscles like to be stretched every day. This keeps them from getting hurt and makes them feel good.	★ Use Disney's *Mousercize* album (especially the "Medley"); after completing the routine, discuss how stretching is good for the body.

Sample Overall Unit Outcome

By the end of elementary school, students should be able to

- apply to their daily lives, as much as possible, the basic concepts of training and conditioning.

TRAINING AND CONDITIONING

Concepts and Skills	Learnable Pieces
It is important to exercise frequently.	
	Your body and your muscles feel best if you play and exercise a little bit every day. (K, 1-2) To be fit you should try to exercise and be active at least three times a week. (3-4, 5-6) If you stop exercising or being active for a long time period, your body can become unfit or out of shape. (5-6)
It is important to exercise long enough.	
	You should try to exercise or be active at least 20 to 30 minutes at a time. (5-6)
You can improve your fitness levels.	
	To improve your fitness, you should exercise a little harder or a little longer. (3-4, 5-6)

GRADES 5-6

Sample Portfolio Task

Ask students to keep a log of their activities for 2 weeks. What do they do each day to be active? for about how long? After 2 weeks they should reflect on their activity levels. Were they active enough? What can they do to be more active?

RUBRIC CLUES **To what extent do students**

- show they understand how frequent activity should be?

Emphasize

It is important to exercise frequently.

To be fit you should try to exercise and be active at least three times a week.

If you stop exercising or being active for a long time period, your body can become unfit or out of shape.

Ideas for Lesson Development

★ Discuss the kinds of things that can keep students from being active: bad weather, homework, not being supervised, and so forth. Talk about possible solutions to these blocks.

Emphasize

It is important to exercise long enough.

You should try to exercise or be active at least 20 to 30 minutes at a time.

Ideas for Lesson Development

★ Discuss how exercising for at least 20 to 30 minutes benefits the heart and muscles the most and builds endurance.

★ Ask students for ideas on fun things they can do to be active for 20 to 30 minutes.

★ Have students chart on a weekly calendar what they do, over a 2-week period, that keeps them moving for over 20 minutes at a time.

Emphasize

You can improve your fitness levels.

To improve your fitness, you should exercise a little harder or a little longer.

Ideas for Lesson Development

★ Discuss how to improve fitness by exercising a little harder or a little longer each new week that you exercise. Give examples, such as walking for 3 more minutes or running a little faster.

Ratliffe: *Making Stronger Muscles*

GRADES 3-4

Sample Portfolio Task

Ask students to participate in one activity during the next week that lasts at least 20 minutes. They should describe in writing what they did, for how long, and how they felt about doing it. Was it hard? Was it easy? fun? Would they try it again the next week?

RUBRIC CLUES **To what extent do students**

- explain the benefits of the activity in terms of fitness?
- show they understand what kinds of activities can help their physical health?

Emphasize

It is important to exercise frequently.

To be fit you should try to exercise and be active at least three times a week.

Ideas for Lesson Development

★ Discuss fun things students can do to be physically active. Encourage them to be active with family members, pets, and friends.

Emphasize

You can improve your fitness levels.

To improve your fitness, you should exercise a little harder or a little longer.

Ideas for Lesson Development

★ Discuss how students may start out being active for only a few minutes, and then increase how long they are active and how hard they exercise to become more fit.

GRADES 1-2

Sample Portfolio Task

Ask students to cut out from a newspaper or magazine or draw pictures of equipment they can be active and play with (e.g., bike, hula hoop, ball) to help stay in shape.

RUBRIC CLUES **To what extent do students**

- show they understand the kinds of activity they can participate in for healthful benefits?

Emphasize

It is important to exercise frequently.

Your body and your muscles feel best if you play and exercise a little bit every day.

Ideas for Lesson Development

★ Discuss how everyone should try to be active and play outside for a little bit every day. Talk about activities that are fun for students to do.

★ Show students how to make equipment, such as newspaper balls (cover with masking tape) or scoops from gallon milk jugs, to play with at home.

KINDERGARTEN

Emphasize	Ideas for Lesson Development
It is important to exercise frequently. Your body and your muscles feel best if you play and exercise a little bit every day.	★ Discuss with students ways they can be active and play at home, such as biking, hula hooping, and jumping rope.

Sample Overall Unit Outcome

By the end of elementary school, students should be able to

- apply to their daily lives, as much as possible, basic concepts relative to nutrition and other healthy habits.

HEALTHY HABITS

Concepts and Skills	Learnable Pieces
Healthy habits are important for health.	
	Healthy habits include exercising, eating properly, brushing your teeth, getting enough sleep, washing well, and saying no to drugs, smoking, and alcohol. (K, 1-2, 3-4)
Eating right is part of being healthy.	
	Food is the source of energy for your body. (1-2)
	Good foods to eat each day are milk and dairy foods, bread and cereal, fruits and vegetables, and meat and fish. (1-2)
	Junk foods that aren't good for you to eat every day include candy, potato chips, and other sweet snacks. (1-2)
Everyone is responsible for his or her healthy habits.	
	You can make and change your habits, even if it is not always easy. (3-4, 5-6)
It is important to have good posture.	
	Good posture helps your bones and body to grow tall and strong. (3-4, 5-6)
Body composition is an important part of fitness.	
	You can get fat from not exercising, not being active, eating too much, or not eating correctly. (3-4)
	Body fat relates to the amount of fat your body has compared to muscles, bones, and organs. (5-6)
	It isn't good to have too much—or too little—body fat. (5-6)
	The amount of body fat you have will likely change as you grow older. (5-6)
	You can control the amount of body fat you have by eating right and exercising. (5-6)
	If you are concerned about how much body fat you have, you should talk to your doctor or PE teacher. (5-6)

(continued)

Concepts and Skills	Learnable Pieces
Wellness and fitness go together.	
	Overall wellness means you do healthy things for your body and your mind. (5-6) Fitness is just one part of wellness. (5-6)
Exercise can help in coping with stress.	
	Stress happens when you worry a lot and feel pressure to do things. (5-6) Exercise, or being active, can help prevent feeling "stressed out" and worried. (5-6)

GRADES 5-6

Sample Portfolio Task

Have students write about an activity that makes them feel good, not only physically related ones. Why do they like these activities? Do they think doing them helps their overall "wellness"? Why?

RUBRIC CLUES **To what extent do students**

- show they understand the definition of wellness?

Emphasize

Everyone is responsible for his or her healthy habits.

You can make and change your habits, even if it is not always easy.

Ideas for Lesson Development

- ★ Discuss how each person has the capability to change or make a habit.
- ★ Ask students to think of some habits they might like to change. Discuss ways that parents, family, and friends can help them change.

Ratliffe: *Goal Setting*

Emphasize

It is important to have good posture.

Good posture helps your bones and body to grow tall and strong.

Ideas for Lesson Development

- ★ Discuss why good posture is important for the body as well as for looks.
- ★ Have students sit slumped over, then ask them to straighten up. Can they feel their muscles work to pull them up? Have them put their hands on the abdominal muscles as they slouch and then straighten to feel how they work.

Emphasize

Body composition is an important part of fitness.

Body fat relates to the amount of fat your body has compared to muscles, bones, and organs.

It isn't good to have too much—or too little—body fat.

The amount of body fat you have will likely change as you grow older.

You can control the amount of body fat you have by eating right and exercising.

Ideas for Lesson Development

- ★ Discuss how people we see on TV and in magazines make us think that having no fat is good, but that everyone needs body fat, which helps give you energy and keeps you from getting sick.
- ★ Talk about how body fat can change naturally as people age, but it also depends on how much they eat, what kinds of foods, and how much they exercise growing up.
- ★ Discuss how eating correctly and getting exercise can help control how much body fat you have.
- ★ Encourage students to talk to their doctors, parents, or teachers if they are concerned about body fat.

Emphasize

If you are concerned about how much body fat you have, you should talk to your doctor or PE teacher.

Ratliffe: *Cookie Lesson; The Balancing Act*

Emphasize

Wellness and fitness go together.

Overall wellness means you do healthy things for your body and your mind.

Fitness is just one part of wellness.

Ideas for Lesson Development

- ★ Discuss how fitness is just one part of overall wellness, and how being fit helps people feel better about themselves and, consequently, their overall wellness.
- ★ Ask students to brainstorm and list on the board different things that help them to be "well," not just fit.
- ★ Ask students if they think someone can be well but not fit. Is this possible?

Emphasize

Exercise can help in coping with stress.

Stress happens when you worry a lot and feel pressure to do things.

Exercise, or being active, can help prevent feeling "stressed out" and worried.

Ideas for Lesson Development

- ★ Discuss the types of things that might stress students: school, grades, homework, parents. Talk about how jogging, bike riding, or taking a walk can help get the mind off things and can make them feel better.
- ★ List and discuss positive ways of dealing with stress; then list negative ways of dealing with stress.

GRADES 3-4

Sample Portfolio Task

Ask students to keep track over the week of all the healthy habits they do each day. At the end of the week, ask them to reflect on their habits. Can they improve them? What can help them to improve their habits? What habits do they need to improve?

RUBRIC CLUES **To what extent do students**

- show an understanding of healthy habits?

Emphasize

Healthy habits are important for health.

Healthy habits include exercising, eating properly, brushing your teeth, getting enough sleep, washing well, and saying no to drugs, smoking, and alcohol.

Ideas for Lesson Development

★ Discuss the healthy habits and why they are important.

Emphasize

Everyone is responsible for his or her healthy habits.

You can make and change your habits, even if it is not always easy.

Ideas for Lesson Development

★ Ask students to think of their good and bad habits. What are some ways they can change bad habits? Can parents, family, and friends help to change these habits?

Ratliffe: *Goal Setting*

Emphasize

It is important to have good posture.

Good posture helps your bones and body to grow tall and strong.

Ideas for Lesson Development

★ Discuss good posture, and how it helps people look and feel good.

Emphasize

Body composition is an important part of fitness.

You can get fat from not exercising, not being active, eating too much, or not eating correctly.

Ratliffe: *Cookie Lesson; The Balancing Act*

GRADES 1-2

Sample Portfolio Task

Have students cut out and glue pictures from magazines or the newspaper onto pages called either Good Foods or Junk Foods.

RUBRIC CLUES **To what extent do students**

- correctly identify the food as being in the good-food or junk-food group?

Emphasize	Ideas for Lesson Development
Healthy habits are important for health. Healthy habits include exercising, eating properly, brushing your teeth, getting enough sleep, washing well, and saying no to drugs, smoking, and alcohol.	★ Discuss why these healthy habits are important and what can happen if they aren't always followed.

Emphasize	Ideas for Lesson Development
Eating right is part of being healthy. Food is the source of energy for your body. Good foods to eat each day are milk and dairy foods, bread and cereal, fruits and vegetables, and meat and fish. Junk foods that aren't good for you to eat every day include candy, potato chips, and other sweet snacks.	★ Cut out or draw pictures of foods and then laminate them. Draw two boxes on the board: good foods and junk foods. After discussing the two types of foods, ask students to physically stick (using tape) a food in the correct box. ★ Play food tag—pick two to four students to be "it." *It* is a *junk food* (the students decide what kind). The junk food tries to catch the *good food* (everyone else); when tagged, a student puts his or her hand up, and must give the name of a good food before they can become untagged.

KINDERGARTEN

Emphasize	Ideas for Lesson Development
Healthy habits are important for health. Healthy habits include exercising, eating properly, brushing your teeth, getting enough sleep, washing well, and saying no to drugs, smoking, and alcohol.	★ Ask students to tell you things that are good for the body, and things that people do that aren't good for the body. Discuss how exercise and playing are good to do.

APPENDIX A

Sample Grade-Specific Unit Outcomes for Selected Physical Education Themes

Body Awareness

By the end of Grades 5-6 students should be able to

- design, refine, and perform dance or gymnastics sequences in a small group focusing on using different body shapes and body movements.

By the end of Grades 3-4 students should be able to

- move the body in the air using various body movements and shapes after jumping off low- or medium-level equipment;
- use different body shapes and body movements to creatively express the various qualities of effort (i.e., force, flow, speed); and
- design, refine, and perform group dance and gymnastics sequences that focus on using symmetrical or asymmetrical body shapes.

By the end of Grades 1-2 students should be able to

- use different body parts required by different challenges, alone and with a partner;
- mirror the symmetrical or asymmetrical shape of a partner;
- use a variety of bases of support (body parts) to balance on;
- make the different body shapes with and without a partner;
- perform different body movements to a series of beats of varying tempos (i.e., fast or slow);
- make the different body shapes in the air when jumping off the ground or low-level equipment; and
- design and perform simple sequences that focus on body shapes or body movements.

By the end of kindergarten students should be able to

- make the different body shapes;
- travel while moving in a variety of body shapes;
- use different combinations of body parts to balance on and travel with; and
- move using various body movements.

Space Awareness

By the end of Grades 5-6 students should be able to

- purposefully use pathways, levels, directions, and extensions to change the continuity or flow and add variety to a gymnastics or dance sequence; and
- purposefully use general space to create or deny space when developing or using game strategies.

By the end of Grades 3-4 students should be able to

- change directions and pathways as they move through general space, in order to not collide with others; and
- define, refine, and perform dance and gymnastics sequences that focus on changes in direction, levels, pathways, and extensions (using one or a combination of two at a time).

By the end of Grades 1-2 students should be able to

- find a self-space in a boundaried area;
- purposefully keep out of others' self-space as they travel with or without an object;
- stop and start traveling at a given signal, showing the ability to stop and travel in their own self-space;
- travel and change from one direction to another at the signal;
- move a variety of body parts and objects into different levels;
- manipulate different objects through different levels;
- travel and change from one pathway to another at the signal;
- design and perform simple sequences that focus on changes in directions, levels, pathways, and shapes (using one or a combination of two at a time); and

- travel in different ways while using large and small extensions.

By the end of kindergarten students should be able to

- show the boundaries or limits to their self-space, when alone and when using equipment;
- find a self-space on their own in a large boundaried area;
- stop and start traveling in response to a signal, showing the ability to travel and stop in a self-space;
- move a variety of ways in different directions;
- put a variety of body parts and objects into different levels; and
- move on straight, curved, and zigzag pathways.

Effort

By the end of Grades 5-6 students should be able to

- use the qualities of force, flow, and speed to creatively express feelings, ideas, and actions of the self, others, or groups of others through the use of body shapes;
- design, refine, and perform gymnastics and dance sequences that show smooth transitions between movements varying in force, flow, and speed; and
- manipulate objects (e.g., kick, throw) using varied amounts of force, flow, and speed appropriate to the given situation.

By the end of Grades 3-4 students should be able to

- move in a variety of ways that focus on accelerating and decelerating their speed;
- move in various ways using definite contrasts of bound and free-flowing movements;
- use the specific qualities of force, flow, or speed to creatively express feelings, ideas, and actions through dance and other expressive movement sequences;
- design, refine, and perform dance and gymnastics sequences that focus on changes in force, flow, and speed; and
- manipulate objects (e.g., kick, throw) using varied amounts of force and speed.

By the end of Grades 1-2 students should be able to

- perform different body movements in time to a signal or music of varying tempos, or speeds;
- manipulate an object in time to a signal or music of varying tempos, or speeds;
- safely change from one speed to another when traveling to a signal or music of varying tempos;
- move in various ways showing definite contrasts of light and strong force;
- express the qualities of light and strong force through a variety of creative dance or gymnastics sequences; and
- express the qualities of fast and slow speed through a variety of creative dance or gymnastics sequences.

By the end of kindergarten students should be able to

- make fast and slow movements with various body parts;
- travel in various ways at fast and slow speeds; and
- travel and change from one speed to another at a signal.

Relationships

By the end of Grades 5-6 students should be able to

- use a variety of relationships with a partner or group when designing, refining, and performing repeatable dance, gymnastics, or rope-jumping sequences (e.g., behind, beside, mirroring, matching); and
- use a variety of relationships with others in order to play or design a small-group game.

By the end of Grades 3-4 students should be able to

- move in a variety of ways in relation to a partner, either with or without a piece of equipment;
- mirror and match the movements of a traveling partner;
- use matching or mirroring and meeting or parting to design and perform dance or gymnastics sequences with a partner or small group; and
- design, refine, and perform a repeatable sequence with a partner in which the movements of an object (e.g., scarf, wand) are matched as clearly as possible.

By the end of Grades 1-2 students should be able to

- move in a variety of ways in relation to a stationary partner or object;
- mirror the shape and movements of a stationary partner; and
- change from a leading to a following position in relation to a partner.

By the end of kindergarten students should be able to

- demonstrate a variety of relationships with a stationary partner or object;
- travel while demonstrating a variety of relationships to stationary objects;
- move different objects in a variety of relationships to the self; and
- lead or follow a partner using a variety of locomotor movements.

Locomotor Movements

By the end of Grades 5-6 students should be able to

- run and leap as far, and as high, as possible;
- run and leap a succession of medium-level obstacles without stopping between;
- design, refine, and perform small-group sequences

comprised of even and uneven rhythmic patterns of locomotor movements, body movements, and the use of an object to groups of three or four beats (3/4 or 4/4 time); and

- follow (solo, with a partner, or with a group) given simple patterns of locomotor skills to 3/4 and 4/4 music from various cultures.

By the end of Grades 3-4 students should be able to

- leap a variety of distances, leading with either the right or left leg;
- run and hurdle a succession of low- to medium-level obstacles, using either leg to lead;
- travel and smoothly change directions or movements to music with sets (measures) of three or four beats;
- combine two or more even locomotor movements into a pattern that can be repeated to music with 3- or 4-beat groupings (i.e., 1, 2, 3, (4); 1, 2, 3, (4); etc.);
- combine two or more even and uneven locomotor movements into a pattern that can be performed to music with 3- or 4-beat groupings (i.e., 1 and 2, 3 (4); 1 and 2, 3 (4); etc.); and
- combine two or more movement patterns based on sets of either 3 or 4 beats into repeatable sequences of traveling, manipulating an object, and space awareness concepts (such as levels or pathways) to a counted-out beat or music.

By the end of Grades 1-2 students should be able to

- travel and change from one locomotor movement to another at the signal;
- travel to a signal or music with an even rhythm (walk, run, hop, jump, and march);
- travel to a signal or music with an even rhythm (slide, gallop, skip);
- perform given or self-designed simple sequences that combine even and uneven locomotor movements into counted-out groups of 3, 4, or 8 beats;
- follow given simple sequences that combine locomotor and body movements to counted-out groups of 3, 4, or 8 beats;
- practice leaping, using either foot to lead;
- jump and hop in place while traveling and in relation to an object; and
- design a simple sequence using locomotor and body movements to counted-out beats.

By the end of kindergarten students should be able to

- march in step to a rhythmical (even) beat;
- jump and hop (using both feet) in place and while traveling;
- gallop forward using a basic or rhythmical galloping pattern;
- slide sideways using a basic or rhythmical sliding pattern;
- skip forward using a basic or rhythmical skipping pattern; and
- leap from one foot to the other.

Jumping and Landing

By the end of Grades 5-6 students should be able to

- jump a self-turned rope using as many different types of jumps as possible (e.g., skier, bell);
- perform jumping skills in 3/4 or 4/4 time, using ropes, tinikling sticks, and so forth; and
- design and refine a repeatable routine with a partner or a small group using various jumping skills, other movements, and objects to 3/4 or 4/4 time.

By the end of Grades 3-4 students should be able to

- jump for distance;
- jump for height;
- jump a self-turned rope using buoyant landings;
- jump a self-turned rope using at least five different types of jumps (e.g., hop, skip, jump, and skier); and
- jump into and out of a turning long rope.

By the end of Grades 1-2 students should be able to

- jump and land using a variety of takeoffs and landings in relation to various equipment (e.g., hoops, low hurdles, rope shapes, carpet squares);
- jump a swinging rope with yielding landings;
- jump a self-turned rope both forward and backward with yielding landings; and
- jump a self-turned rope in at least three different ways (e.g., forward, backward, skip step, fast (buoyant), running-skip step).

By the end of kindergarten students should be able to

- jump and land using a variety of takeoff and landing patterns (two feet to two feet; 2-1; 1-2; 1-1; 1-other); and
- jump a slowly swinging long rope using a two feet to two feet pattern.

Chasing, Fleeing, and Dodging

By the end of Grades 5-6 students should be able to

- cooperatively devise strategies to keep opponents from reaching a specified area, person, or object; and
- cooperatively play a designed or given small-group game with opponents that involves throwing and catching with dodging, chasing, and fleeing.

By the end of Grades 3-4 students should be able to

- travel and dodge stationary opponents; and
- use dodging skills in a small-group situation to avoid a thrown soft, lightweight object.

By the end of Grades 1-2 students should be able to

- follow a fleeing partner's pathways to catch or overtake them;

- flee from a partner as quickly as possible at a signal;
- travel and change pathways as quickly as possible at a signal;
- travel and change directions as quickly as possible at a signal; and
- quickly perform dodging skills at a signal.

By the end of kindergarten students should be able to

- travel and make straight, curved, and zigzag pathways;
- travel around stationary obstacles without touching them; and
- follow the pathway that their partner makes.

Rolling

By the end of Grades 5-6 students should be able to

- roll smoothly in a forward and backward direction;
- use different shapes to begin and end rolls when rolling in different directions;
- balance in a variety of upright or inverted positions, move smoothly into a roll, then balance again;
- travel, jump over low equipment, land, and roll;
- travel, jump, land, and roll over low equipment (starting the roll with or without hands on the floor);
- jump off the ground or low equipment to catch an object thrown directly to them, land, and roll;
- roll forward or backward on low equipment (bench, beam, table); and
- design, refine, and perform repeatable sequences (with a partner or in a small group) involving rolling and other skills (such as traveling, balancing, and weight transfers).

By the end of Grades 3-4 students should be able to

- roll, starting and ending in different shapes and using different speeds;
- roll forward over a low hurdle, starting with hands on or off the floor;
- jump off low equipment, land, and roll; and
- design, refine, and perform (alone or with a partner) simple sequences involving rolling, weight transfers, balances, and concepts (levels, shapes, directions, speed).

By the end of Grades 1-2 students should be able to

- roll smoothly and consecutively in a sideways direction;
- rock smoothly and repeatedly back and forth on the back;
- roll forward smoothly;
- roll in at least two different directions;
- starting from a squatting position, rock backward, placing hands in the appropriate position behind; and
- jump, land, and roll in any direction.

By the end of kindergarten students should be able to

- roll sideways consecutively; and
- on the back, rock back and forth and side to side.

Balancing

By the end of Grades 5-6 students should be able to

- balance on low equipment (tables, benches) in positions using a variety of bases of support; and
- balance with partners using principles of counter-balance (pushing) and counter-tension (pulling).

By the end of Grades 3-4 students should be able to

- balance in a symmetrical or asymmetrical shape on large gymnastics equipment (e.g., beams, tables, benches);
- move smoothly from one balanced position to another in a variety of ways;
- balance on a variety of moving and other balancing objects (e.g., stilts, balance boards) (dynamic balance);
- balance in inverted positions using the least number of bases of support possible;
- balance in a variety of positions using different bases of support and directions when on large gymnastics equipment; and
- cooperatively balance as part of a small group by connecting with or supporting each other's body weight.

By the end of Grades 1-2 students should be able to

- balance on different numbers of bases of support;
- balance using a variety of symmetrical and asymmetrical body shapes, either with or without a partner;
- balance using a variety of inverted symmetrical or asymmetrical body shapes;
- balance using different bases of support on low equipment;
- balance while traveling and changing directions and levels on low- or medium-level equipment; and
- design and perform simple sequences involving balancing along with other skills (weight transfers, rolling) or concepts (levels, shapes).

By the end of kindergarten students should be able to

- balance on a variety of combinations of body parts;
- travel and stop in balanced positions; and
- follow different pathways while moving forward and sideways on the ground or on low equipment.

Weight Transfer

By the end of Grades 5-6 students should be able to

- travel and smoothly move into transfers of weight from feet-to-hands;

- travel into a spring takeoff and then transfer weight onto a large apparatus (e.g., bars, beam, vault box);
- transfer weight off low apparatus (beam, bench, table) using a variety of body actions, starting with hands and feet stationary on the apparatus (e.g., stretching, twisting, turning); and
- transfer weight in a variety of ways along low- to medium-level apparatus (beam, benches) in a variety of ways, using changes in directions, levels, speeds, and body shapes.

By the end of Grades 3-4 students should be able to

- transfer weight from one body part to another (hands, knees, feet) in a variety of ways when on a large apparatus (e.g., climbing apparatus, bars);
- use safe methods to recover from unstable feet-to-hand transfers of weight;
- use a variety of body actions to move into and out of a variety of transfers of weight from feet-to-hands with large extensions (e.g., stretching legs wide; torso twisting; rolling, curving feet over to land on one or two feet);
- step into transfers of weight from feet-to-hands over low equipment or apparatus (e.g., box, crate, beam);
- transfer weight in various ways off low equipment or apparatus (beam, bench, box) onto floor level, starting with hands on the floor;
- use balances to move smoothly into and out of different transfers of weight;
- travel into a spring takeoff and then transfer weight from the feet-to-hands onto low- to medium-level equipment or apparatus (e.g., beam, bench, table, large tire); and
- transfer weight onto low- to medium-level equipment or apparatus by placing the hands on equipment and springing off from two feet (land on hands and feet or knees).

By the end of Grades 1-2 students should be able to

- transfer weight from one set of body parts to another in a variety of ways (e.g., twist, rill, turn);
- transfer weight over low equipment (e.g., hurdles, hoops, mats) in a variety of ways, beginning with hands on the opposite side of the hurdle;
- transfer weight from feet-to-hands in a variety of ways;
- transfer weight from feet-to-hands, making the legs land in different places around the body;
- transfer weight across a mat in as many ways as possible; and
- transfer weight by traveling into a spring takeoff.

By the end of kindergarten students should be able to

- transfer weight from one body part to another in a variety of ways, using rocking, rolling, and feet-to-hand actions with small extensions; and
- take weight momentarily onto the hands by transferring weight from feet-to-hands with large extensions.

Dribbling With the Hands

By the end of Grades 5-6 students should be able to

- dribble while traveling in a group (in a large boundaried area) without touching others or stationary objects;
- dribble and smoothly change from one direction to another without stopping;
- dribble and change from one speed to another without stopping;
- dribble continuously while stopping and starting traveling at the signal;
- dribble and then throw a leading pass to a moving partner using a chest or bounce pass;
- travel, dribble, and pivot on one foot to begin dribbling in another direction;
- shoot toward an appropriate-height goal from different distances;
- dribble and keep the ball away from an opponent in a 1-on-1 situation;
- dribble and pass in a small-group keep-away game; and
- cooperate and play a small-group game using passing, receiving, and shooting toward an appropriate-height goal.

By the end of Grades 3-4 students should be able to

- dribble a ball in self-space using one, then the other, hand;
- dribble while moving to the right or left;
- dribble and change direction at the signal;
- dribble and change from one speed to another at the signal;
- dribble and change the pathway, moving on at the signal;
- dribble while keeping the ball away from stationary opponents; and
- travel, dribble, and chest- and bounce-pass the ball to a stationary partner.

By the end of Grades 1-2 students should be able to

- dribble a ball in self-space using one, then the other, hand;
- dribble a ball in self-space while switching from one hand to the other;
- dribble a ball in self-space at the different levels;
- dribble while slowly traveling in different directions; and
- dribble while slowly traveling on different pathways.

By the end of kindergarten students should be able to

- use two hands to bounce and catch a large playground ball; and

- use two hands to bounce and catch a ball while slowly traveling forward.

Kicking and Punting

By the end of Grades 5-6 students should be able to

- dribble and change speeds at the signal;
- dribble with a group in a boundaried area, without losing control of the ball and while avoiding contact with others or opponents;
- use the inside of the foot to dribble and kick a leading pass to a moving partner;
- punt a ball using a 2- or 3-step approach;
- punt a ball to targets at varying distances;
- collect a thrown or kicked ball using the thigh and chest;
- defend a goal by catching or deflecting balls kicked to them with appropriate force;
- dribble and pass in a small-game keep-away situation; and
- cooperate to play a designed or given small-group game involving dribbling, passing, kicking, or punting to keep the ball away from opponents and to reach a goal area.

By the end of Grades 3-4 students should be able to

- run and kick a ball that is moving slowly toward and away from them, using the instep;
- use the insides or outsides of the feet to slowly dribble the ball;
- dribble while changing pathways and directions at the signal;
- dribble in a group in a boundaried area without losing control of the ball or colliding with others;
- dribble around stationary opponents and avoid losing the ball;
- dribble and then kick the ball to a large target area from a distance of choice, using the instep;
- dribble and then kick the ball to a target or stationary partner while using the inside of the foot;
- use the inside of the foot to collect a ball coming toward them; and
- punt a ball as high and as far as possible.

By the end of Grades 1-2 students should be able to

- kick a slowly rolling ball by using the instep;
- run up to and kick a stationary ball as far as possible with the instep;
- kick a stationary ball along the ground toward a stationary partner or target while using the inside of the foot;
- dribble and slowly jog while using the inside of either foot;
- dribble and slowly jog around stationary obstacles while using the insides of each foot;
- trap a slowly moving ball rolling toward and away from them, contacting the ball with the ball of the foot; and
- punt a ball into the air using the instep.

By the end of kindergarten students should be able to

- walk and "roll" the ball forward, using the inside of either foot;
- from a stationary position kick a stationary large playground ball, using any part of the foot; and
- move up to and kick a stationary ball, using any part of the foot.

Throwing and Catching

By the end of Grades 5-6 students should be able to

- throw to a partner or target, using varying degrees of force and speed;
- throw and catch a Frisbee;
- using a variety of objects, throw a leading pass overhand to a moving partner;
- catch objects of different sizes and weights while moving toward a specified area;
- move in order to throw to a (stationary) partner while being guarded in a small-group keep-away situation; and
- throw and catch in a self-designed or given small-group game to keep the ball away from opponents or to reach a goal area.

By the end of Grades 3-4 students should be able to

- throw a variety of objects to target areas using a smooth underhand motion;
- throw as far as possible using a smooth overhand motion;
- throw balls of various sizes and weights to an appropriate target or partner using a smooth overhand motion;
- throw, using an overhand throw, so that the ball travels in different pathways in the air and covers different distances;
- catch a ball, tossed by themselves or by others, at different levels;
- move in different directions to catch a ball thrown by a partner; and
- move to catch an object in a small-group (2-on-1) keep-away situation.

By the end of Grades 1-2 students should be able to

- catch a self-tossed yarn or other soft ball;
- catch a softly thrown ball at different levels;
- catch a ball thrown softly to different places around the body;
- throw a variety of objects using an underhand motion;
- throw as far as possible using an overhand motion; and

- throw (underhand) to themselves and catch, using a scoop or other implement.

By the end of kindergarten students should be able to
- catch a softly rolled large ball;
- catch a self-tossed yarn or other soft ball;
- throw to a variety of large targets using an underhand throwing motion; and
- throw a yarn or other soft ball using an overhand arm motion.

Volleying

By the end of Grades 5-6 students should be able to
- cooperate in a group to strike a lightweight ball with various body parts while keeping it off the ground;
- underhand-strike a lightweight ball over a medium-level net or rope (from an appropriate distance);
- overhead-volley a lightweight ball back and forth with a partner across a medium-level net or rope;
- move to bump-pass or overhead-volley a lightweight ball back to a partner;
- bump-pass a lightweight ball to an area different from where the ball was tossed from;
- bump-pass a lightly tossed lightweight ball back to a partner across a medium-level rope or net;
- use underhand and overhead volleys and bump passes to cooperatively keep a ball in play over a medium-level net or rope with a partner or a small group; and
- use underhand and overhead volleys and bump passes in a given or self-designed small-group game.

By the end of Grades 3-4 students should be able to
- strike a lightweight ball in succession using at least two different body parts, keeping it in self-space;
- strike a lightly tossed lightweight ball back to a partner using a variety of body parts;
- underhand-strike a lightweight ball back and forth across a line or low net to a partner after one bounce;
- overhead-volley a self-tossed lightweight ball to a wall or partner (to an appropriate height, if desired); and
- bump-pass a lightly tossed lightweight ball back to a partner.

By the end of Grades 1-2 students should be able to
- strike a lightweight ball with at least three different body parts (e.g., knee, foot, elbow) keeping it in self-space;
- underhand-strike a soft, lightweight ball or balloon upward with the hand, keeping it in self-space; and
- travel slowly and underhand-strike a soft, lightweight ball or balloon upward with the hand or other body parts.

By the end of kindergarten students should be able to
- using both right and left hands, continuously push a balloon upward with the hands, keeping it off the ground; and
- using the palm, strike a balloon underhand (upward) continuously.

Striking With Short-Handled Implements

By the end of Grades 5-6 students should be able to
- strike a rebounding ball with a paddle or lightweight racket from a wall using a forehand stroke;
- strike a gently tossed ball from a partner, using a backhand motion;
- repeatedly strike a rebounding ball from a wall using forehand or backhand strokes, moving back to a ready position in between strokes; and
- strike a self-dropped ball with a racket over a low-level line or net to various designated areas, using a forehand stroke.

By the end of Grades 3-4 students should be able to
- bounce and then strike a small object to a wall or across a low net using an underhand motion with a lightweight paddle or racket;
- bounce and then strike a small object using a forehand motion with a lightweight paddle or racket;
- strike a small object with a forehand motion using both strong and light force; and
- bounce and then strike a small object using a backhand motion with a lightweight paddle or racket.

By the end of Grades 1-2 students should be able to
- strike a small, lightweight ball upward with a hand or lightweight paddle, letting it bounce between strikes (i.e., bounce, strike, bounce);
- continuously strike a small, lightweight ball upward using a hand or lightweight paddle;
- continuously strike a suspended ball, using a forehand motion, with either a hand or lightweight paddle; and
- bounce then strike a small, lightweight ball using a hand or other paddle.

By the end of kindergarten students should be able to
- repeatedly strike a balloon upward using a hand or lightweight paddle; and
- repeatedly strike a small suspended ball with a hand or other lightweight paddle.

Striking With Long-Handled Implements

By the end of Grades 5-6 students should be able to
- strike a gently tossed ball using a bat;

- in a large group, use a hockey stick to control-dribble a ball so as to not collide with others or obstacles;
- use a hockey stick to dribble a ball around stationary obstacles without losing control of the ball;
- dribble and then strike a ball to a stationary target or partner, using a hockey stick;
- strike a ball toward large target areas from an appropriate distance using a golf club or hockey stick; and
- design and play small-group keep-away games involving dribbling and shooting with a hockey stick toward a goal area.

By the end of Grades 3-4 students should be able to

- strike a softly pitched ball with a bat as far as possible;
- dribble a Wiffle-type ball with a hockey stick and change directions and pathways at the signal;
- strike a Wiffle-type ball along the ground to a stationary partner using a hockey stick; and
- strike a Wiffle-type ball in the air using a golf club or hockey stick.

By the end of Grades 1-2 students should be able to

- strike a Wiffle-type ball off a tee with a bat;
- use an underhand swing to strike a Wiffle-type ball with a hockey stick or golf club; and
- travel slowly in different directions and dribble a Wiffle-type ball with a hockey stick.

By the end of kindergarten students should be able to

- strike a small playground ball off a tee or cone using the hand.

APPENDIX B

NASPE Physical Education Benchmarks

Examples of Benchmarks—Sixth Grade

As a result of participating in a quality physical education program it is reasonable to expect that the student will be able to

5-6, #1. Throw a variety of objects demonstrating both accuracy and distance (e.g., Frisbees, deck tennis rings, footballs)

5-6, #2. Continuously strike a ball to a wall or a partner, with a paddle, using forehand and backhand strokes

5-6, #3. Consistently strike a ball, using a golf club or a hockey stick, so that it travels in an intended direction and height

5-6, #4. Design and perform gymnastics and dance sequences that combine traveling, rolling, balancing, and weight transfer into smooth, flowing sequences with intentional changes in direction, speed, and flow

5-6, #5. Hand dribble and foot dribble while preventing an opponent from stealing the ball

5-6, #6. In a small group keep an object continuously in the air without catching it (e.g., ball, foot bag)

5-6, #7. Consistently throw and catch a ball while guarded by opponents

5-6, #8. Design and play small-group games that involve cooperating with others to keep an object away from opponents (basic offensive and defensive strategy) (e.g., by throwing, kicking, or dribbling a ball)

5-6, #9. Design and refine a routine, combining various jump-rope movements to music, so that it can be repeated without error

5-6, #10. Leap, roll, balance, transfer weight, bat, volley, hand and foot dribble, and strike a ball with a paddle, using mature motor patterns

5-6, #11. Demonstrate proficiency in front, back, and side swimming strokes

5-6, #12. Participate in vigorous activity for a sustained period of time while maintaining a target heart rate

5-6, #13. Recover from vigorous physical activity in an appropriate length of time

Note. *From* Outcomes of Quality Physical Education Programs *by M. Franck, G. Graham, H. Lawson, T. Loughrey, R. Ritson, M. Sanborn, and V. Seefeldt (the Outcomes Committee of NASPE), 1992, Reston, VA: National Association for Sport and Physical Education. Copyright 1992 by NASPE. Reprinted by permission.*

5-6, #14. Monitor heart rate before, during, and after activity

5-6, #15. Correctly demonstrate activities designed to improve and maintain muscular strength and endurance, flexibility, and cardiorespiratory functioning

5-6, #16. Participate in games, sports, dance, and outdoor pursuits, both in and outside of school, based on individual interests and capabilities

5-6, #17. Recognize that idealized images of the human body and performance, as presented by the media, may not be appropriate to imitate

5-6, #18. Recognize that time and effort are prerequisites for skill improvement and fitness benefits

5-6, #19. Recognize the role of games, sports, and dance in getting to know and understand others of like and different cultures

5-6, #20. Identify opportunities in the school and community for regular participation in physical activity

5-6, #21. Identify principles of training and conditioning for physical activity

5-6, #22. Identify proper warm-up, conditioning, and cool-down techniques and the reasons for using them

5-6, #23. Identify benefits resulting from participation in different forms of physical activities

5-6, #24. Detect, analyze, and correct errors in personal movement patterns

5-6, #25. Describe ways to use the body and movement activities to communicate ideas and feelings

5-6, #26. Accept and respect the decisions made by game officials, whether they are students, teachers, or officials outside of school

5-6, #27. Seek out, participate with, and show respect for persons of like and different skill levels

5-6, #28. Choose to exercise at home for personal enjoyment and benefit

Examples of Benchmarks—Fourth Grade

As a result of participating in a quality physical education program it is reasonable to expect that the student will be able to

3-4, #1. While traveling, avoid or catch an individual or object

3-4, #2. Leap, leading with either foot

3-4, #3. Roll in a backward direction, without hesitating or stopping

3-4, #4. Transfer weight, from feet to hands, at fast and slow speeds, using large extensions (e.g., mulekick, handstand, cartwheel)

3-4, #5. Hand dribble and foot dribble a ball and maintain control while traveling within a group

3-4, #6. Strike a softly thrown, lightweight ball back to a partner using a variety of body parts and combinations of body parts (e.g., the bump volley as in volleyball, the thigh as in soccer)

3-4, #7. Consistently strike a softly thrown ball with a bat or paddle, demonstrating an appropriate grip, side to the target, and swing plane

3-4, #8. Develop patterns and combinations of movements into repeatable sequences

3-4, #9. Without hesitating, travel into and out of a rope turned by others

3-4, #10. Balance with control on a variety of moving objects (e.g., balance boards, skates, scooters)

3-4, #11. Jump and land for height as well as jump and land for distance, using a mature motor pattern

3-4, #12. Throw, catch, and kick using mature motor patterns

3-4, #13. Demonstrate competence in basic swimming strokes and survival skills in, on, and around the water

3-4, #14. Maintain continuous aerobic activity for a specified time

3-4, #15. Maintain appropriate body alignment during activity (e.g., lift, carry, push, pull)

3-4, #16. Support, lift, and control body weight in a variety of activities

3-4, #17. Regularly participate in physical activity for the purpose of improving skillful performance and physical fitness

3-4, #18. Distinguish between compliance and noncompliance with game rules and fair play

3-4, #19. Select and categorize specialized equipment used for participation in a variety of activities

3-4, #20. Recognize fundamental components and strategies used in simple games and activities

3-4, #21. Identify ways movement concepts can be used to refine movement skills

3-4, #22. Identify activities that contribute to personal feelings of joy

3-4, #23. Describe essential elements of mature movement patterns

3-4, #24. Describe healthful benefits that result from regular and appropriate participation in physical activity

3-4, #25. Analyze potential risks associated with physical activities

3-4, #26. Design games, gymnastics, and dance sequences that are personally interesting

3-4, #27. Appreciate differences and similarities in others' physical activity

3-4, #28. Respect persons from different backgrounds and the cultural significance they attribute to various games, dances, and physical activities

3-4, #29. Enjoy feelings resulting from involvement in physical activity

3-4, #30. Celebrate personal successes and achievements and those of others

Examples of Benchmarks—Second Grade

As a result of participating in a quality physical education program it is reasonable to expect that the student will be able to

1-2, #1. Travel in a backward direction and change direction quickly, and safely, without falling

1-2, #2. Travel, changing speeds and directions, in response to a variety of rhythms

1-2, #3. Combine various traveling patterns in time to the music

1-2, #4. Jump and land using a combination of one- and two-foot takeoffs and landings

1-2, #5. Demonstrate skills of chasing, fleeing, and dodging to avoid or catch others

1-2, #6. Roll smoothly in a forward direction without stopping or hesitating

1-2, #7. Balance, demonstrating momentary stillness, in symmetrical and asymmetrical shapes on a variety of body parts

1-2, #8. Move feet into a high level by placing the weight on the hands and landing with control

1-2, #9. Use the inside or instep of the foot to kick a slowly rolling ball into the air or along the ground

1-2, #10. Throw a ball hard demonstrating an overhand technique, a side orientation, and opposition

1-2, #11. Catch, using properly positioned hands, a gently thrown ball

1-2, #12. Continuously dribble a ball, using the hands or feet, without losing control

1-2, #13. Use at least three different body parts to strike a ball toward a target

1-2, #14. Strike a ball repeatedly with a paddle

1-2, #15. Consistently strike a ball with a bat from a tee or cone, using a correct grip and side orientation

1-2, #16. Repeatedly jump a self-turned rope

1-2, #17. Combine shapes, levels, and pathways into simple sequences

1-2, #18. Skip, hop, gallop, and slide, using mature motor patterns

1-2, #19. Move each joint through a full range of motion

1-2, #20. Manage own body weight while hanging and climbing

1-2, #21. Demonstrate safety while participating in physical activity

1-2, #22. Participate in a wide variety of activities that involve locomotion, nonlocomotion, and the manipulation of various objects

1-2, #23. Recognize similar movement concepts in a variety of skills

1-2, #24. Identify appropriate behaviors for participating with others in physical activity

1-2, #25. Identify changes in the body during physical activity

1-2, #26. State reasons for safe and controlled movements

1-2, #27. Appreciate the benefits that accompany cooperation and sharing

1-2, #28. Accept the feelings resulting from challenges, successes, and failures in physical activity

1-2, #29. Be considerate of others in physical activity settings

Examples of Benchmarks—Kindergarten

As a result of participating in a quality physical education program it is reasonable to expect that the student will be able to

K, #1. Travel, in different ways, in a large group without bumping into others or falling

K, #2. Travel, in forward and sideways directions, and change direction quickly in response to a signal

K, #3. Demonstrate clear contrasts between slow and fast speeds while traveling

K, #4. Distinguish between straight, curved, and zigzag pathways while traveling in various ways

K, #5. Make both large and small body shapes while traveling

K, #6. Travel, demonstrating a variety of relationships with objects (e.g., over, under, behind, alongside, through)

K, #7. Place a variety of body parts into high, middle, and low levels

K, #8. Without falling, walk forward and sideways on the length of a bench

K, #9. Roll sideways (right or left) without hesitating or stopping

K, #10. Toss a ball and catch it before it bounces twice

K, #11. Demonstrate the difference between an overhand and underhand throw

K, #12. Kick a stationary ball, using a smooth, continuous running approach prior to the kick

K, #13. Continuously jump a swinging rope held by others

K, #14. Form round, narrow, wide, and twisted body shapes alone and with a partner

K, #15. Walk and run using a mature motor pattern

K, #16. Sustain moderate physical activity

K, #17. Participate daily in vigorous physical activity

K, #18. Identify selected body parts, skills, and movement concepts

K, #19. Recognize that skill development requires practice

K, #20. Recognize that physical activity is good for personal well-being

K, #21. State guidelines and behaviors for the safe use of equipment and apparatus

K, #22. Identify feelings that result from participation in physical activities

K, #23. Enjoy participation alone and with others

K, #24. Look forward to physical education lessons

References

Barlin, A.L. (1979). *Teaching your wings to fly.* Los Angeles: Learning Through Movement.

Belka, D. (1994). *Teaching children games: Becoming a master teacher.* Champaign, IL: Human Kinetics

Brandt, R. (1992a). On outcome-based education: A conversation with Bill Spady. *Educational Leadership*, **50**(4), 66-70.

Brandt, R. (1992b). On performance assessment: A conversation with Grant Wiggins. *Educational Leadership*, **50**(8), 35-37.

Buschner, C. (1994). *Teaching children movement concepts and skills: Becoming a master teacher.* Champaign, IL: Human Kinetics.

Council on Physical Education for Children. (1992). *Developmentally appropriate physical education practices for children.* Reston, VA: National Association for Sport and Physical Education

Franck, M., Graham, G., Lawson, H., Loughrey, T., Ritson, R., Sanborn, M., & Seefeldt, V. (1992). *Outcomes of quality physical education programs.* Reston, VA: National Association for Sport and Physical Education.

Frazier, D.M., & Paulson, F.L. (1992). How portfolios motivate reluctant writers. *Education Leadership*, **50**(8), 62-65.

Graham, G. (1992). *Teaching children physical education: Becoming a master teacher.* Champaign, IL: Human Kinetics.

Graham, G., Holt/Hale, S., & Parker, M. (1993). *Children moving* (3rd ed.) Mountain View, CA: Mayfield.

Hebert, E. (1992). Portfolios invite reflection—From students and staff. *Educational Leadership*, **50**(8), 58-61.

Kentucky Department of Education (1991). *Kentucky Education Reform Act: Goal 1.* Frankfort: Author.

Meyer, C. (1991). *What's in a label? Performance assessment or authentic assessment.* Prepublication draft. Beaverton, OR.

Purcell, T. (1994). *Teaching children dance: Becoming a master teacher.* Champaign, IL: Human Kinetics.

Ratliffe, T., & Ratliffe, L. (1994). *Teaching children fitness: Becoming a master teacher.* Champaign, IL: Human Kinetics.

Schiemer, S. (1993). Beyond the traditional skills test. *Teaching Elementary Physical Education*, **4**(2), 9-10.

Spady, W.G. (1988). Organizing for results: The basis of authentic restructuring and reform. *Educational Leadership*, **46**(2), 4-8.

Weikart, P. (1989). *Teaching movement and dance* (3rd ed.). Ypsilanti, MI: High Scope Press.

Werner, P. (1994). *Teaching children gymnastics: Becoming a master teacher.* Champaign, IL: Human Kinetics.

Wiggins, G. (1992). Creating tests worth taking. *Educational Leadership*, **50**(8), 26-33.

Wolf, D.P., LeMahieu, P.G., & Eresh, J. (1992). Good measure: Assessment as a tool for educational reform. *Educational Leadership*, **50**(8), 8-13.

Suggested Readings

American Heart Association. (1982a). *Putting your heart into the curriculum. Intermediate level grades: Three-Five.* AHA National Center, 7320 Greenville Avenue, Dallas, TX 75231.

American Heart Association. (1982b). *Putting your heart into the curriculum. Primary level grades: Kindergarten-Two.* AHA National Center, 7320 Greenville Avenue, Dallas, TX 75231.

Dauer, V., & Pangrazi, B. (1991). *Dynamic physical education for children* (10th ed.). New York: Macmillan.

Diez, M.E., & Moon, C.J. (1992). What do we want students to know? . . . and other important questions. *Educational Leadership*, **50**(4), 38-41.

Ferguson, S. (1992). Zeroing in on math abilities. *Learning*, **21**(3), 38-41.

Foster, E.R., Hartinger, K., & Smith, K.A. (1992). *Fitness fun*. Champaign, IL: Human Kinetics.

Gallahue, D.L., Werner, P., & Leudke, G.C. (1972). *Moving and learning: A conceptual approach to the physical education of young children.* Dubuque, IA: Kendall/Hunt.

Gustafson, M.A., Wolfe, S.K., & King, C. (1991). *Great games for young people*. Champaign, IL: Human Kinetics.

Hammett, C. (1992). *Movement activities for early childhood*. Champaign, IL: Human Kinetics.

Herman, J. (1992). What research tells us about good assessment. *Educational Leadership*, **50**(8), 74-78.

Holt/Hale, S. (1993). *On the move: Lesson plans for children moving.* Mountain View, CA: Mayfield.

Joyce, M. (1980). *First steps in teaching creative dance to children* (2nd ed.). Mountain View, CA: Mayfield.

King, J.A., & Evans, K.M. (1991). Can we achieve outcome-based education? *Educational Leadership*, **49**(2), 73-75.

Logsdon, B., Barrett, K., Ammons, M., Broer, M., Halverson, L., McGee, R., & Roberton, M.A. (1984). *Physical education for children: A focus on the teaching process*. Philadelphia: Lea & Febiger.

McDonald's Corporation. (1975). *Nutrition action pack*. St. Charles, IL: McDonald's Education Resource Center.

McDonald's Corporation. (1979). *Moving learning action pack*. St. Charles, IL: McDonald's Education Resource Center.

McDonald's Corporation. (1992). *Healthy growing up*. St. Charles, IL: McDonald's Education Resource Center.

Mitchell, R. (1992). *Testing for learning: How new approaches to evaluation can improve American schools*. New York: Free Press.

Morris, D., & Stiehl, J. (1992). *Changing kid's games*. Champaign, IL: Human Kinetics.

National Dairy Council. (1988). *Get moving, get eating, get fit*. Rosemont, IL: Author.

O'Neil, J. (1992). Putting performance assessment to the test. *Educational Leadership*, **50**(2), 14-19.

Pica, R. (1990). *More music for moving & learning*. Champaign, IL: Human Kinetics.

Pica, R. (1991a). *Early elementary children moving & learning*. Champaign, IL: Human Kinetics.

Pica, R. (1991b). *Special themes for moving & learning*. Champaign, IL: Human Kinetics.

Redding, N. (1992). Assessing the big outcomes. *Educational Leadership*, **50**(8), 49-53.

Sanders, S.W. (1992). *Designing preschool movement programs*. Champaign, IL: Human Kinetics.

Spady, W.G., & Marshall, K.J. (1991). Beyond traditional outcome-based education. *Educational Leadership*, **49**(2), 67-72.

Thomas, J.R., Lee, A.M., & Thomas, K.T. (1988). *Physical education for children: Concepts into practice*. Champaign, IL: Human Kinetics.

Tierney, R. (1992). Setting a new agenda for assessment. *Learning*, **61**(2), 62-64.

Vogel, P., & Seefeldt, V. (1988). *Program design in physical education*. Indianapolis, IN: Benchmark Press.

Wenk, B. (1992). *Holiday games and activities*. Champaign, IL: Human Kinetics.

Werner, P., & Burton, E. (1979). *Learning through movement*. St. Louis: Mosby.

Wessel, J.A., & Kelly, L. (1986). *Achievement-based curriculum development in physical education*. Philadelphia: Lea & Febiger.

Wickstrom, R. (1983). *Fundamental movement patterns*. Philadelphia: Lea & Febiger.

Wiggins, G. (1988, Winter). Rational numbers. *American Educator*, 20-25, 45-48.

Wiggins, G. (1989, May). A true test: Towards more authentic and equitable assessment. *Phi Delta Kappan*, 703-713.

About the Author

Christine Hopple is the resource development director of the United States Physical Education Association (USPE) and former editor of the USPE newsletter *Teaching Elementary Physical Education (TEPE)*. She previously was an elementary physical education specialist at Marion County's College Park Primary School, Florida's first Elementary Physical Education Demonstration School.

Christine received her master's degree in elementary physical education pedagogy at Virginia Polytechnic Institute and State University in 1994. She received her bachelor's degree in physical education from The Florida State University, where she was a 1984 recipient of the Southern District Alliance for Health, Physical Education, Recreation and Dance's Student Honor Award.

Christine is a member of the United States Physical Education Association, the National Association for Sport and Physical Education (NASPE), and the Illinois Alliance for Health, Physical Education, Recreation and Dance. As an active member of NASPE's Council on Physical Education for Children (COPEC), she helped coauthor COPEC's *Developmentally Appropriate Physical Education Practices for Children* document.